GAINSBOROUGH'S FAMILY ALBUM

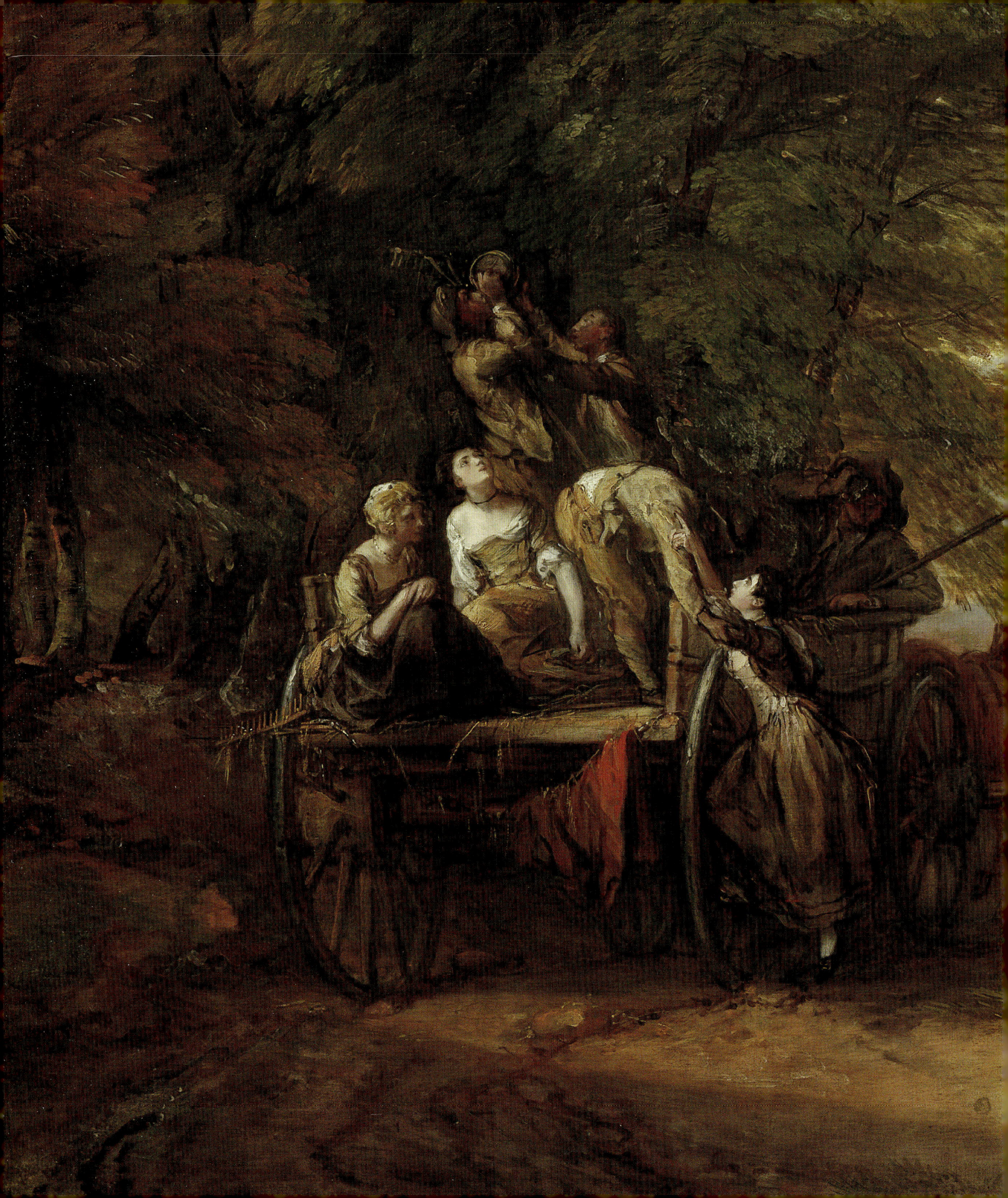

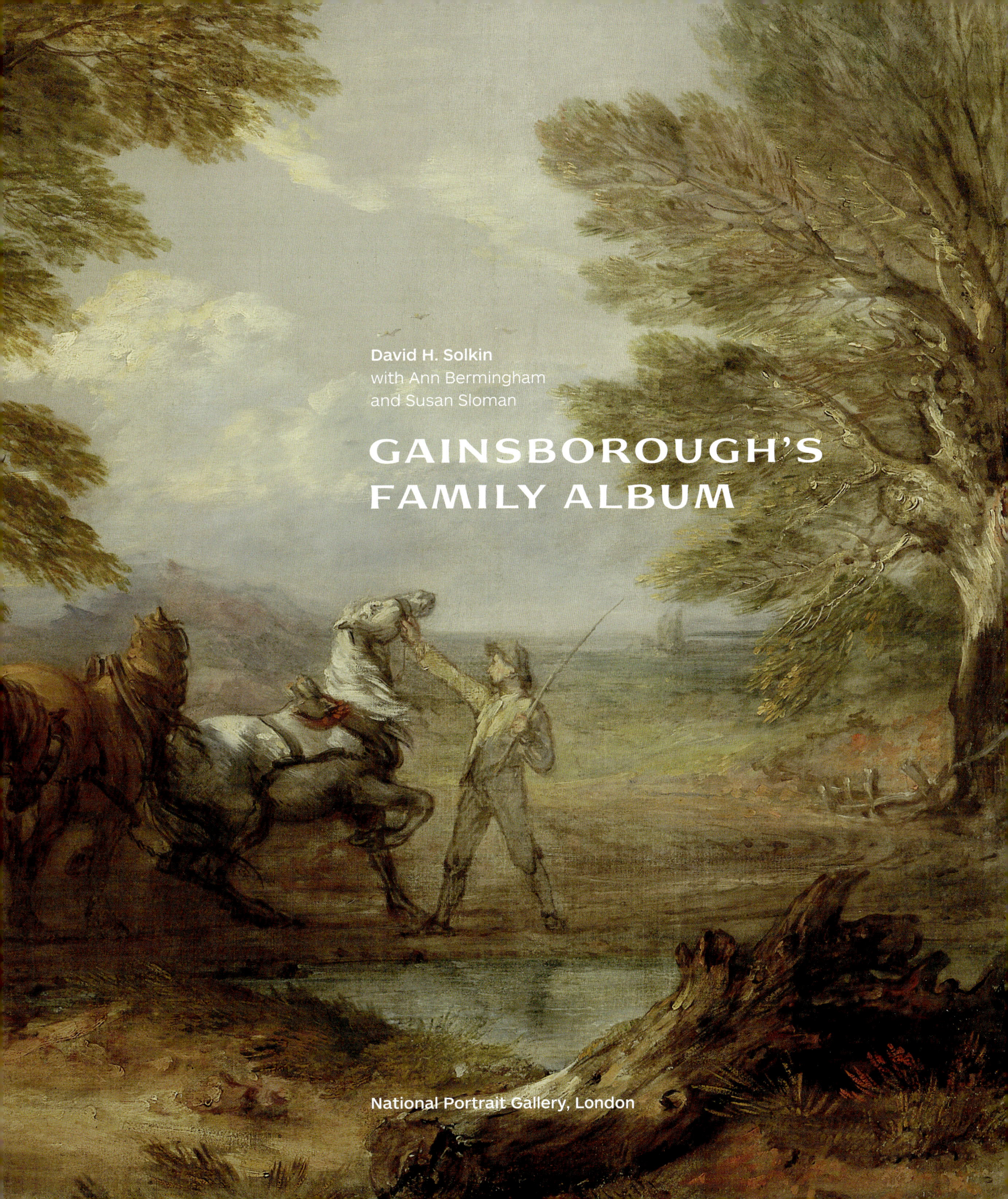

David H. Solkin
with Ann Bermingham
and Susan Sloman

GAINSBOROUGH'S
FAMILY ALBUM

National Portrait Gallery, London

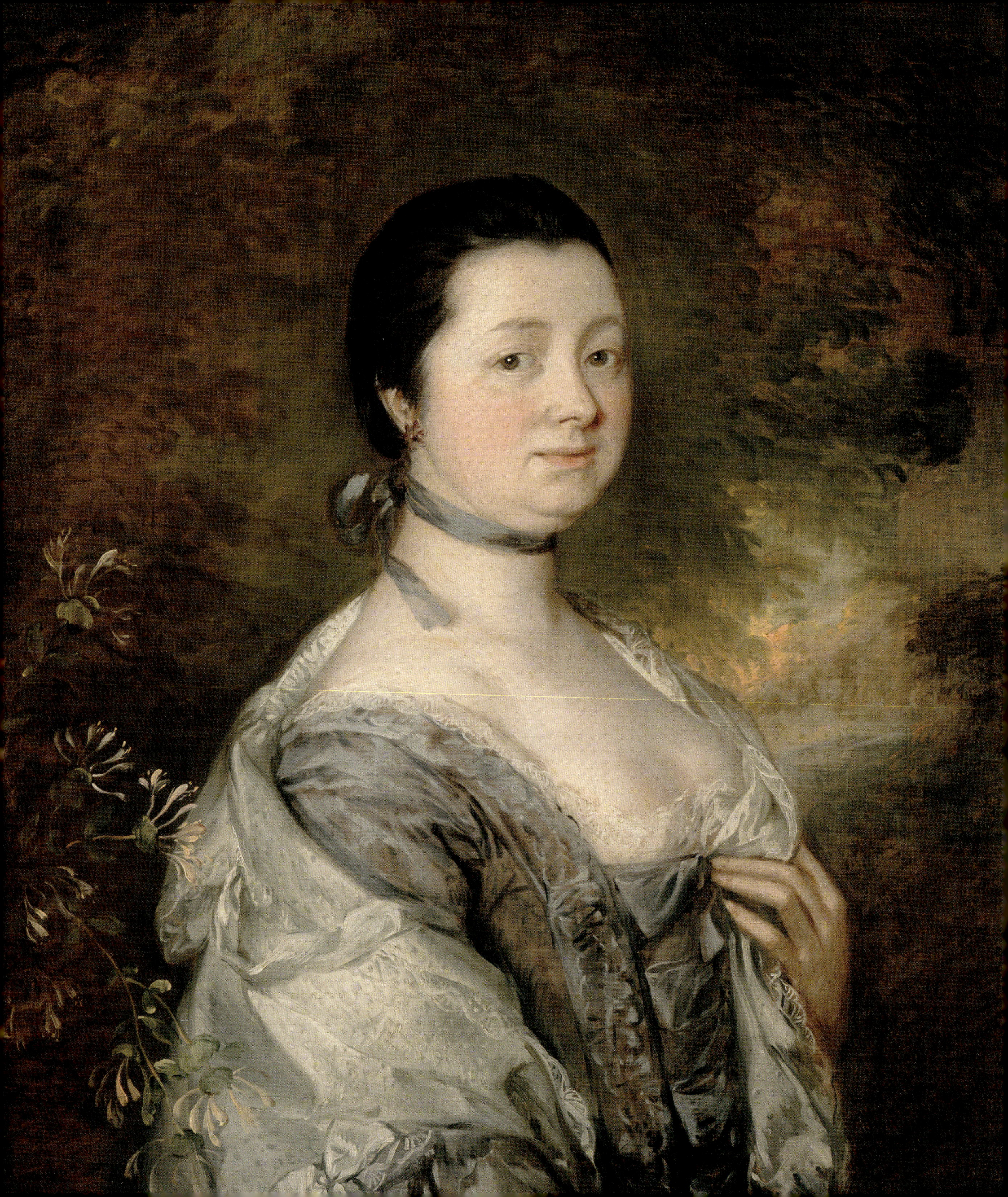

CONTENTS

DIRECTOR'S FOREWORD

The eighteenth-century master Thomas Gainsborough once famously complained, in a letter to his friend William Jackson, that he was sick and tired of painting portraits, an activity that he likened to the confinement inflicted on a horse in harness, compelled against its natural free inclinations 'to follow the track'. Despite frustration at the business of portraiture, Gainsborough painted and drew over fifty portraits of his extended family. A passion for portraying family may seem natural to us, but this predilection made Gainsborough unique in his own time and practically unprecedented in the history of western art. In consequence, I am delighted that the National Portrait Gallery has been able to reunite Gainsborough's 'family album' for the very first time.

This exhibition juxtaposes some of the artist's best loved works of art with little known and rarely seen portraits. Proposing a new way of considering Gainsborough, it tells the story of a provincial artist's rise to metropolitan fame and fortune as part of a wider kinship network of blood relations, in-laws and friends, comprising, amongst others, an artist, his wife and business manager, their daughters, an artist's assistant, a clothes merchant turned postmaster, a milliner and a carpenter, what makes this ensemble particularly remarkable is that it depicts an ordinary family at a time when portraiture was almost exclusively confined to the rich, the famous and the upper classes.

Asking why Gainsborough was driven to depict his family members on so many occasions, Professor David H. Solkin and his collaborators show that if some of these portraits were an outlet for the artist's emotions, they also served his social and professional ambitions. Uncomissioned family portraits provided the opportunity for experiment. There are six stunning double portraits of his daughters, each of which can be related to a seminal moment in Gainsborough's artistic development. Similarly, the portraits of his nephew Dupont enabled Gainsborough to cultivate his artistic reputation and explore his beliefs about great art. Together these intertwined narratives of public and private offer new insights into the life, motivations and work of one of Britain's greatest artists.

Professor Solkin is among the principal authorities on the history of British art and we are sincerely grateful for his intellectual leadership, research and vision in curating *Gainsborough's Family Album* for the National Portrait Gallery and Princeton University Art Museum. Since he proposed the project in 2012, David has worked intensively with Dr Lucy Peltz, the National Portrait Gallery's Senior Curator of 18th Century Collections and Head of Collections Displays (Tudor to Regency), in the development and realisation of the exhibition and publication. The role of the portraits in illuminating Gainsborough's professional and personal relationships, first with his daughters and then with his wife and sisters, are thoughtfully interrogated by Professor Ann Bermingham and Dr Susan Sloman in their respective contributions to the catalogue. A ubiquitous and nagging question raised by this scholarly project is the complex relationship that portraiture has with biography. So I am delighted to acknowledge the support of the Paul Mellon Center for Studies in British Art, and Professor Mark Hallett and Ella Fleming in particular, for funding and organising a two-day conference at which this question will be discussed by an international gathering of scholars.

Gainsborough's Family Album is the result of many people's hard work. At the Gallery, I would like to express my sincere gratitude to Sarah Tinsley, Director of Exhibitions and Collections, and Rosie Wilson, Head of Exhibitions, who have been closely involved in the development of the exhibition from the outset. Collaborating with the Gallery's Curator Lucy Peltz, Eloise Stewart, Exhibitions Manager, and Ulrike Wachsman, Exhibitions Officer, have skillfully led the exhibition's production in consort with Jude Simmons, Head of Design and Andrea Easey, Interpretation Manager. This elegant publication has been overseen by Amelia Collins working with Ruth Müller-Wirth as the publication Production Manager and Mark Lynch as the Picture Researcher.

Other colleagues at the National Portrait Gallery I wish to acknowledge are Melanie Aram, Pim Baxter, James Cunninghame Graham, Helena Cuss, Kara Green, Richard Hallas, Susie Holden, Jess Litwin, Karl Lydon and his team, Rab MacGibbon, Laura McKechan, Alison Smith, Fiona Smith, Liz Smith, Anna Starling, Louise Stewart, Ben Weaver, Helen Whiteoak. Outside the Gallery, we thank Anjali Bulley, Patricia Burgess, Hilary Bird and Ocky Murray who have all been involved in the design and production of the publication. At Princeton University Art Museum, we are grateful to their Director, Dr James Steward, and the Exhibition team including T. Barton Thurber, Alexia Hughes and Elizabeth Aldred.

The vast majority of Gainsborough's family portraits remained with the family until many years after his death. Now they are spread far and wide. Consequently, we extend our warmest thanks to the many museums and private collectors who have generously agreed to share important and much loved works. These loans have allowed the reassembling and reappraisal of Gainsborough's family album which, I sincerely hope, will be enjoyable, surprising and moving in both its London and Princeton evocations.

Nicholas Cullinan, Director
National Portrait Gallery, London

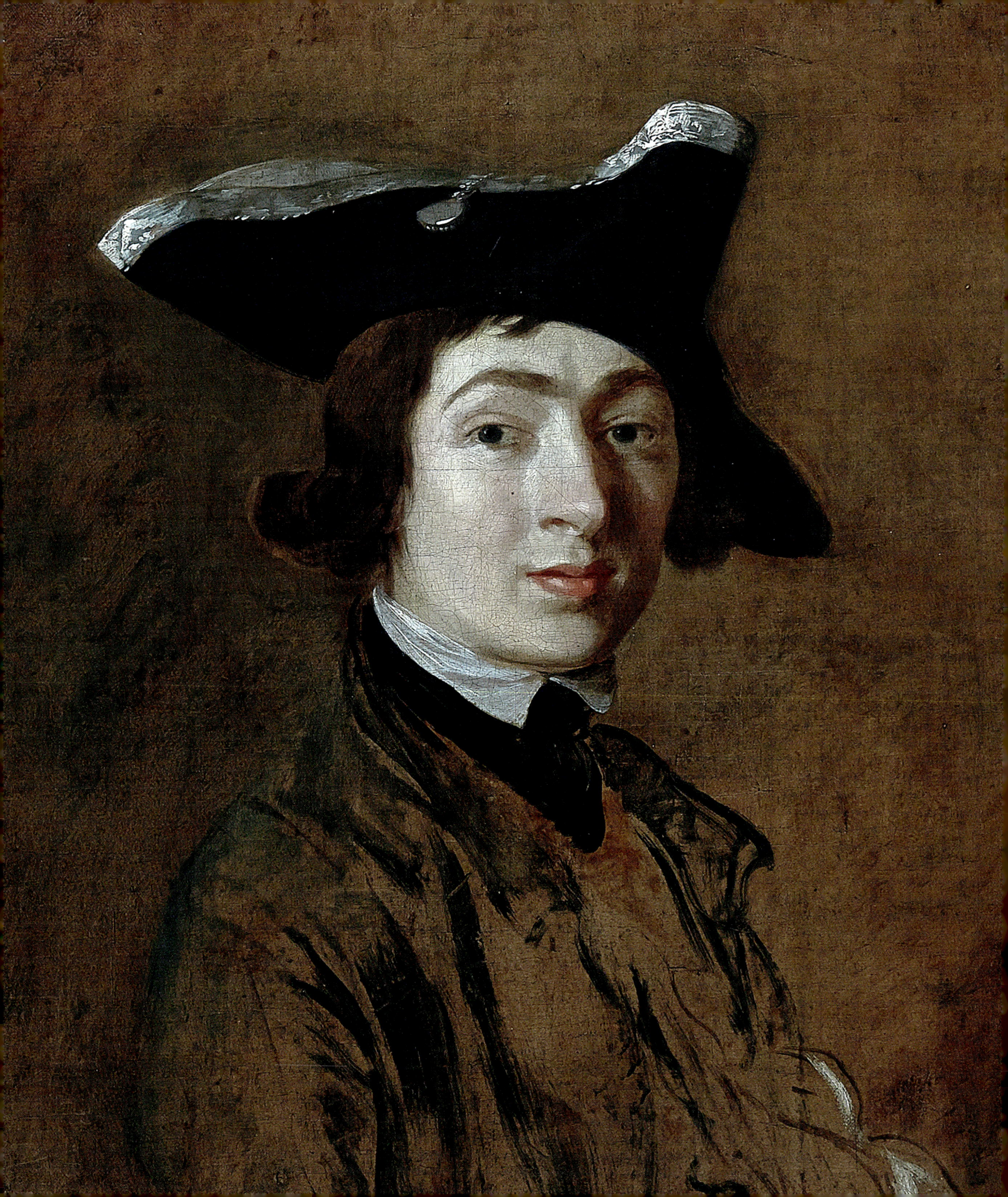

CURATOR'S FOREWORD

Thomas Gainsborough was one of eighteenth-century Britain's most successful portraitists, but he paid a high price for his popularity. His private correspondence makes it clear that he chafed under the tyranny of his vain and wealthy sitters, whose incessant demands he blamed for stifling his creativity as an artist and demeaning his dignity as a gentleman. He also lamented that the need to earn his living from catering to an endless parade of 'damnd Faces' prevented him from pursuing his devotion to landscape, the branch of art he most loved but that sadly did not pay. Yet, despite these feelings of profound frustration, Gainsborough nonetheless found the time, the energy and (perhaps most surprisingly) the desire to paint and draw more portraits of his family members than any other artist of his or any earlier period is known to have produced – nearly fifty likenesses in total. So how might we account for his seemingly paradoxical and decidedly unusual behaviour? And what can these pictures teach us about the painter, his world, and perhaps even ourselves?

These were the principal questions I had in mind when I approached the National Portrait Gallery with the idea for *Gainsborough's Family Album* several years ago, and since then I have learned not to expect any simple answers. Gainsborough's portraits notoriously resist easy reading even when a great deal is known about their subjects and about the circumstances of the paintings' production and reception. Also, as the introductory essays will at times make apparent, a critical consensus proves even harder to achieve where such historical evidence is lacking. Since all but one or two of his family pictures stayed entirely out of the public eye until long after the artist's death, these portraits only rarely prompted written comments during his lifetime, or at least any that can now be traced. Compounding the problems caused by this lack of comment on the part of Gainsborough and his contemporaries is the concise economy of the pictorial rhetoric that he almost invariably adopted for depictions of his kinfolk. Given that he was not being paid for his labours, it is easy to understand why the painter's main priorities tended to be simplicity and speed – although this has made the challenge facing later interpreters all the more difficult by leaving images that, as a rule, have little

beyond the obvious to say about themselves. The fact is that they did not
have to do more, if only for the simple reason that they were intended for
an audience of relatives and friends, people who knew the sitters (and the
painter) well. Not only are we not privy to that intimate knowledge, but today
we can merely guess at what it must have been like to view Gainsborough's
'family album' in its original setting. Largely confined in the eighteenth
century to a small network of domestic households, the pictures now inhabit
spaces of very different kinds across the world. Bringing these scattered works
together under one roof presents a unique opportunity to reveal the full
richness of their meanings, as individual objects and as a visual ensemble, and
to see what further questions they suggest.

If one primary purpose of this book, and of the exhibition it accompanies,
is to offer a new perspective on Thomas Gainsborough the portraitist, another
is to challenge our thinking about his era and its relationship to our own. It
is for that reason that I have deliberately chosen an anachronistic title. While
the 'family album' per se may be a more modern invention, if we look back
I believe we can begin to trace its origins in the historical circumstances that
shaped Gainsborough's precursor of the genre. The term 'family album',
therefore, should not be taken literally, but instead as an invitation to think
about the past alongside the present and to juxtapose a seemingly prescient
example of artistic practice with what has in recent decades become our
own habitual, even obsessive, devotion to photographing ourselves and our
networks of relations, friends and acquaintances. Yet if here there is common
ground to be explored, we shall soon discover that there is alien territory as
well. Whereas our own experience might lead us to expect Gainsborough's
pictures to conform to twenty-first-century ideas of privacy and informality,
instead we find that in the main these representations are anything but
casual, and that most are concerned less with expressing feelings of intimate
attachment than with making claims to social status. That being said, those
aims may not be as foreign to the world of selfies posted online as we might at
first be inclined to admit.

A resonance with the sexual politics of today may well come as a
greater surprise. Although Gainsborough was about as far from being a
feminist as one could imagine, an admiration for strong women (albeit
sometimes begrudgingly expressed) emerges as a striking feature of his
correspondence, and informs more than one portrait of his female relations.
His attitudes must have been shaped by personal experience, as Susan Sloman
demonstrates in her essay. She explains how the two most important women
in Gainsborough's adult life, his wife Margaret and his sister Mary Gibbon,
each played a key role in supporting the business side of his career. Their
examples may in turn have prompted Gainsborough's ambitions to educate
his two daughters – also a Mary and a Margaret – so that they could earn
their keep as professional landscape painters, though in the end they never
did so. Instead, their visibility in the history of art derives chiefly from the
part they played as the models for some of their father's most experimental
canvases. These pictures, as Ann Bermingham argues, have considerably more

to tell us about Gainsborough's aspirations than they do about the girls; yet even here – perhaps especially here – the sisters' own voices can still be heard, intermingled with echoes of their mother's, and of the family chorus at large. The conviction that artists act not alone, but in concert with the people closest to them, lies at the very heart of *Gainsborough's Family Album*.

Curating, too, invariably entails collaboration. The exhibition I envisioned would never have become a reality without the unwavering encouragement of Lucy Peltz, who has kept a firm hand on the project's tiller throughout our long journey together. Likewise, I am hugely grateful to my two co-authors for agreeing to contribute to this book and for their replies to numerous questions, not least because each has immeasurably more experience of Gainsborough than I would ever dare claim for myself. All three of us have built on the foundations of research carried out by countless others, but above all by Hugh Belsey, the pre-eminent expert on the artist's portraits, who organised an earlier, if less comprehensive, display of Gainsborough's family pictures precisely thirty years ago. I would like to express my personal appreciation to my former colleague Aileen Ribeiro, for advice on all matters relating to eighteenth-century dress, and to Mark Hallett for, amongst other things, a useful critical reading of the first draft of my essay. Thanks are also due to Brian Allen, Mark Bills, Director of Gainsborough's House, Andrew Clayton-Payne, Katie Coombs and Nicola Costaras at the Victoria and Albert Museum, Harriet Drummond, of Christie's, Mark Hedges, Editor of *Country Life*, David Moore-Gwyn of Sotheby's, Anthony Mould, and to Martin Myrone and Greg Sullivan at Tate Britain. Working with the National Portrait Gallery has been a pleasure and a privilege, thanks not just to Lucy, but also to Tanya Bentley, Dustin Frazier McKinley and Louise Stewart for much essential information-gathering, to Christopher Tinker, Kara Green and Amelia Collins for their editorial guidance and to a succession of equally enthusiastic Directors, first Sandy Nairne and now Nicholas Cullinan. But it is only fitting that these acknowledgements should end with an expression of gratitude to the people I most cherish, whose images fill the pages of my own family albums. Where would any of us be without our families?

David H. Solkin, FBA
Emeritus Professor of the History of Art
The Courtauld Institute of Art

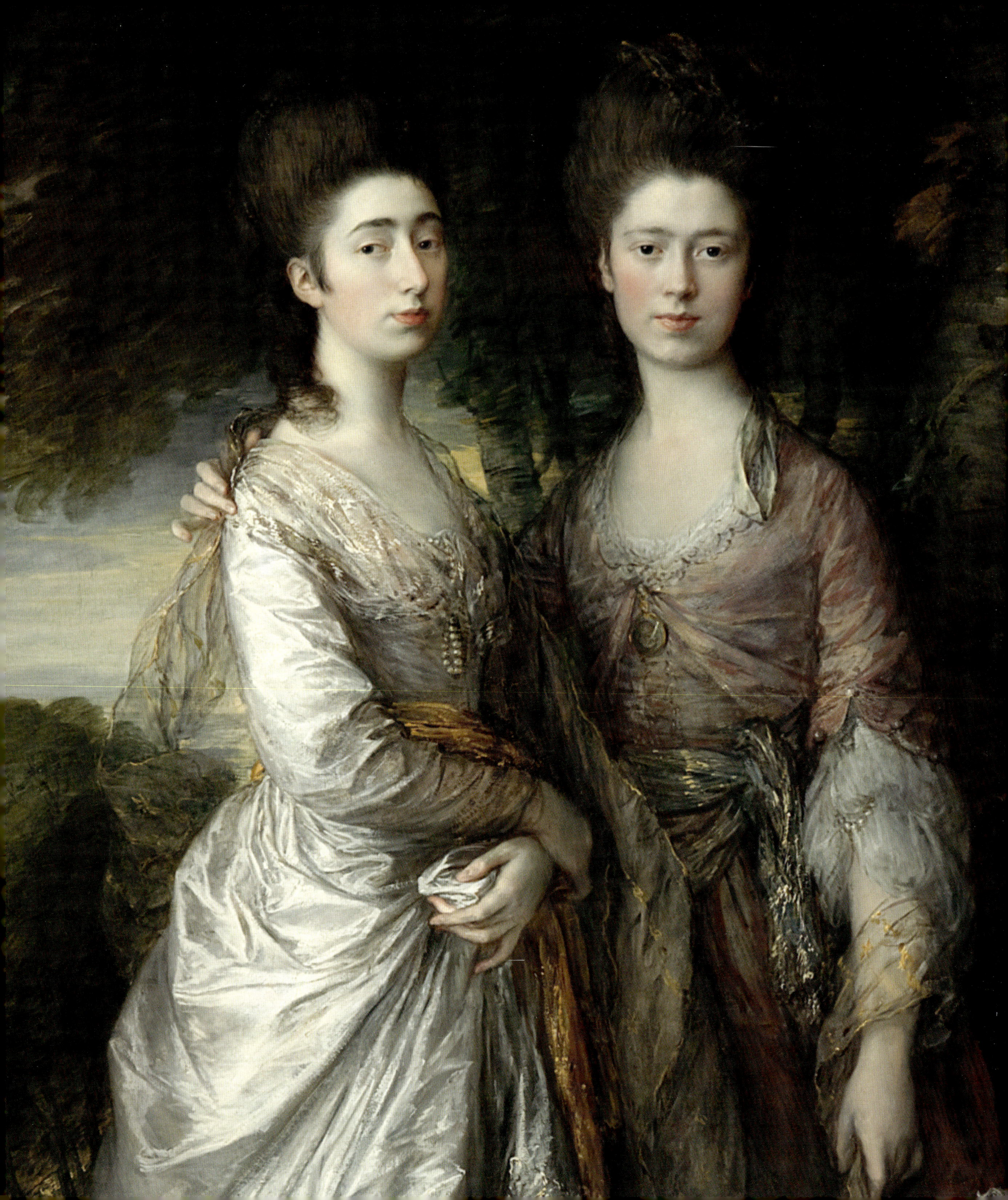

CHRONOLOGY

1727
Born in Sudbury, Suffolk, the fifth son of John Gainsborough and Mary Burrough; baptised on 14 May.

Margaret Burr (the future Mrs Gainsborough) born in London (?); possibly the person of that name baptised at St James's, Westminster on 15 October.

c.1740
Begins apprenticeship with Hubert-François Gravelot in London.

1743–4
Establishes an independent studio in Hatton Garden, London, at 2 Little Kirby Street.

1746
On 15 July, marries Margaret Burr, illegitimate daughter of Henry, 3rd Duke of Beaufort and an unidentified Scottish woman (possibly Margaret Burr, née Aikman) in a clandestine ceremony at St George's Chapel, Curzon Street, London. Margaret is likely to have been pregnant at the time of their marriage.

Late 1746 or early 1747
Birth of his first daughter, Mary.

1747
By March, living at 67 Hatton Garden, London, where the Gainsboroughs reside until 1749. He travels back and forth to Suffolk throughout this period.

1748
Probable date of *The Artist with his Wife and Eldest Daughter Mary* (cat. 2).

On 1 March his first daughter Mary is buried at the parish church of St Andrew Holborn.

On 29 October his father John Gainsborough dies in Sudbury.

1749
By spring, the Gainsboroughs have relocated to Sudbury.

1750
Birth of his second daughter Mary, who is baptised at All Saints' Church, Sudbury, on 3 February.

1751
Birth of his third daughter, Margaret, who is baptised at St Gregory's Church, Sudbury, on 22 August.

1752
The Gainsboroughs move to Ipswich, to a house opposite the Shire Hall.

1754
Paints unfinished self-portrait (cat. 4).

Gainsborough Dupont born in Sudbury to the artist's sister Sarah and her carpenter husband Philip Dupont, and baptised 28 April.

c.1756
Paints first double portrait of his daughters, depicting them chasing a butterfly (cat. 9).

1758
Between 2 and 7 October, arrives in Bath, where he remains for the next six months before returning temporarily to Ipswich.

1759
On 22/3 October, holds sale in Ipswich of all his household goods, 'with some PICTURES, original DRAWINGS in the Landskip way'.

Moves to Bath.

1760
From June, occupies house belonging to the Duke of Kingston in Abbey Street, Bath, which he leases at £150 per annum.

1763
Recovers from a serious illness. Lets out rooms in Abbey Street house to lodgers, while retaining use of his studio and showroom. Moves with his family to Lansdown Road, Bath.

1766
Around Christmas, moves up the hill to the Circus, while retaining the lease on the Abbey Street house.

1767
Exhibits *The Harvest Wagon* (cat. 20) at the Society of Artists in London.

1768
In December, appointed a founder member of the Royal Academy.

1772
On 12 January, signs the papers of indenture that contract his nephew Gainsborough Dupont to serve a seven-year term as his apprentice.

1773
Paints oval portrait of Dupont in Van Dyck dress (cat. 26) in a single one-hour sitting, before giving the picture to Philip Thicknesse.

1774
When the lease on Abbey Street house comes to an end, moves to London; here the Gainsboroughs rent west wing of Schomberg House, Pall Mall.

1780
On 21 February, Mary Gainsborough marries the musician Johann Christian Fischer, but the marriage fails within a few years, and she returns to live with her parents.

1780–81
Paints his first portraits of George III and Queen Charlotte; exhibits these full-lengths at the Royal Academy in 1781.

1784
After quarrelling with the Royal Academy, withdraws his paintings from the exhibition and never shows there again. From this year onwards, exhibits his work annually in his Schomberg House studio.

In August, after the death of Allan Ramsay, is appointed Principal Painter to the King.

1788
In July, knowing that he is terminally ill, holds final conversation with Sir Joshua Reynolds. Dies on 2 August.

In December, Reynolds delivers his fourteenth *Discourse* to the Royal Academy as a tribute to Gainsborough.

1797
Death of Gainsborough Dupont, who is buried beside his uncle at St Anne's, Kew.

1799
Death of Mrs Margaret Gainsborough.

1820
Death of Margaret Gainsborough.

1826
Death of Mary Fischer, née Gainsborough.

Note: All dates are given in the New Style (Gregorian) calendar, which came into effect in Britain on 1 January 1752. Previously, under the Julian calendar, the year began on Lady Day (25 March).

THE GAINSBOROUGH FAMILY TREE

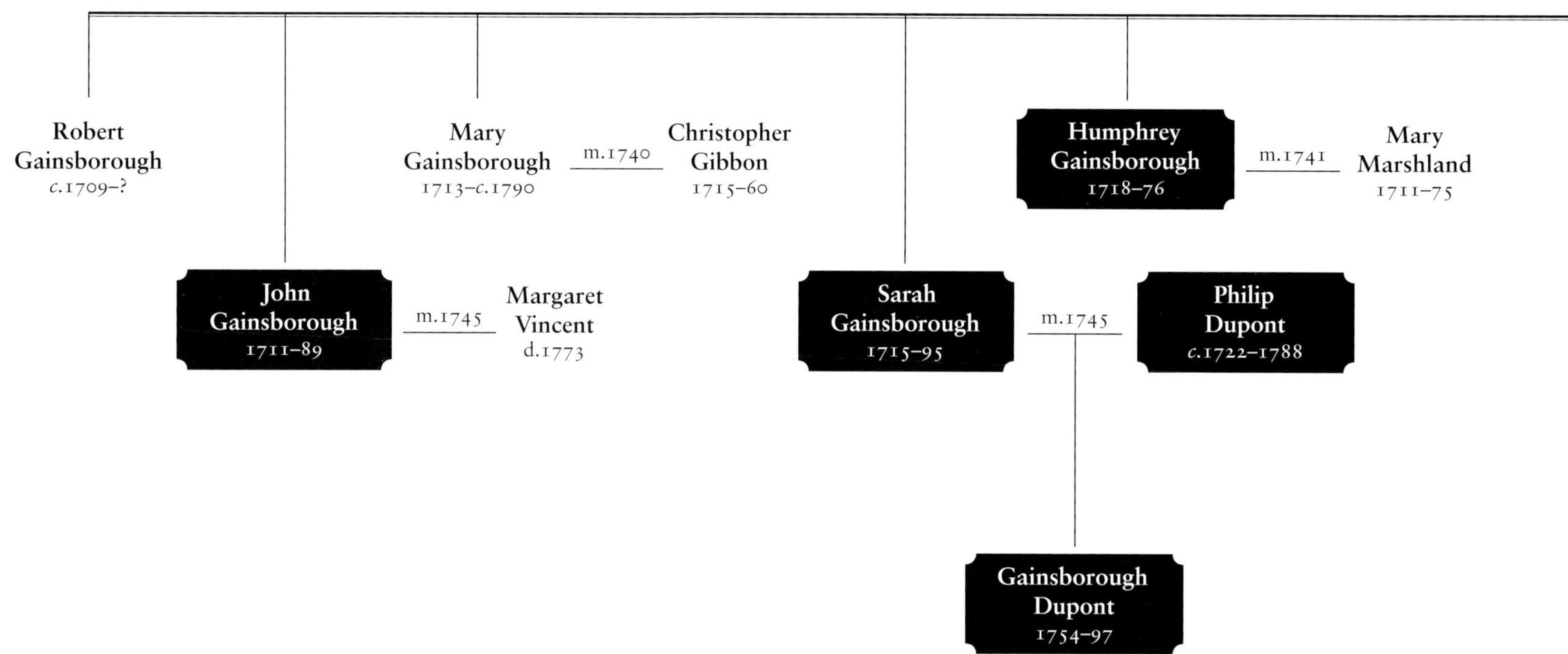

Names outlined in black are of persons included in *Gainsborough's Family Album*

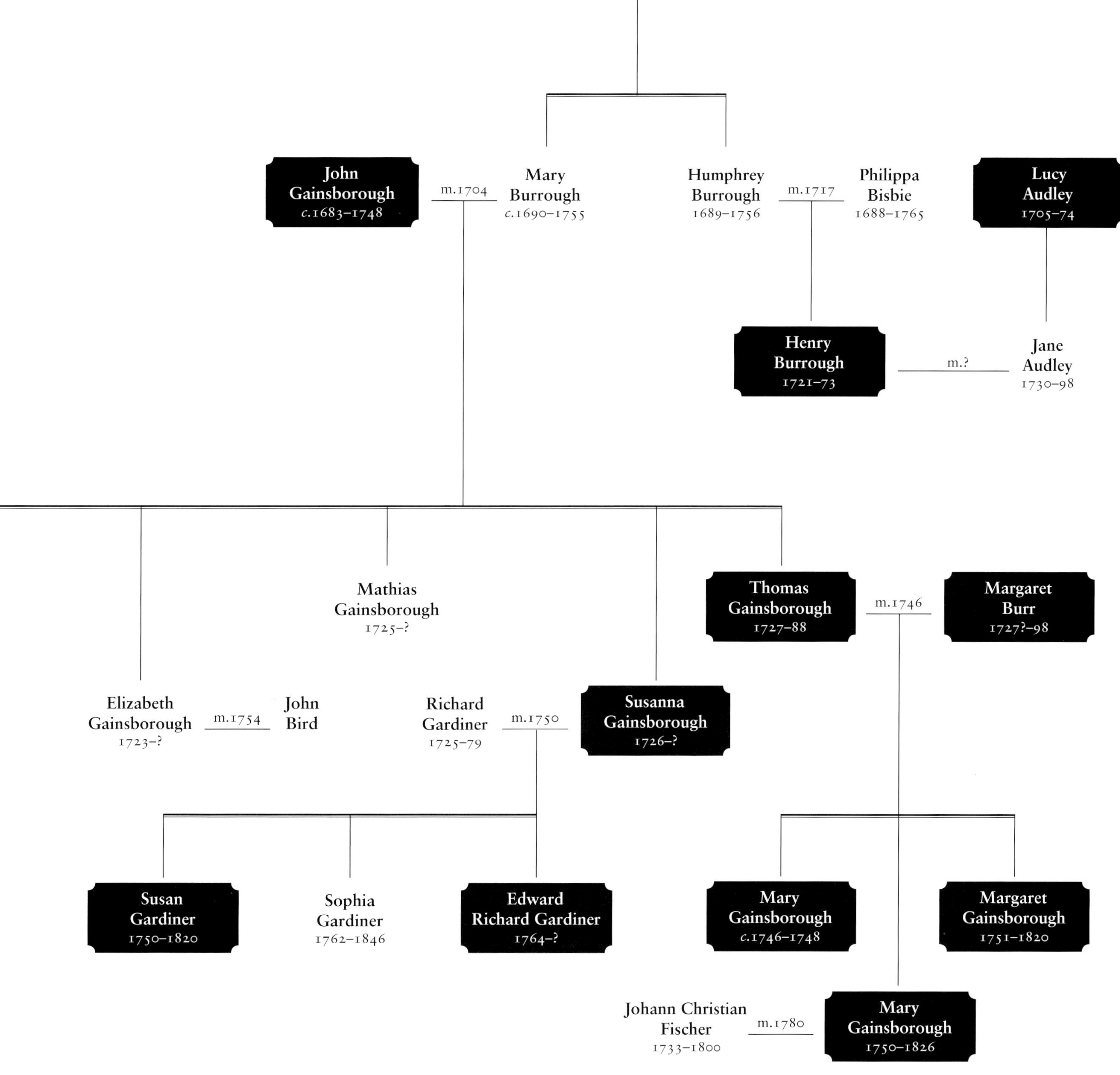

John
Gainsborough
c.1683–1748
m.1704
Mary
Burrough
c.1690–1755
Humphrey
Burrough
1689–1756
m.1717
Philippa
Bisbie
1688–1765
Lucy
Audley
1705–74
Henry
Burrough
1721–73
m.?
Jane
Audley
1730–98
Mathias
Gainsborough
1725–?
Thomas
Gainsborough
1727–88
m.1746
Margaret
Burr
1727?–98
Elizabeth
Gainsborough
1723–?
m.1754
John
Bird
Richard
Gardiner
1725–79
m.1750
Susanna
Gainsborough
1726–?
Susan
Gardiner
1750–1820
Sophia
Gardiner
1762–1846
Edward
Richard Gardiner
1764–?
Mary
Gainsborough
c.1746–1748
Margaret
Gainsborough
1751–1820
Johann Christian
Fischer
1733–1800
m.1780
Mary
Gainsborough
1750–1826

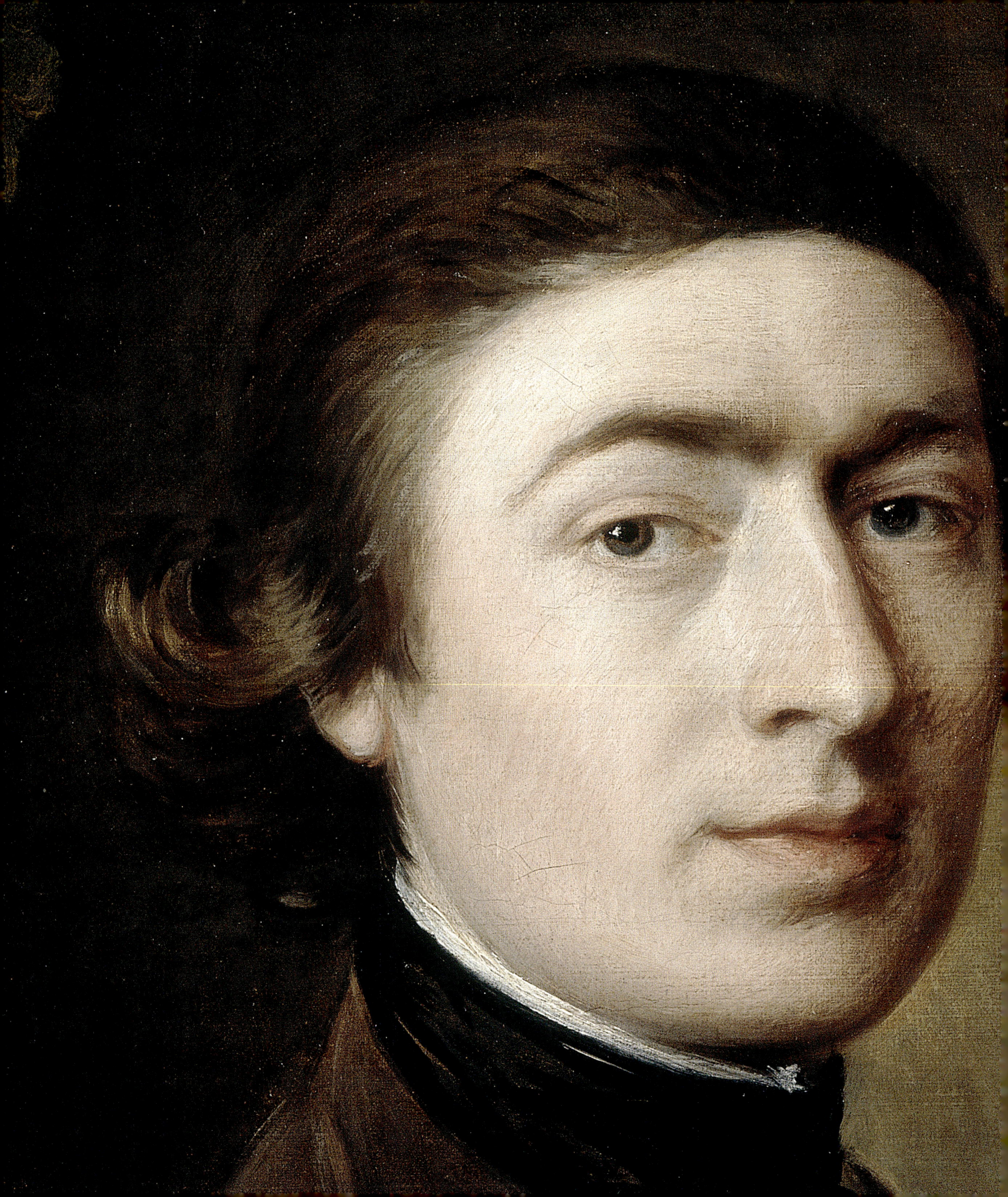

PRIVATE AND PUBLIC RELATIONS

David H. Solkin

PRIVATE AND PUBLIC RELATIONS: GAINSBOROUGH'S FAMILY ALBUM

David H. Solkin

Nowadays we have become so accustomed to making and accumulating images of ourselves and of those closest to us that we tend to forget just how recently this practice became possible. From ancient times up until fewer than two hundred years ago, the representation of individual human likenesses almost invariably required the employment of a skilled and costly specialist – that is to say, a portraitist. As a consequence, only the wealthiest families – usually noble or (more often) royal dynasties – possessed the means to acquire and retain significant groups of pictures of themselves. Lower down the social scale, the same capacity was almost exclusively limited to families of professional artists; but before the modern period only a very few painters and sculptors had either the time or the inclination to produce more than the odd self-portrait, or the occasional image of a spouse or a child.

One rare exception to this pattern is the major eighteenth-century English artist Thomas Gainsborough. Over a career spanning four decades, Gainsborough produced nearly fifty portraits of himself and his family members – his father, his wife, his daughters, two sisters and two brothers, a brother-in-law, two nephews, one niece, and a few more distant connections, not to mention his pet dogs. The vast majority of these works stayed with the family throughout the painter's lifetime, by the end of which he had single-handedly created an unusually comprehensive visual record of an eighteenth-century British kinship network, with several of its key players shown more than once, at different stages in their lives.

Apart from the factor of Gainsborough's authorship, what makes this ensemble unlike any other is its focus on a family of ordinary private individuals – among them a Suffolk clothes merchant, two clergymen, a milliner, a failed inventor, a carpenter, a lodging-house keeper, two portraitists (Thomas and his nephew Gainsborough Dupont), and several young children. This cast of characters, in other words, consists of just the sort of working- and middle-class individuals who would reappear in the family albums that began to proliferate throughout Europe and elsewhere in the second half of the nineteenth century, once the spread of commercial photography made portraiture accessible to people on relatively

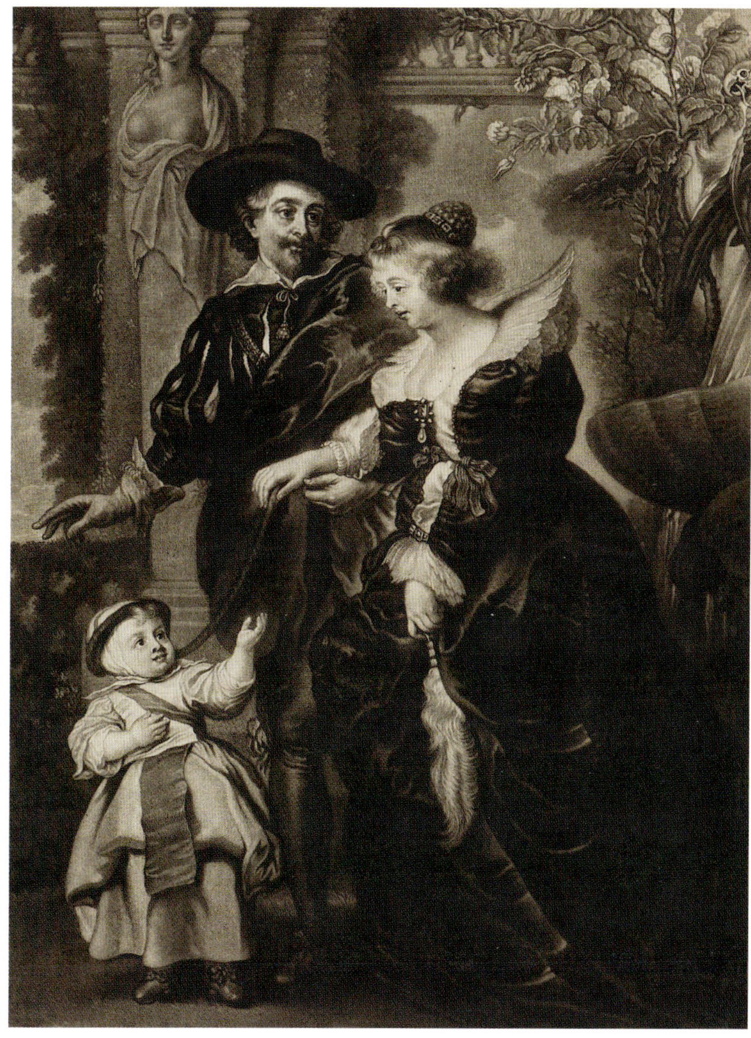

modest incomes. Later the invention of affordable and easy-to-use portable cameras would make it possible for millions of private citizens not just to collect, but also to create pictures of themselves, their relatives, and friends. More recently, the advent of the digital age, exemplified above all by the smartphone, has made such collections infinitely and easily expandable, and accessible to view anywhere in a matter of seconds. Of course, the technologies of representation available to Gainsborough were far more limited, and even in his wildest dreams – or more likely, nightmares – he could never have anticipated the culture of the selfie, never mind the endless circulation of portraits via the Internet. Nonetheless, in one fundamental respect he used his own 'family album' in much the same way as we do – to document the people with whom he shared his life. But for Gainsborough these portraits fulfilled another purpose of at least equal importance; they served his ambitions as well as his affections.

Gainsborough was not the first European artist to portray himself and his kindred on multiple occasions, although he could have known of only a very few precedents. Principal among these was Sir Peter Paul Rubens, the renowned Flemish painter of religious, allegorical and historical subjects, whose enormous output also included dozens of depictions of high-born patrons, as well as a substantial number of likenesses (more than twenty-five are now known) of his immediate and extended family.[1] Unlike his autonomous self-portraits, which were designed to project his public image as a courtly artist of consummate elegance and panache, Rubens's pictures of those closest to him were never intended for display outside the family circle. While some have rightly been described as 'private' images, in the main they are of a scale and ambition befitting the status of their producer, his sitters and their viewers as prominent members of the Antwerp elite. Such is certainly the case with Rubens's self-portrait with his second wife Helena Fourment, and one of their children, either Clara Johanna or Frans, from the first half of the 1630s. Gainsborough would certainly have been familiar with this elaborate full-length, either in the original at Blenheim Palace or through James McArdell's mezzotint (fig. 1).[2] But whereas Rubens executed several finished portraits of his immediate family members at full-length and life-size, Gainsborough brought only one work of this type to completion: significantly, it was that which announced his daughters' entrance into fashionable society as fully adult young women (cat. 30). No other image of Mary and Margaret, or indeed of any of their relations, aspires to anything like the formality of this grand double full-length. The remainder of the 'album' consists of some half a dozen drawings and around forty modestly sized oils, around half of which would have been considered unfinished by normal eighteenth-century standards.

The question of 'finish' – or rather the lack thereof – in regard to this group of paintings is a complex one, discussed more fully later on. All that needs to be said for now is that by the middle of the eighteenth century, leaving a likeness in oils of a relation or friend palpably incomplete had become one way of signalling its status as the product and expression of a personal connection between artist and sitter – as distinct from a commodity done on commission, and measurable in terms of its commercial value.[3] This is one of the points implied in a self-portrait of the mid 1660s by the earlier Suffolk-born portraitist Mary Beale, where she has depicted her own figure in a manner calculated to demonstrate the full range of her skills to potential patrons; by contrast, propped up beside her is an unframed canvas bearing the unfinished likenesses of her two sons, signifying their private, filial character (fig. 2). Beale also produced a number of incomplete small-scale studies in oils of the boys individually, as well as several of her studio assistants and her husband Charles. From one of the latter's notebooks we learn that these works were done by his wife for her 'study and improvement',[4] though 'friendship' – a term with far broader reach in the seventeenth and eighteenth centuries than now, and clearly of great importance to the Beales – must also have been a motivation. The same two reasons take us some way towards explaining the unfinished character of such a high proportion of Gainsborough's portraits of his near relations; but before developing this line of enquiry, we need to ask ourselves why he painted so many pictures of them (and himself) in the first place.

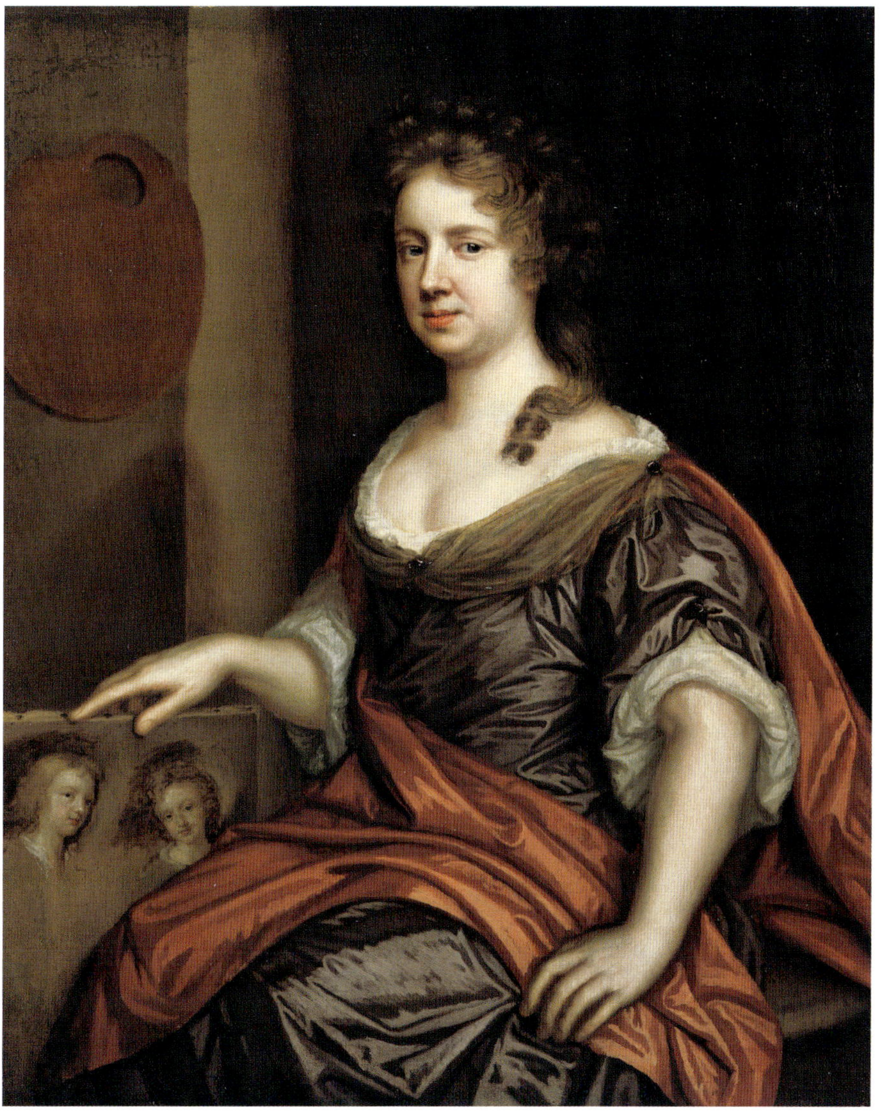

Mary Beale
Self-portrait, c.1665/6
Oil on canvas
1092 x 877mm

National Portrait Gallery,
London

Several interrelated factors – less personal, perhaps, than commercial and artistic – can help to explain his highly unusual behaviour.[5] To begin with, one key driver must simply have been the desire to secure social status. At a time in history when only a small minority of people could afford to have their portraits painted, to sit to a professional artist was implicitly to assert a claim to membership of an affluent and honourable elite. For the aristocracy and gentry, this was a straightforward matter of confirming an established position of dominance, but any 'middling' citizens with aspirations to gentility faced a considerable array of obstacles – prejudices that portraiture promised to help them overcome. The painters of portraits may have possessed the means to do so on their own behalf, but by comparison with other professional groups, the challenges they confronted were especially daunting. Not only did portraitists have to acquire a patina of good breeding if they were to secure the patronage of the beau monde, they also had to overcome the stigma attached to any paid employment that relied on a manual skill. Around the turn of the eighteenth century, the 3rd Earl of Shaftesbury revealed the class-driven basis of this

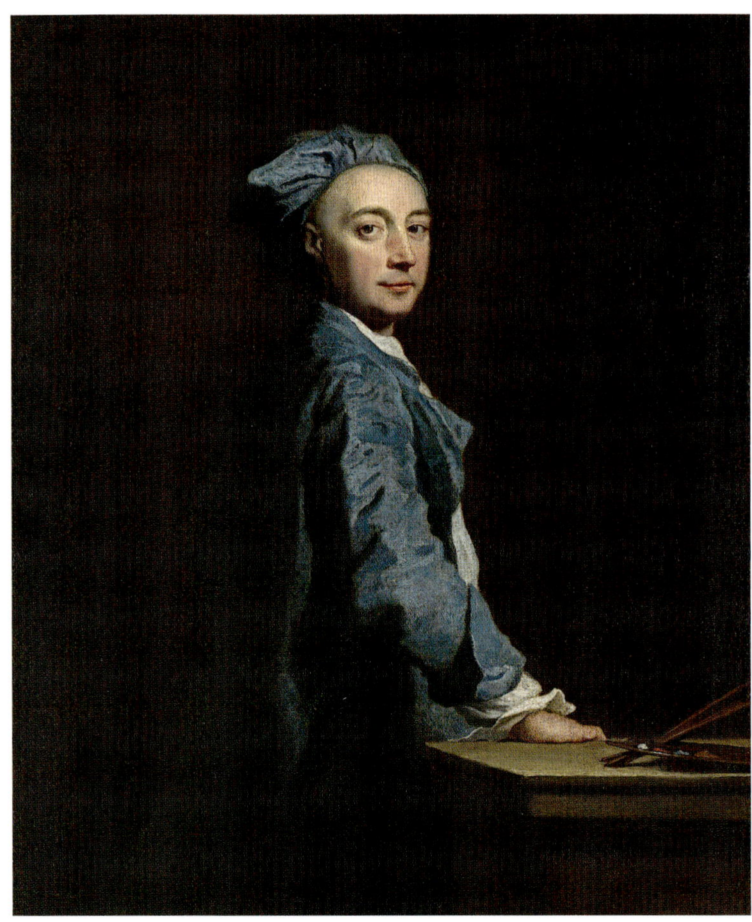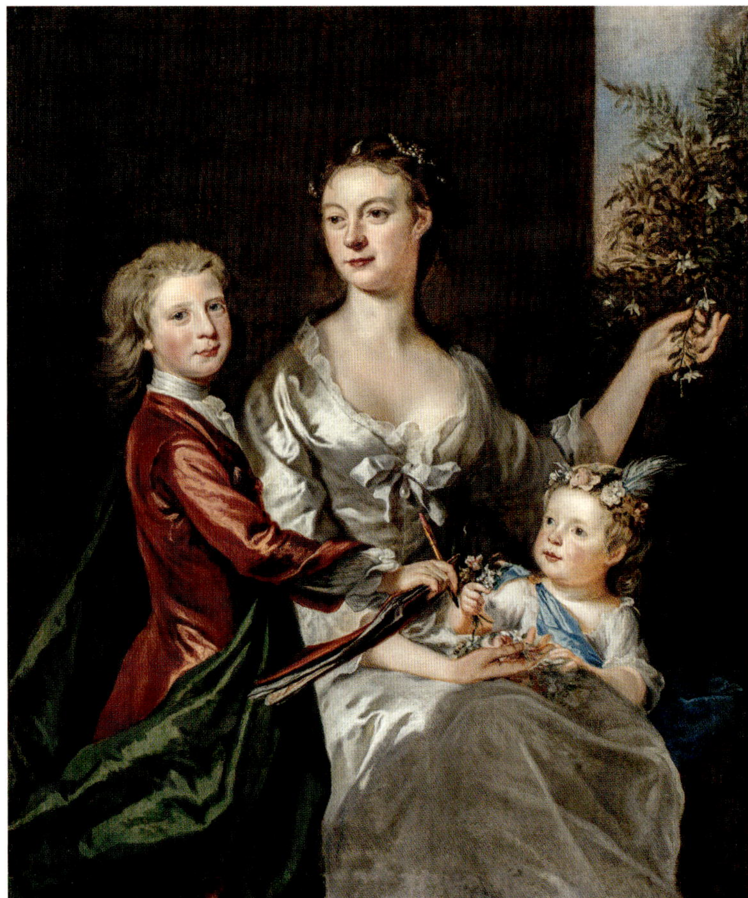

condescending attitude by expressing the commonly held view that portraiture was 'not so much a liberal art nor to be so esteemed, as requiring no liberal knowledge, genius, education, converse, manners, moral-science, mathematics, optics, but merely practical and vulgar'. This was because the 'mere face-painter … copies what he sees, and minutely traces every feature and odd mark. 'Tis otherwise with men of invention and design.'[6]

There was only a limited amount that British portraitists could do to change perceptions of their art as a fairly mundane exercise in copying the particular appearances of their subjects, or to remove it from the taint of both venality and flattery; but at least they could use their own talents to represent themselves – and their family members – in paint, and in so doing to fashion a visible argument for their genteel status.

Joseph Highmore offers the best case in point among artists of the generation previous to Gainsborough's. The well-educated son of a London coal merchant, Highmore initially trained as a lawyer, and in 1716 he married an heiress – factors that help to explain why he took such pains to project himself as being superior to the run-of-the-mill artist. These ambitions assumed a particularly striking visual form in a pair of half-length portraits that Highmore executed in the late 1720s, one showing himself sporting a turban and a matching blue satin banyan, a luxuriant dressing gown identified with an affluent man of leisure – while its pendant (companion-piece), which

FIG. 3
Joseph Highmore
Self-portrait, c.1727–8
Oil on canvas
1264 x 1010mm
National Gallery of Victoria, Melbourne

FIG. 4
Joseph Highmore
Susanna Highmore, the Artist's Wife, with their Children Anthony and Susanna, c.1727–8
Oil on canvas
1260 x 1017mm
Art Gallery of South Australia, Adelaide

positively shouts its reliance on the courtly art of Sir Anthony van Dyck, represents his wife and children in garb of equal elegance, albeit of markedly greater formality (figs 3, 4). Around two decades later, Highmore would follow up this family group with individual likenesses of his offspring (figs 5, 6). Here he depicts his son Anthony as a fine, well-mannered gentleman, bewigged and carrying a three-cornered hat under his arm at just the proper angle. His daughter Susanna, meanwhile, is shown bedecked in pearls, satin, and lace, but also (and rather more unusually) holding a portrait miniature – presumably of her own creation[7] – for the viewer's inspection, in an interior featuring numerous signs of an enlightened upbringing: a book of cut-out dolls, a wall-mounted toy theatre, two tortoiseshell cats on an ornate table, and a parrot in a cage. Elements of the same iconography, drawn from the northern European genre of fancy pictures (see page 48), would reappear not long afterwards in Gainsborough's depictions of his own daughters.

His and Highmore's circumstances were in fact not that dissimilar. Gainsborough also came from solid tradesman's stock; and although his father John (cats 1, 3), a clothes merchant turned postmaster, had gone bankrupt in the early 1730s, he had been prevented from falling into poverty by a wealthy nephew, who was evidently a man of considerable influence in the Suffolk locality.[8] Somewhat less is known about the background of the painter's mother, Mary, although the fact that her brother was a Cambridge-educated clergyman and the master of Sudbury grammar school (which in the 1730s counted the future painter among its pupils) suggests that her social status may have been somewhat higher than her husband's. More pertinently, perhaps, at the age of nineteen Thomas married Margaret Burr, an illegitimate daughter of the 3rd Duke of Beaufort. Margaret was not only in receipt of a £200 annuity from her father's family (from 1745 until her death), but the noble connection that she brought to the marriage was to assist in the advancement of Gainsborough's career.[9] Notwithstanding that illegitimacy carried a considerable stigma in eighteenth-century Britain, both money and aristocratic blood served as powerful counterweights, and there is evidence that Mrs Gainsborough took considerable pride in her ducal ancestry.

Whether or not her husband entirely shared these sentiments, the problematic circumstances of his wife's birth and his own parents' history of financial difficulty may well have contributed to the awareness he showed throughout his life of the importance of establishing his credentials as a gentleman – something considered essential for success as a portraitist, but also universally acknowledged as socially desirable. This helps to explain why, within two years of his marriage, and while still resident in London's Hatton Garden, Gainsborough elected to paint himself and his wife as individuals of quality, fashionably taking their ease in a tranquil rustic idyll. Soon afterwards he added the figure of their first child Mary, who died early in 1748 (cat. 2). Although the sheet of paper that Thomas holds in this portrait may originally have borne the traces of a sketch, all that would have signified within this context was a genteel interest in the arts rather than just denoting a professional man and his spouse. The couple's rural situation, relaxed poses

and fine clothing combine to convey the overwhelming impression that they
are the social equals of any of Gainsborough's wealthy landed patrons of the
late 1740s and early 1750s. Nevertheless, a closer inspection reveals certain
features that one would not expect to find in a commissioned portrait, starting
with the provocative glimpse through her muslin apron of the pink flesh
of Margaret Gainsborough's right calf. If this is one marker of the image's
private character (and of the risqué sensibility that colours more than one
of Gainsborough's surviving letters), another is the fact that the picture was
never finished. Note especially the numerous visible pentimenti (revisions) in
and around the figure of the artist's wife, the unresolved passages in her (and
her daughter's) arms and feet, and the absence of her left hand. Although the
young Gainsborough is known to have sold at least one portrait with a detail
left to be resolved,[10] surely no paying customer would have accepted a painted
likeness that was so obviously incomplete.

Of the next six paintings to enter the 'family album', all from
Gainsborough's time in Ipswich (1752–58/9), only two are finished to a
degree found in his contemporary commissioned portraits.[11] Presumably,
it is not coincidental that these works – depicting his cousin the Reverend
Henry Burrough and his niece Susan Gardiner (cats 8, 10) – are also
alone in representing relations from outside the artist's immediate family
(including his siblings). As works that were destined to assume their place
in the world outside his studio, these portraits had to meet the standards
conventionally expected of the genre. Indeed, Burrough later commissioned
a copy (more slickly polished than the original) that he presented, by way
of self-promotion, to his old Cambridge college.[12] It is impossible to know
whether Gainsborough volunteered his services to his clerical kinsman –
perhaps with a view to advertising his talents among the members of the
Reverend's circle[13] – or if it was the sitter who took the initiative. Likewise,
there is no telling whether Susanna Gardiner (cat. 42) asked her brother to
paint a portrait of her daughter, or if it was his spontaneous decision to do
so, perhaps as a parting gift for his sister on the eve of his move to Bath.[14] On
either or both occasions a reciprocal obligation may well have been involved,
as we know happened in other instances when Gainsborough refused payment
for a portrait.[15] In eighteenth-century Britain it was customary practice for
members of tradesmen's families to exchange goods and services with one
another on a contractual basis,[16] and the surviving evidence suggests that the
Gainsboroughs were no exception.

Apart from a profile of his brother Humphrey (cat. 7), finished to a
reasonably high level except in the area of the linen cravat, the other family
portraits that survive from Gainsborough's time in Ipswich are of himself
and his daughters, and he left all of these in an incomplete state (cats 4, 9,
11). The sole self-portrait in oils never progressed much beyond the study of
a head and a three-cornered hat on a bare expanse of primed canvas. All we
see below the artist's neck is a series of deft brushstrokes in black, brown and
blue that roughly approximate the forms of the upper body, with a dash of
white cuff to indicate the conventional hand-in-waistcoat pose. At a stage in

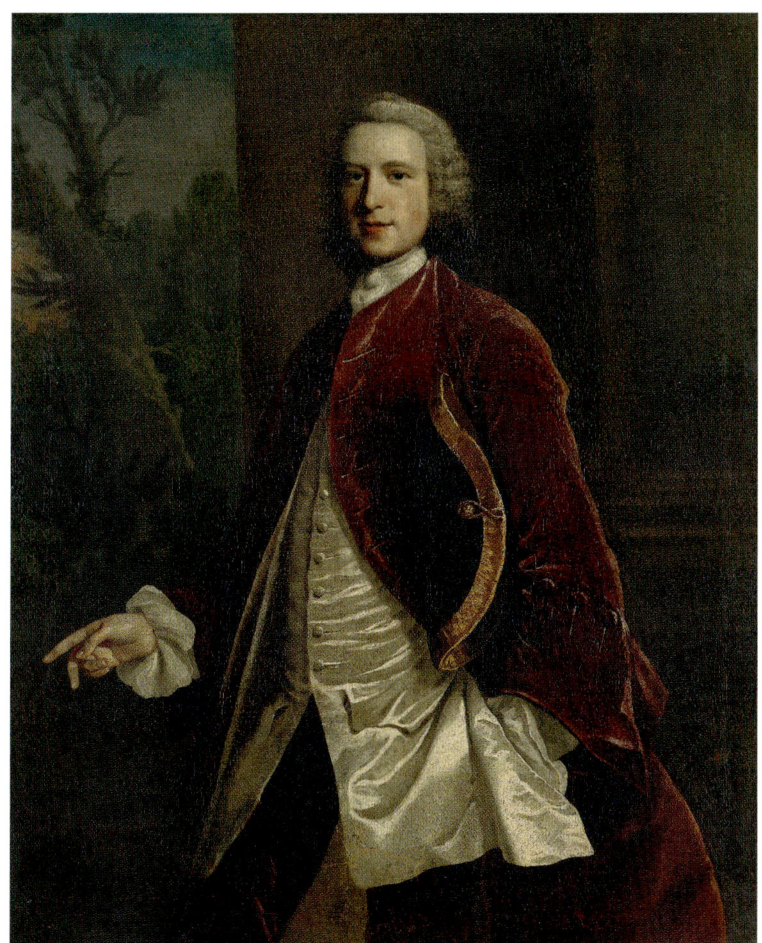

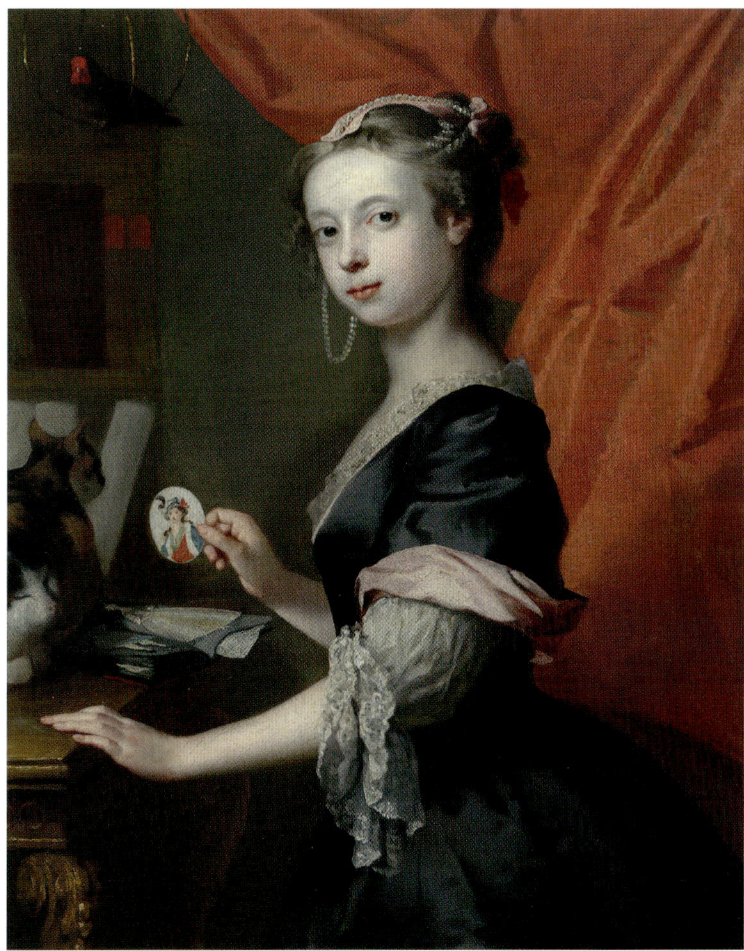

his career when Gainsborough was making the transition from 'painting in little' to portraiture on the scale of life, this self-portrait probably served as a useful training exercise. To have taken it any further would have been a waste of valuable time far better spent on the commissioned side of his portrait business.

The absence of any economic imperative, allied with a desire to expand his artistic repertoire, may likewise help to explain why Gainsborough evidently devoted so much thought and effort to the earliest double portrait of his daughters (cat. 9), but neglected to bring the picture to completion. Although this may not have been his first attempt to depict two sitters in a single composition on something approaching the scale of life,[17] he had never previously tried to show such figures moving through a landscape. Both the ensemble and its manner of execution embodied a radical departure from the far smaller, more static and much more tightly painted conversation pieces he was producing for his Suffolk paying clientele. As more than one scholar has observed,[18] when fashioning likenesses of his nearest and dearest, Gainsborough enjoyed the freedom to experiment. Liberated from the tyranny of patronage, he could pursue novel effects and technical challenges that interested him as an artist, and that he could later incorporate into his commissioned work. On this occasion it was the integration of figures into nature that would provide one of the key foundations for Gainsborough's mature approach to portraiture, together with a freedom of handling (in his word, 'pencilling') that he would go on to develop as arguably *the* defining hallmark of his signature style.

Of course there can be no denying that *The Artist's Daughters Chasing a Butterfly* (cat. 9) is also a deeply affectionate image; in eighteenth-century middling families sentiment and usefulness went hand in hand, and often sustained one another. On this occasion, the use to which Gainsborough put a picture of the girls he fondly referred to as 'Molly and the Captain' went beyond providing him with an opportunity for artistic innovation; for instead of retaining what to our eyes looks like a highly personal memento, he apparently let go of it before leaving Ipswich for Bath in the autumn of 1759. Somewhere around that point this large, unfinished portrait of a provincial artist's children became the property of the Reverend Robert Hingeston, the headmaster of Ipswich School – just the sort of person who could well have appreciated the composition's moral message, as Ann Bermingham has observed.[19] Other scholars have suggested that Hingeston may have purchased the canvas[20] as a modern fancy picture, but this seems unlikely. While Gainsborough's sale of his household goods just prior to his departure did include 'some PICTURES, original DRAWINGS in the Landskip way',[21] it is almost inconceivable that an artist 'desirous of leaving' a good impression on his 'friends' would have set a price on a painting of his daughters – never mind one in an incomplete state – or that anyone would have thought such an object worth paying for. The idea that *Chasing a Butterfly* was presented gratis to a close acquaintance and next-door neighbour makes far more sense, especially since the Hingestons were prominent members of a community to which Gainsborough wished to retain close ties even after leaving Ipswich.

The artist's gift of so personal a painting would also have been entirely in keeping with contemporary attitudes towards generosity, especially on the part of tradesmen. In *The Apprentice's Vade Mecum; or Young Man's Travel Companion*, first published in 1734, the printer and soon-to-be bestselling novelist Samuel Richardson strongly advised his readers always to put their own interest first, 'yet that you should so pursue it as should shew you were not sordidly attached to it, so as to be incapable of a generous Action, when it will be of little or no *Prejudice* to your self. This conduct will engage your many Friends, who, as they grow up with you into Life and Business, may be of very great Service to you. You will also hereby gain the name of a *generous* and *Gentleman-like* Man.'[22] Gainsborough would have lost little by giving away the picture of his daughters, and (apart from ridding himself of the inconvenience of having to transport it to Bath) may well have gained much more in return. He was to make a lifetime habit of bestowing pictures on his friends (cat. 26 being another example), and while it would be quite wrong to suggest that he did so with a cynical view to 'reflect[ing] Honour' on his 'Name and Family', he belonged to a world where generous actions lost none of their moral value if they also brought reputational benefits to the giver.

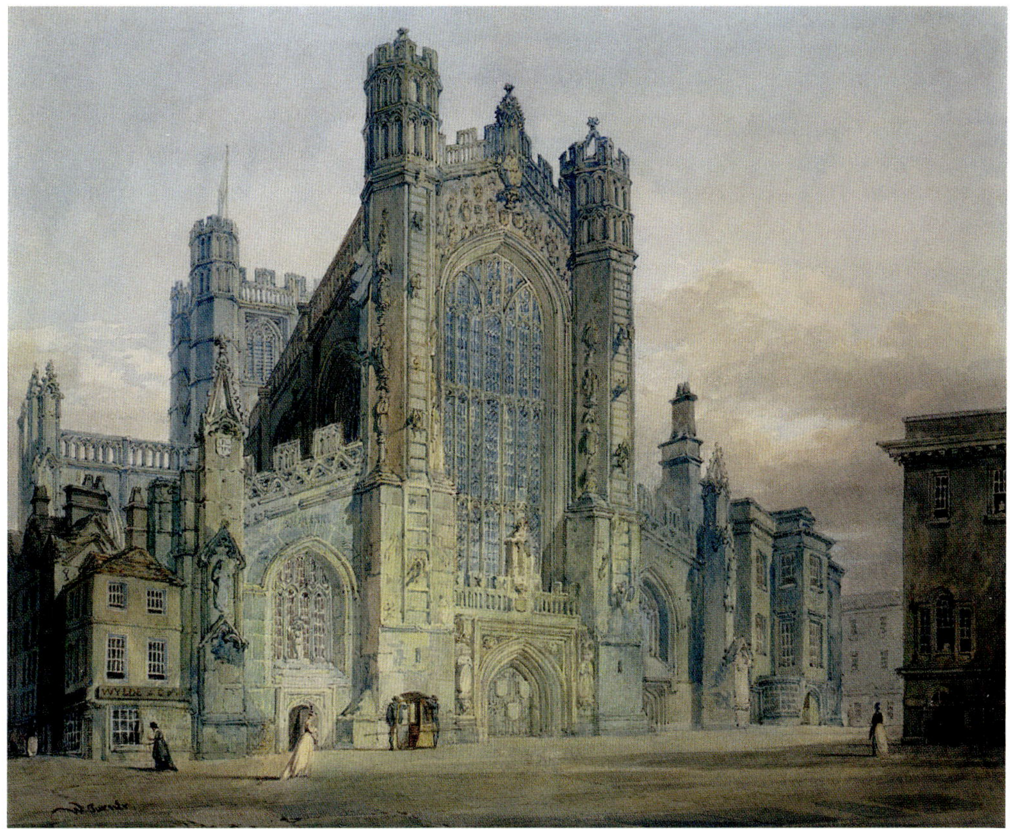

In 1750s England, as William Hogarth's friend Jean André Rouquet observed at the time, no portraitist could have any realistic expectation of succeeding with the highest levels of society unless he or she gained acceptance as a 'person of distinction'.[23] Rouquet identified the essential prerequisites to achieving this end as 'some powerful friend', a 'fine house' and exuding an 'air of importance and superiority' over rival artists – all things Gainsborough knew full well. After settling in Bath, he set about building a patronage network by exploiting his wife's links to the Duke of Beaufort, and within a year had taken on the lease of a splendid Abbey Street house, right in the centre of town (fig. 7). In the nation's premier spa resort, public image counted for everything, so it cannot be coincidental that Gainsborough executed his first finished portraits of himself and his wife just around the time of their arrival (cats 12, 13, now split between London and Berlin).

There are several features of these two 'three-quarter' (i.e. 762 x 635mm; 30 x 25") canvases that lend support to the hypothesis that they were conceived with a view to promoting the couple's efforts to establish themselves in a competitive new marketplace. Most obviously, perhaps, they represent the painter and his spouse as 'persons of distinction' – that is to say, as socially on a par with Bath's affluent, cosmopolitan clientele. Thus, just as he had done four or five years earlier in Ipswich (cat. 4), Gainsborough chose to depict himself not as an artist, but as a well-dressed country gentleman, whose standard hand-in-waistcoat pose is a model of refined deportment. However, the transfer of his hat from his head to the crook of his arm suggests a more

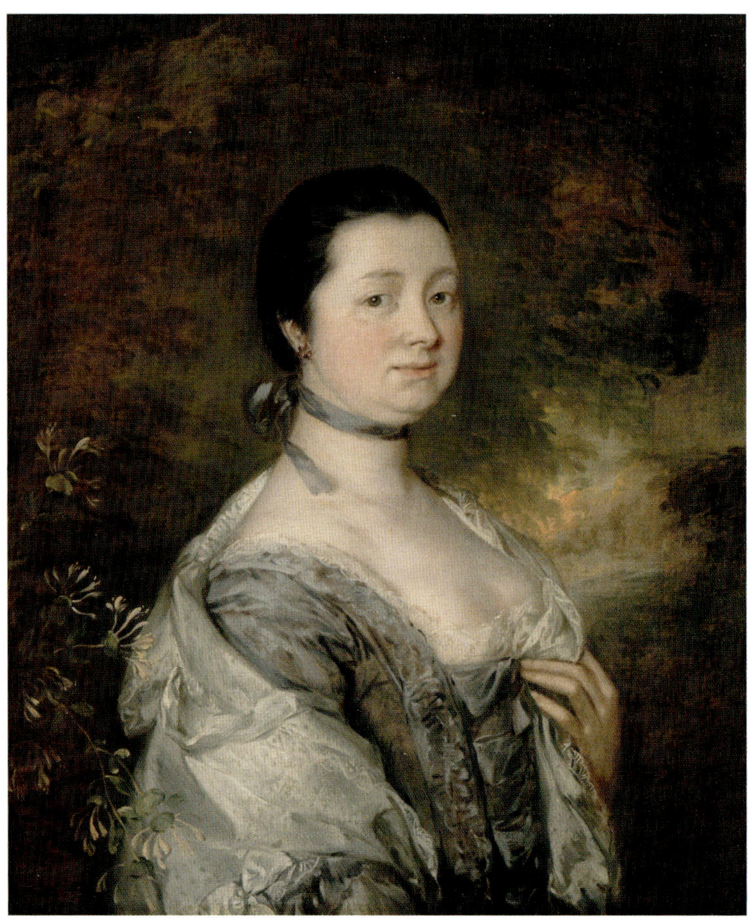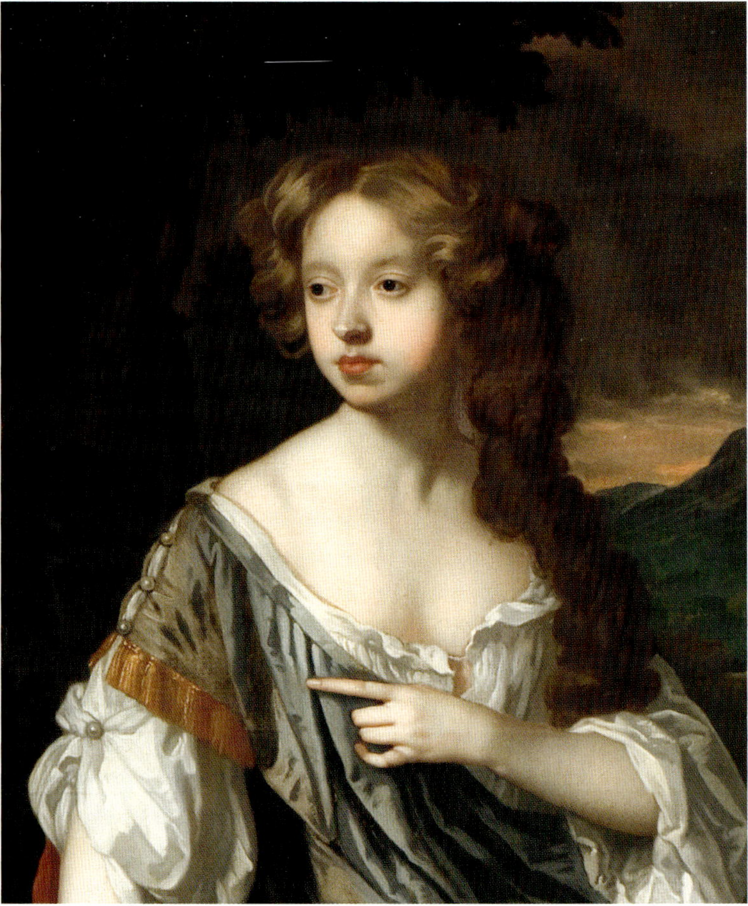

formal encounter with the viewer – an impression further reinforced by the painting's fully finished state. Seen alongside – or, more likely, opposite or below[24] – the image of her husband, the portrait of his wife (fig. 8) presented her to visitors as an opulently dressed lady of high rank, reminiscent of the courtly beauties immortalised by Sir Peter Lely (fig. 9) or Van Dyck; her sensuality is underlined by the presence of honeysuckle, a flower traditionally symbolic of love. Neither of these pendants hints even obliquely at the fact that together they represent the joint operators of a successful commercial business that would soon expand to letting rooms (in their Abbey Street premises), as well as the production and sale of works of art. Around a decade later, Thomas's friend Philip Thicknesse would describe the artist as someone who 'knows, as well how to act, and think, like a gentleman, as he does to contemn and despise those who dare to treat him in any other light'.[25] We can sense something of the same steely determination from Gainsborough's letters, and from the only pair of portraits he ever completed of Margaret and himself.

Another, more mundane function of these two pictures may have been to convince potential sitters of their creator's ability to achieve a good likeness. By the middle of the eighteenth century it had become a well-established practice among British portraitists to decorate the parlours or showrooms where they received their clients with pictures of people who were bound to be recognised, even if the painter ran the risk of being criticised for failing to get their features right. Gainsborough quickly proved himself a master of this particular gambit. By early December 1758, barely two months after he had initially arrived in Bath to test out the marketplace, he was already gaining plaudits for the accuracy of his portraiture: 'We have a painter here,' the poet William Whitehead wrote to Viscount Nuneham, 'who takes the most exact likenesses I ever saw. … [His] name is Gainsborough.'[26] Further confirmation of this point comes from the miniaturist Ozias Humphry, who was based in Bath from 1760 to 1764. Many years later Humphry recalled that, 'Exact resemblance in his Portraits … was Mr Gainsborough's constant Aim, to which he invariably adhered'[27] – and of which he frequently boasted to his patrons. He could hardly have devised a more effective means to flaunt his confidence in his own mimetic powers than by displaying the painted replicas of his own and his wife's features in immediate proximity to the living originals.

The pendants of Thomas and Margaret would also have been well suited to serve as templates for commissioned works, and appear to have done so with considerable success.[28] Perhaps more than anything else, what made them effective as sample commodities was an astute blending of familiarity and innovation; that is to say, they would have told potential customers that Gainsborough knew how to compose modestly sized portraits in a reassuringly conventional way, but that he also brought something new to the mix. While the idea of posing a half-length figure within a natural setting was hardly without precedent, the novelty of Gainsborough's portrait-in-a-landscape lay in his ability to merge the format's two constituent elements into a unified whole through the skilful orchestration of colouring and chiaroscuro. If the *Thomas* and the *Margaret Gainsborough* each conveyed this point on its own, they would have done so with even greater force when seen together. Simultaneously, though, the same juxtaposition also highlighted the stylistic differences between Gainsborough's likenesses of men and women. For his male sitters, to infer from the evidence of the self-portrait, the artist could be expected to employ the broad brushwork and sober colouring that by the 1750s had come to be identified as the characteristically 'English' way of painting established by Sir Godfrey Kneller, and subsequently championed by William Hogarth. This approach was further associated with the qualities of plainness and manliness, in contrast to the delicate, fluttering, 'feminine' manner commonly identified with contemporary French art, with which the Berlin *Margaret Gainsborough* asked to be compared.

It is this portrait of the artist's wife, to a greater extent than her husband's, that showcases the salient features of what Gainsborough would go on to develop as his signature style. Its foundations lay in his visible commitment to painting each of his portraits in its entirety – i.e. not just the head, but the clothing and background as well – instead of following the conventional practice (as adopted by Sir Joshua Reynolds, for example) of assigning these secondary elements to one or more hired specialists. While Gainsborough's approach may have added to his workload, it also gave him the opportunity to express his own artistic identity within the constrained arena of commissioned portraiture. This was achieved less through the treatment of

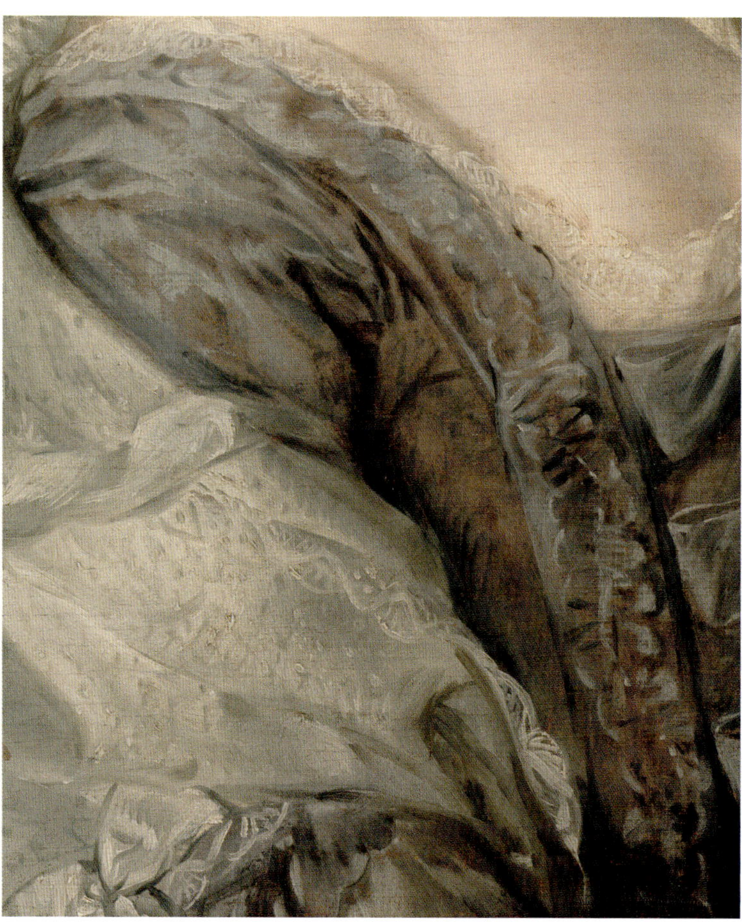

his sitters' facial features, where the tyranny of likeness held sway, than in his rendering of landscape elements and the ornate forms of female dress. As a modern art historian has perceptively observed, it is not just in the natural settings of his portraits that Gainsborough parades his 'loose, confident virtuoso handling'; the 'collective inventory of [women's] fashionable attire' is another 'pictorial terrain where he foregrounds his emphatic marks, where the seductive and substantial daubs, scribbles, streaks and stains announce … that we are looking at a painting – indeed a painting by Gainsborough'(fig. 10).[29]

After his long-time rival's death some thirty years later, Reynolds would speak with admiration (mixed with a certain unease) of those 'odd scratches and marks, which, on a close examination, are so observable in Gainsborough's pictures'[30] and that the early *Margaret Gainsborough* may well have introduced to his Bath clientele. A comparison with the artist's commissioned female portraits from the years immediately following suggests that he initially had difficulty persuading his paying customers that such free handling was acceptable in a finished portrait. Leaving large areas of reddish-brown ground visible through thin layers of coloured pigment, as found throughout the blues of Margaret's dress, was not what artists were supposed to do. No wonder that Whitehead characterised Gainsborough's painting as 'coarse and slight'; 'but', he went on to add, it 'has ease and spirit'.[31]

The rather more ambivalent phrase that Reynolds would use to describe the same visual qualities was 'the appearance of chance and hasty negligence'. This he recognised as – paradoxically – the hard-won reward of many years of 'diligence', including countless evenings Gainsborough devoted to his favourite pastime of drawing landscapes. [32] Even before leaving Ipswich, he had begun to seek out ways of transferring the freedom he enjoyed as a landscape draughtsman into his commissioned portraiture, and ultra-fashionable Bath, with its culture of spectacular social display, seems to have inspired a redoubled effort on his part to imbue the society portrait with what he called a 'Variety of lively touches and surprising Effects to make the Heart dance'.[33] If figure drawing and landscape painting helped Gainsborough achieve this aim, so too did his continuing experiments with group portraiture, using members of his family as his subjects.

At some point around 1760 he appears to have toyed with the idea of executing a grand full-length of Margaret holding each of her daughters by the hand, but this probably never progressed beyond the stage demarcated by a single drawing (cat. 14), which is all that survives of Gainsborough's second and last attempt to portray his wife in her maternal role. On a much more considerable scale, and of much greater consequence, are the two roughly contemporaneous double portraits of the girls (cats 15, 16), along with the fragment of a third (cat. 17). We can only speculate as to the reasons why this cluster of unfinished oils came into being at this particular juncture, perhaps just after the family moved into their grand Abbey Street residence in June 1760. While it is tempting to conclude that Gainsborough created these works solely for reasons of private pleasure when he had time to spare, the early history of *The Artist's Daughters Chasing a Butterfly* (cat. 9) leaves open the possibility that its Bath-period successors may also have enjoyed a degree of public exposure, perhaps as a demonstration of their creator's technical virtuosity. Although Reynolds had Gainsborough's later finished works in mind, few, if any, eighteenth-century British portraits more eloquently project 'the appearance of chance and hasty negligence' than *The Artist's Daughters Playing with a Cat* (cat. 16) or *Margaret Gainsborough … as a Gleaner* (cat. 17).

These experiments with the unfinished also need to be understood in the context of Gainsborough's growing interest in developing a public style expressive of effortless ease – an aesthetic rooted in the Italian Renaissance idea of *sprezzatura*. Originally coined by Baldassare Castiglione in *The Book of the Courtier* (1528) as a way of describing the nonchalant performance of exquisite manners by the noble attendants to a prince, this notion soon entered into pan-European artistic discourse as a means of describing how the dazzling and seemingly careless brushwork of painters such as Titian, Rubens, Velázquez and Van Dyck brought the forms of nature to life.[34] The opposite of excessive diligence, *sprezzatura* in art came to be prized by connoisseurs, who associated it with the Italian term *non finito* (sketchiness), and with a fluid painting technique that highlighted a master's quasi-magical ability to conjure up natural appearances with just a few quick strokes of the brush. Such an

achievement on Gainsborough's part went hand in hand with his ongoing
efforts to promote himself as both an artist and a gentleman.

Perhaps the single greatest hindrance to those efforts lay in portraiture
itself, which, as the demand for the painter's services grew steadily during
the 1760s, left him feeling increasingly frustrated by the constraints imposed
upon him by those 'damn Gentlemen'[35] and ladies who pestered him for
sittings. 'If the People with their damnd Faces would but let me alone a
little,' he lamented to his friend James Unwin in 1768.[36] However, the same
circumstances also prompted him to speed up the production process, a
change that offered Gainsborough the further advantage of diverting attention
away from the subjects of his portraits in favour of highlighting the masterful
character of his art. In this enterprise the members of his family – and one
member in particular – had a particularly important role to play.

In 1772 Gainsborough took on the only apprentice he would ever employ
– his nephew Gainsborough Dupont. The son of the artist's sister Sarah and
her husband, the carpenter Philip Dupont (cats 38, 39), the boy is reported
to have joined his uncle's household at an early age, perhaps (as was then
common) under the terms of an oral agreement stipulating an exchange of
his labour for room, board and clothing. At the age of seventeen he signed
the articles of indenture that initiated a seven-year term of formal training,
for which he paid the token sum of five shillings (at a time when £20–£30
seems to have been the normal minimum). But within three years, after he
had moved with the family to London, and a few months before entering the
Royal Academy Schools, Dupont's role appears to have evolved into that of
a paid studio assistant,[37] an arrangement that would remain in place until
Thomas's death fourteen years later. There are numerous aspects of their
familial-cum-business relationship that are worthy of comment, none more
curious than the fact that Gainsborough produced at least five portraits (four
painted, one drawn) of his nephew over a period of around five years, from
the early to mid 1770s.

What may well be the earliest picture in this sequence is a small, unfinished
head study (cat. 48 and see page 37). Far better known at the time of its
production, however, was an oval bust-length image of Dupont wearing blue
Van Dyck dress (now at Waddesdon Manor, Buckinghamshire; cat. 26),[38]
which Philip Thicknesse would later single out, just after Gainsborough's
death, as one of the artist's outstanding achievements: 'the finest head he ever
painted, was that of his nephew, Mr. Dupont, and that was never touched but
once, and that once the work of one hour. … [The picture] is in the possession
of Lord Bateman, to whom I had the honor to present it, for the instant I saw
it, I asked for it, and there was nothing I could ask of Gainsborough, which
he could give (*except my own Portrait*) that he would have refused me.'[39] A
letter written by Thicknesse fifteen years previously shows just how impressed
he had been on first seeing the painting: 'Gainsbro has given me a head of his
young Nephew painted I think better than ever Painter painted one before – it
is more like the work of God than man, the face tho very like has a Divine
Countenance'[40] (fig. 11).

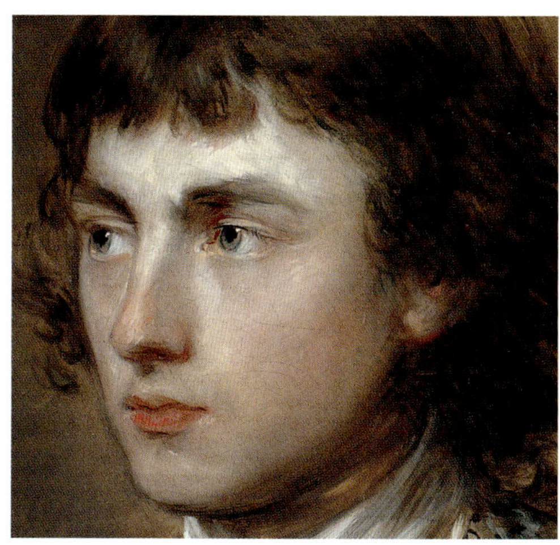

Thomas Gainsborough
Gainsborough Dupont,
the Artist's Nephew, 1773
(detail)
Oil on canvas
520 x 390mm
Waddesdon (Rothschild Family)

What this fascinating account tells us, amongst other things, is that Dupont's presence in the studio offered his uncle a useful opportunity once again to prove to his clients that his powers as 'your Likeness Man'[41] remained without parallel. But the image itself, supported by Thicknesse's reference to its 'Divine Countenance', suggests that Gainsborough was also aiming to demonstrate something more: how his creative powers could give a common (albeit strikingly handsome) apprentice the 'divine' air of a seventeenth-century aristocrat, and in so doing elevate portraiture to the level of great art. He must have been pleased to see these claims gain Thicknesse's immediate endorsement, and no less delighted to learn of the painting's subsequent acquisition by the 2nd Viscount Bateman, a great favourite of George III, who may well have supported Gainsborough's efforts to gain royal patronage after moving to London in 1774. By then (or shortly afterwards)[42] the picture had found a prestigious home in the Batemans' well-appointed residence on the corner of Park Lane – not because its owners cared a fig about Dupont, but because they wished to demonstrate their taste for Gainsborough, and for modern painting at its finest.

What made the oval of *Dupont* all the more remarkable was that it had reputedly been executed in a single hour[43] – a performance that effectively earned Gainsborough the right to attach his name to a long and noble line of virtuoso British portraitists who had 'painted with an amazing quickness',[44] reaching back through Sir Godfrey Kneller to the 'swift hand'[45] of Van Dyck himself. On its own, the fast and fluid manner of the picture's brushwork may well have prompted comparisons with the seventeenth-century Flemish master's 'thin brilliant pencilling style';[46] but even for viewers with minimal expertise, the artistic origins of Dupont's costume and luxuriant curls would have been easy to identify. Moreover, this was not the first such exercise that Gainsborough had attempted: three years earlier he had publicly announced his ambitions to emulate Van Dyck by exhibiting the 'Portrait of a Young Gentleman' – almost certainly the work now known as *The Blue Boy* (fig. 12) – to great acclaim at the Royal Academy. It may well be that *The Blue Boy* also represents Dupont, though the case for that identification remains tantalisingly inconclusive.[47]

With the Waddesdon oval of Dupont, however, there can be absolutely no doubt that we are dealing with a picture from the 'family album' which almost immediately lost its familial connotations, and – once it had left the painter's studio – assumed a quite different, entirely *artistic* identity. The same cannot be said of the half a dozen or so other portraits of Gainsborough's relations that he is believed to have painted towards the end of his time in Bath. All of these are simple head-and-shoulders compositions, none on a canvas larger than the standard three-quarter size that Gainsborough used for the smallest of his commissioned likenesses; indeed, a few are considerably smaller. Judging from the consistently summary treatment of forms – the sitters' faces only partially excepted – it is doubtful that any of these pictures took much time to produce. This is hardly surprising, perhaps, given that the painter was not being paid for his labours, and was struggling to cope with the pressures of a thriving

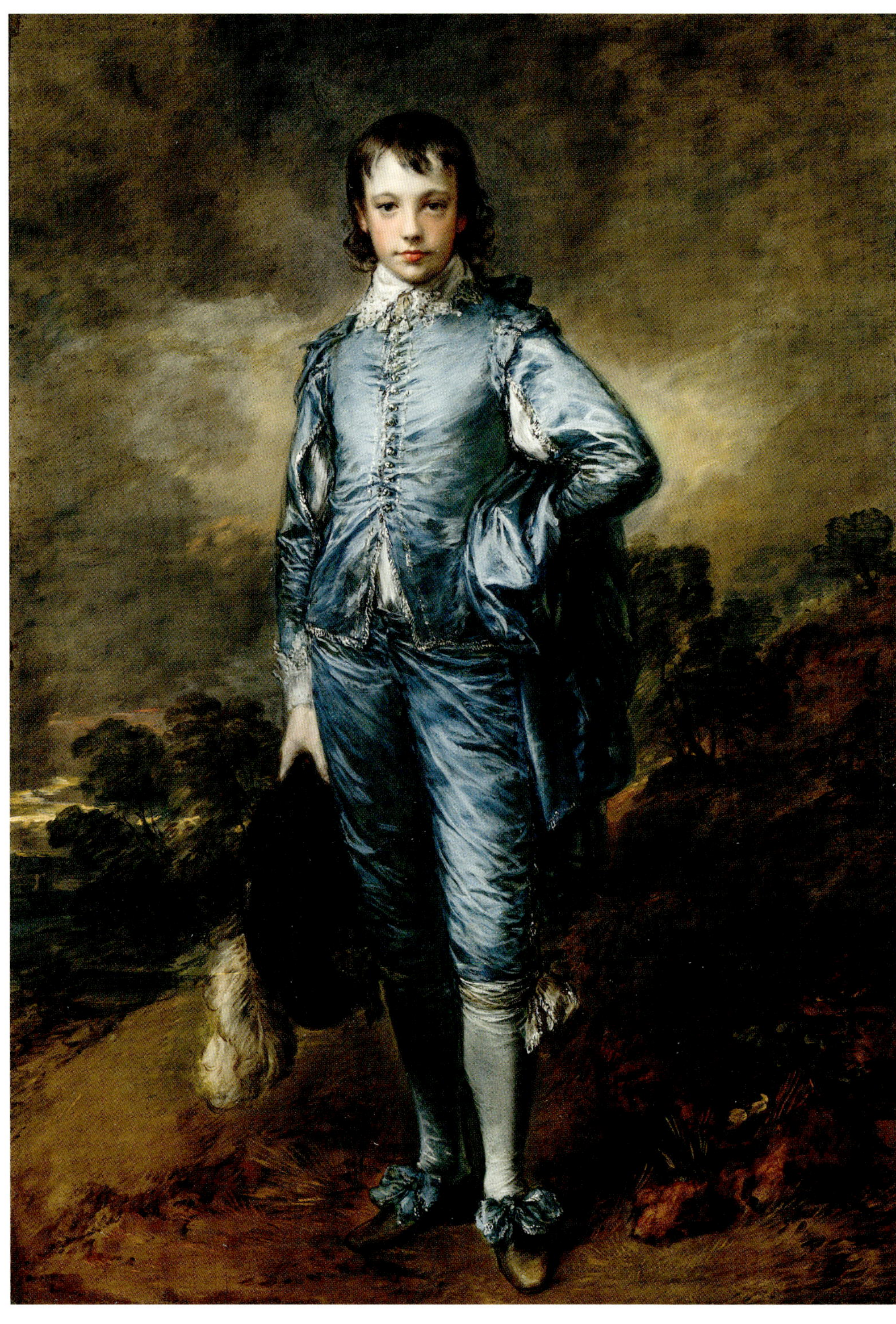

portrait business of which he had grown increasingly tired. Having been appointed a founding member of the Royal Academy in 1768, Gainsborough was by now firmly established as one of Britain's leading artists, and as a public figure of considerable importance. Thus, it is only to be expected that various family members wished to bask in his reflected glory by having him paint their pictures to display on their walls. Given that kinship in eighteenth-century Britain entailed expectations of solidarity and mutual support, Gainsborough may well have felt himself duty-bound to put his brush in the service of his siblings and a few more far-flung connections. The unfinished passages present in so many of these likenesses also point to affection, as opposed to money, being the artist's motivation. Certainly, it is hard to imagine why else he took the time to portray Fox and Tristram, the family's pet dogs, as an amusing study in contrasting canine characters (cats 23, 41).

One suspects that Gainsborough approached the task of painting what would prove to be the final double portrait of his daughters (cat. 30) with feelings of a far more complicated nature. As Ann Bermingham observes (see page 55), this is his only properly finished painting of Mary and Margaret – it is easy to imagine them nagging him to get it done! – as well as the sole example that looks to all intents and purposes like one of their father's commissioned works. Pointedly absent now, for the first time in the entire sequence of six images going back to the sisters' childhood, is any sense of Gainsborough's emotional intimacy with his offspring. What we encounter instead is the rather stiff formality expected of a grand likeness at whole length. Such a portrait would undoubtedly have looked at home in the opulent setting of Schomberg House in Pall Mall, where the family took up residence in the autumn of 1774.

The move from Bath to London brought with it a rise in prominence and status that appears to have prompted a corresponding shift in the character of subsequent additions to the 'family album' (though there are certain exceptions). In Gainsborough Dupont's case, the Van Dyck dress and flowing locks modelled by the teenaged apprentice give way to the fine tailoring and powdered wig of an urbane young gentleman (cat. 32 and fig. 36). Similarly, his first five years back in the capital also saw Gainsborough produce what is arguably the most complex of all the portraits of his wife, possibly to mark the occasion of her fiftieth birthday, in 1777 (cat. 34).

By then, around twenty years may have passed since Margaret had last sat to her husband for a depiction in oils, and he seized the opportunity to produce what can be described as both a deeply personal record and a likeness of exceptional intellectual ambition.[48] In both respects the image is not quite like any other in his portrait oeuvre. Although Gainsborough often exploited the bust-length format to create the fiction of an intimate encounter between sitter and spectator, the prerequisite of 'modesty' as a social norm for respectable women demanded that such intimacy be qualified. Consequently, most comparable commissioned portraits by the artist either show their subjects turned (or at least glancing) slightly to one side, or – more typically – they place the sitter within an illusionistic painted oval, which keeps the spectator at a distance. But, on this occasion, Gainsborough has arranged his wife's hands, head and drapery to suggest the presence of that feigned oval, and in so doing has given her an air of unusual immediacy that is reinforced by the frontality of her gaze. In eighteenth-century England, women were meant to reserve this sort of look exclusively for their spouses. 'I would have the husband firmly persuaded,' Eliza Haywood advised married women in a conduct book of 1773, 'that his bride has a great fund of tenderness in her

heart [but that she is incapable of] bestow[ing] the least part of it on any
other than himself.'[49] In the Courtauld portrait, Margaret Gainsborough
seems perfectly 'composed' to play this role. Holding back her black satin
and lace cloaking to reveal her face, with just perhaps the hint of a smile, her
expression of tenderness is both limited and temporary, a moment of intimacy
that functions only to dramatise a commitment to modesty, which is signified
by the enclosing mantle and the concealing bows.

This is the 'story' the image tells, of an action poised uncertainly between
veiling and unveiling, performed by a matronly yet fashionable wife for her
attentive painter-husband. But there is more to the portrait than that, for the
tranquil posture Margaret adopts – her right hand fingering the edge of her
mantilla while her left crosses her abdomen beneath – clearly derives from a
famous antique statue, the Vatican *Pudicity* (from the Latin *pudicitia*, meaning
'modesty' or 'chastity'). In a book by the eighteenth-century historian Joseph
Spence, a copy of which we know Gainsborough had in his library, this
sculpture (fig. 13) is identified as a representation of Juno Matrona, Jupiter's
queen, 'who was antiently looked on as the great patroness of marriage and
a wedded life'. Yet while the Romans may have revered Juno as a paragon of
spousal virtue, according to Spence, her 'most obvious and striking character'
was 'that of an imperious haughty wife'.[50] Surely Gainsborough must have
been aware of the dual associations of the pose he had chosen, and of their
relevance to a woman whom he clearly loved, but whose 'Pride and insolence,
and eternal Obraiding [upbraiding] & reflections'[51] drove him at times to
distraction. Did Margaret have any idea that her portrait bore this deeply
ambivalent subtext? One suspects that her husband was having a gentle
private joke at her expense. Another target in his sights may well have been
his rival Reynolds, who had a habit – as Gainsborough did not – of enriching
his portraits with witty quotations from classical art.

According to an old family tradition of somewhat dubious reliability, was
that over the course of many years Gainsborough always painted his wife's
likeness on their wedding anniversary.[52] If this story contains a kernel of
truth, the period in question is likely to have coincided with the family's time
in London, from which five portraits in oils of Margaret can now be traced.
The last two of these, probably from the mid to late 1780s, are hardly bigger
than large miniatures, and both show her wearing a mob-cap, a head covering
worn indoors by fashionable wives of the period. But even more than the
domestic connotations of Mrs Gainsborough's headwear, it is the scale and
swift brushwork of these little images that demarcate them as intimate tokens
of the artist's affection for the 'Dear Good Wife'[53] who had managed his
accounts and put up with his foibles throughout the previous four decades.

By now, and with the two self-portraits that date from Gainsborough's
final years (cats 46, 47), his engagement with the 'family album' was nearly
at an end. But in 1788, when he realised that he had only a short time left
to live, the painter made one last curious intervention. Some thirty years
later his niece Sophia Lane recalled that 'on his easel when he died' was a
head of his nephew Gainsborough Dupont, which had since come into her

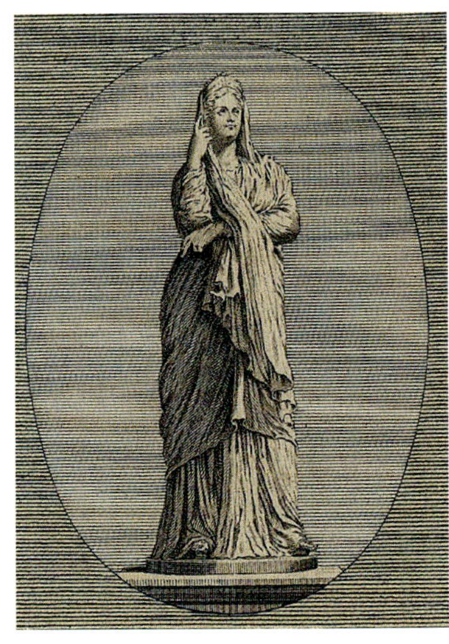

possession. As William T. Whitley, an early twentieth-century writer on art, was the first to point out, this can only have been the small unfinished study that over a century later found its way into the Tate's collection (cat. 48).[54] Here, both Dupont's youthful appearance and the stylistic evidence suggest that it is a product of the early 1770s (maybe with some later touches?), a fact that immediately prompts us to ask why the dying Gainsborough retrieved this seemingly unimportant canvas from the various old pictures presumably scattered around his studio, and gave it pride of place on his easel.

Of course it is possible that his action was of little or no consequence, nothing more than a step idly taken while the artist's painting room was closed to visitors, with the exception of a few intimates, among them Dupont himself. But given our knowledge of the great care that Gainsborough took in arranging the stage for his impending demise – for instance, by turning two of his self-portraits (probably cats 46, 47) to the wall, and specifying which of these was to be engraved for posterity[55] – a far stronger likelihood is that he was making a calculated gesture with a view to shaping the way he and his art would be remembered by posterity. But remembered how, exactly? The safest way to explore this highly speculative territory is to be guided by the small portrait of Dupont, and by three of its aspects in particular: its unfinished state, its allusions to Van Dyck, and the sitter's relationship to the artist.

Whether or not any of the brushstrokes that model Dupont's features or his clothing were actually applied by Gainsborough in his final days, the canvas, by virtue of its placement, assumed a deeply significant role – that of 'the last picture [he] ever painted'.[56] In so doing, it claimed its place within a long and illustrious history of painters' unfinished final works that had been objects of fascination going at least as far as back as the time of Pliny the Elder. The key passage in the English translation of Pliny's *Natural History* most commonly used in the eighteenth century reads as follows:

> But one thing more there is, of rare admiration and worthie to be remembred [sic], That the last peeces of excellent Painters, and namely such tables [i.e., pictures] as bee left unperfect, are commonly better esteemed than those that bee fully finished … for in these and such like imperfect tables, a man may (as it were) see what traicts [traits] and lineaments remayne to be done, as also the very desseignes and cogitations of the Artificers: and as these beginnings are attractive allurements to move us to commend those hands that began such Draughts: so the conceit that they now be dead and missing, is no small griefe to us … [57]

Of all the words in this well-known statement, it is the adjectives 'unperfect' and 'imperfect' that probably hold the key to understanding why Gainsborough chose the hasty sketch of Dupont to represent him at his passing. Earlier in his life, he may well have cherished such pictures for what they said about his boasted speed of execution, or the virtuosity of his brush. But during the final weeks of his illness, there is evidence that Gainsborough's unfinished paintings acquired a different significance in his eyes, as the objects of a melancholic awareness that, as an artist, he had failed to realise the full

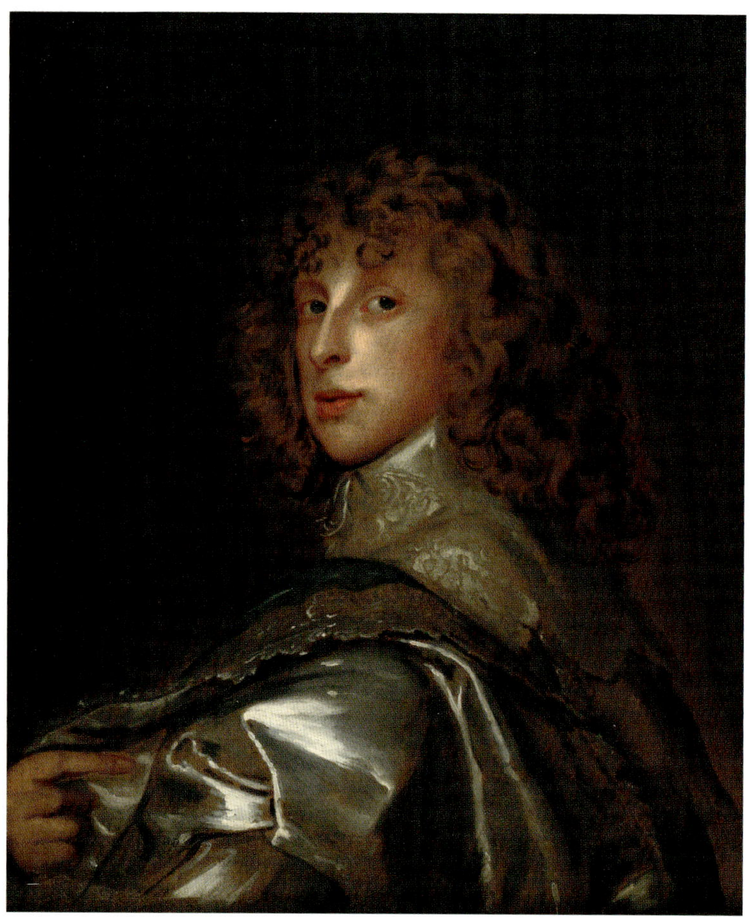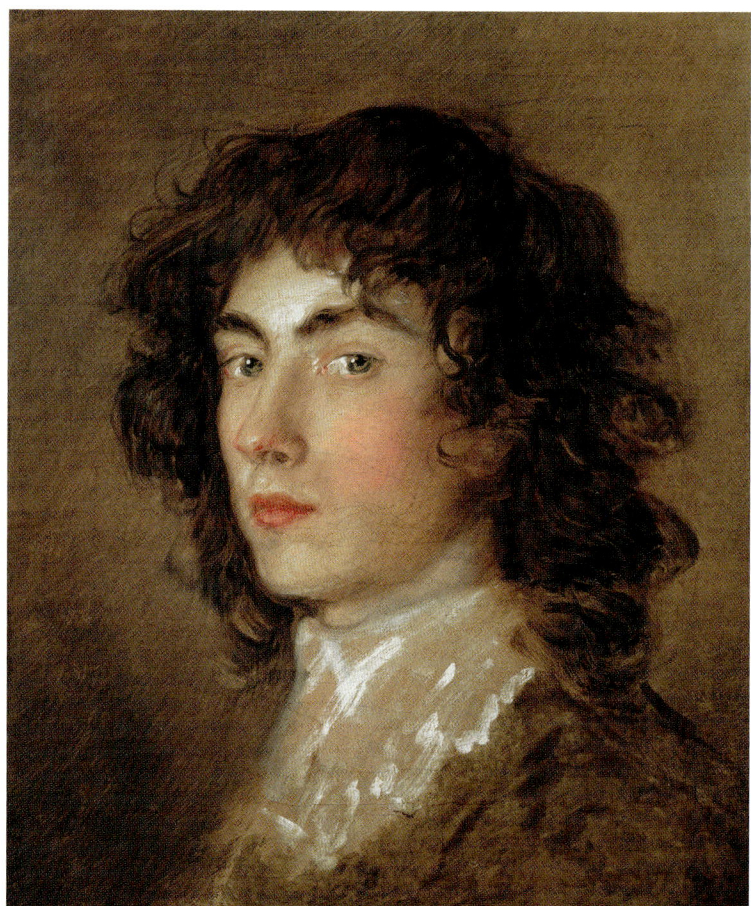

extent of his talents. During his last meeting with Reynolds, to whom he
had written to request a final conversation, Gainsborough confessed that his
principal 'regret at losing life' was 'the regret at leaving his art; and more
especially as he now began … to see what his deficiencies were'.[58] On the same
occasion, in July 1788, he is said to have had 'many of his unfinished canvases
brought to his bedside' so that he could discuss them with Reynolds.[59] It is
probably too much to hope that one of the works the two men talked about
was the little *Dupont*, yet it hardly matters whether or not that was the case.
For, even if encountered in isolation on the painter's easel, the incomplete
canvas of Gainsborough's nephew-cum-assistant would have made the dying
artist's poignant self-assessment clear enough: that at his death he still had
work remaining to be done.

More specifically, or so his 'last picture' was charged with communicating,
Gainsborough left it to posterity to judge how close he had come to fulfilling
his desire to stand beside Van Dyck among the ranks of the immortals.
The English painter's dying words may not quite have been 'We are all
going to heaven, and Van Dyck is of the company', as his friend William
Jackson would subsequently claim.[60] According to a more reliable source,
he simply stated, 'Van Dyck was right'.[61] In either case, however, there can
be no mistaking the essence of the sentiment. And surely it is the *Dupont*,
(fig. 15 and cat. 48) with its multiple allusions to both the manner and the

matter of Van Dyck's portraits (in particular to one he had copied more than once – fig. 14),[62] that provides by far the most eloquent confirmation of Gainsborough's terminal preoccupation with the Old Master whose art he had worshipped for so long.

But if the small portrait Gainsborough propped up in his soon-to-be deserted studio looked back to the art of the past, it also looked forward, to the anticipated continuation of his legacy by the only pupil he had ever taught, his sister's son. Gainsborough Dupont had been by his uncle's side for over fifteen years; he had learned to paint in his style; he had assisted him on several important commissions and would soon be tasked with completing some of the works left unfinished at his death (including one self-portrait, cat. 33); he would handle the sale of the contents of the studio; act as chief mourner at his funeral; inherit all his painting materials; and be buried alongside him in 1797. Hence it was only fitting that, at the end of his life, Gainsborough assigned Dupont's image a place of honour in his painting room, and in so doing anointed his long-time assistant as his artistic heir.[63] But the same gesture also served, intentionally or otherwise, to acknowledge a larger truth: that Thomas Gainsborough's own career had formed the centrepiece of a larger family business – a collective enterprise in which not just his nephew, but also his wife, his daughters, his sisters and other relations had had important parts to play. Nowadays, more often than not, we tend to think of artists as autonomous social actors; yet for all of Gainsborough's efforts to cultivate his own individuality, his 'family album' tells quite a different story of one painter's rise to fame, a tale in which he features as just one player among many.

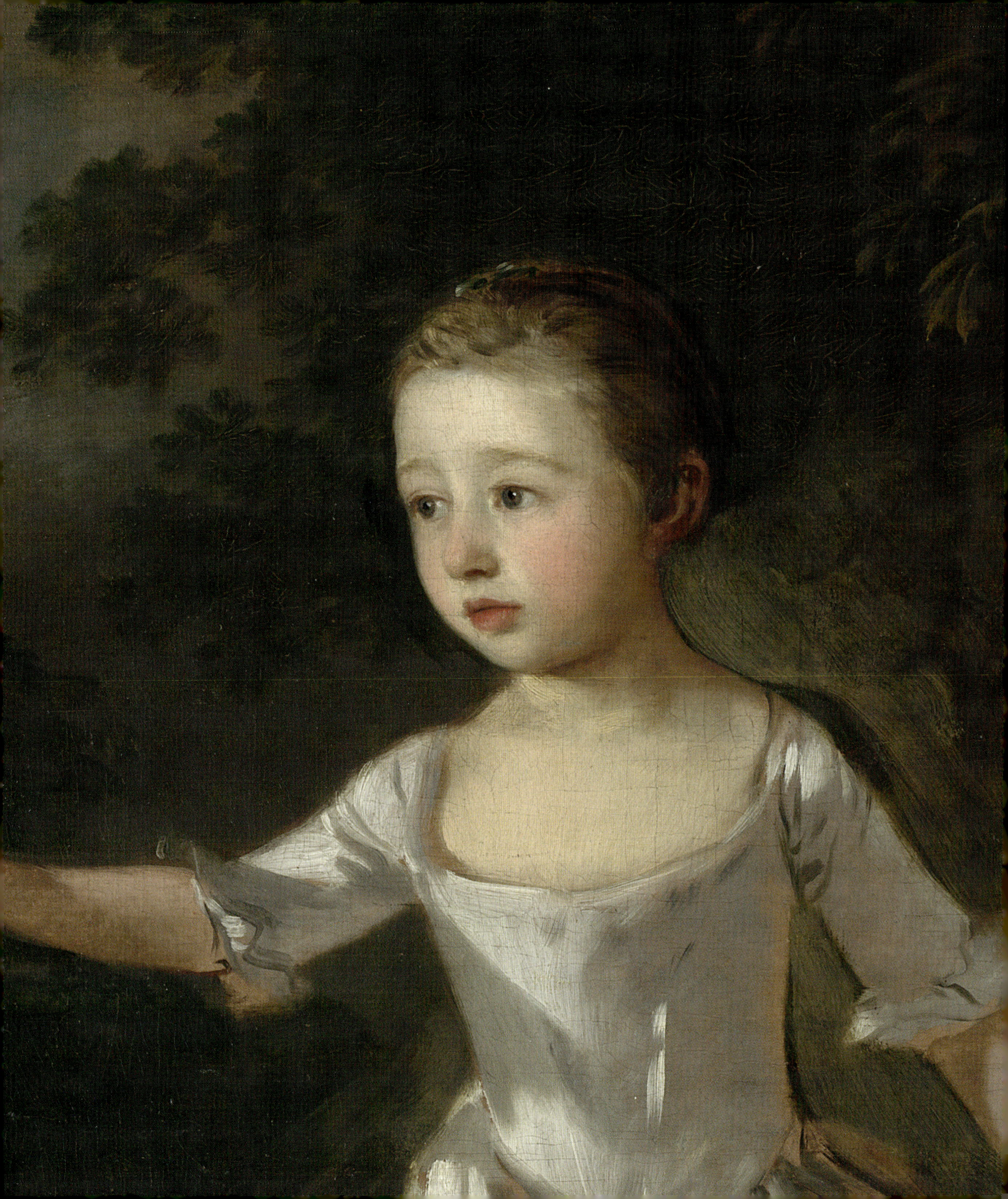

DAUGHTERS
AND SISTERS

Ann Bermingham

DAUGHTERS AND SISTERS: GAINSBOROUGH'S PORTRAITS OF MARY AND MARGARET

Ann Bermingham

… when a man is called to paint a girl
He paints all of himself.
Gbenga Adesina[1]

As the poet Gbenga Adesina reminds us, a portrait is more than a simple reflection of the sitter's appearance; it is also a projection of the artist's selfhood. Feelings, memories, hopes and desires awakened in the artist by the sitter are transported to the image on the canvas. An adult male artist painting the portrait of a girl exists at two removes from his subject, he being neither female nor young. Distance, however, can enable fantasy; the artist can imagine whatever he likes about his subject.[2]

It is in the context of the portrait as a site of sentiment and imagination that this essay examines the six double portraits that Thomas Gainsborough painted of his daughters, Mary and Margaret, over roughly twenty years between the mid 1750s and the early 1770s (cats 9, 15, 16, 17, 19, 30). During this period Mary and her younger sister Margaret not only posed for their numerous likenesses, but also occasionally appeared as country girls in their father's fancy pictures and rustic landscapes, such as *The Harvest Wagon* (fig. 16 and cat. 20).[3] Gainsborough is one of a very few major artists to paint numerous portraits of his family, in particular his children. Perhaps the only others comparable to him in this respect are Sir Peter Paul Rubens and Pablo Picasso, though in the case of Gainsborough's double portraits of his daughters, the works played a singular role in his artistic development.

For a good portion of the time in question, Gainsborough lived in the city of Bath.[4] The family moved from Ipswich to Bath in the autumn of 1759, when Mary and Margaret were quite young, and remained there until 1774, when the family moved to London.[5] Bath was a sophisticated spa town frequented from October to May by aristocrats, gentry, merchants, doctors, fortune hunters, aspiring artists, writers and performers, and, occasionally, the truly ill. Gainsborough's Bath period is credited with his mature formation as an artist, a time when his portrait style began to change in response to the works of Sir Anthony van Dyck and Rubens, which he now had the

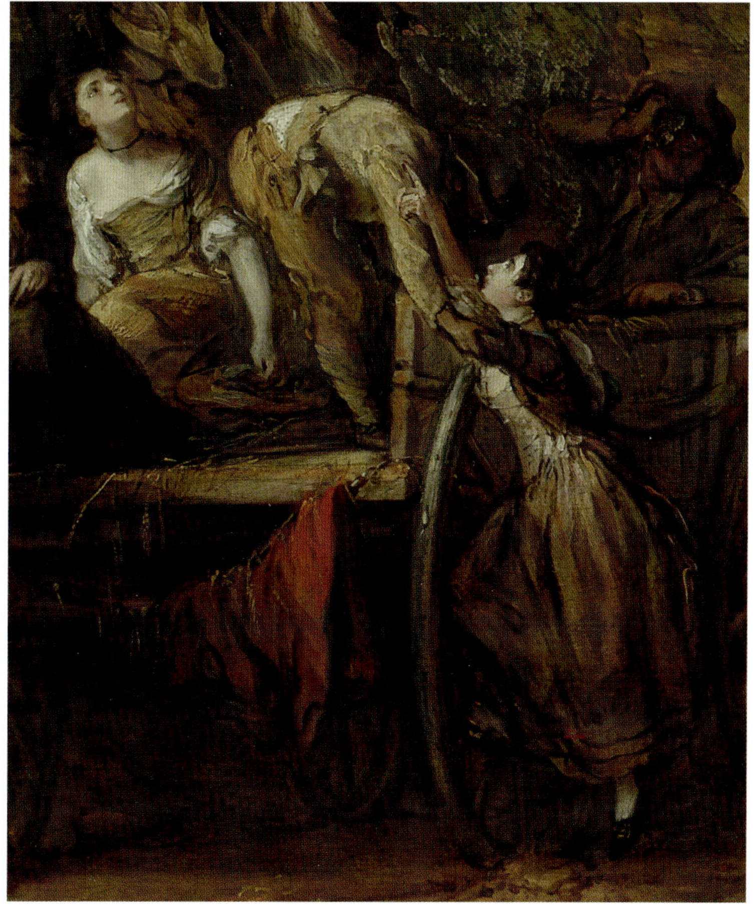

opportunity to study in local collections. From 1761 he sent his work to be exhibited in London, first at the Society of Artists, and then, from 1769, at the newly founded Royal Academy. During this time, Gainsborough also indulged his passion for landscape painting and was first recognised by his friends as particularly gifted in this genre.

Family Matters

Margaret Burr, the mother of Mary and Margaret, was the illegitimate daughter of Henry Somerset, 3rd Duke of Beaufort.[6] Upon her father's premature death in 1745, she received an annuity of £200 from his estate. It was the diarist and Royal Academician Joseph Farington who first reported this, when in 1799 he noted that Gainsborough's daughter Margaret had revealed to him her mother's patrimony.[7] Mrs Gainsborough had recently died and Margaret was trying to secure, unsuccessfully as it turned out, the Beaufort annuity for herself and her older sister Mary. Their mother's descent from a duke explains the story that is often told of her, that on one occasion she justified her extravagant dress by whispering to her niece, Sophia Gardiner: 'I have some right to this, for you know, my love, I am a prince's daughter.'[8]

His wife's heritage is never discussed in Gainsborough's surviving letters. Nevertheless, her annuity provided him with a source of comfort and financial security, allowing him to pursue his love for landscape painting and drawing which, unlike portraiture, did not pay well. Despite this, Gainsborough valued his landscapes highly both as works of art and as a source of private income. Whereas all profits from portraiture were given over to his wife, who managed the family finances, those from landscape remained the artist's alone.[9] As a sign either of the high value he placed on his landscapes or his need for pocket money, or more likely both, there were occasions in Bath when Gainsborough charged as much as £80 for a landscape at a time when his rate was £100 for a full-length portrait.[10]

Gainsborough married Margaret Burr in London in July 1746. It has recently been discovered that she was pregnant at the time with their first-born daughter Mary, who died in 1748 and was buried on the 1st March at the church of St Andrew Holborn.[11] In a painting probably completed shortly before her death, Mary is shown as a toddler with her parents in a landscape (cat. 2). Perhaps in an effort to find a more salubrious environment, Gainsborough moved his wife from London to his hometown of Sudbury in Suffolk sometime during her second confinement, while he returned to London.[12]

Gainsborough's feelings about his marriage occasionally emerge in his letters. In the autumn of 1763, when overwork and over-indulgence resulted in a physical breakdown that nearly took his life, Gainsborough wrote from his sickbed to his good friend the lawyer James Unwin: 'My Dear Good Wife has sat up every night til within a few and has given me all the Comfort that was in her power. I shall never be a quarter good enough for her if I mend a hundred degrees.'[13] Writing to Unwin on another occasion, however, Gainsborough referred to his wife as 'Old Margaret', a pejorative expression suggesting that he felt he was being henpecked.[14] To his sister Mary Gibbon, a milliner who set up in Bath, he confessed, '… my wife is weak but good, and never much formed to humour my Happiness'.[15] From his friend Philip Thicknesse we hear that Gainsborough was loath to entertain at home for fear Margaret would object to the expense.[16] Add to this, Gainsborough's eye for the ladies together with his fondness for conviviality and the company of his musician friends, it is possible to conclude that, while affectionate, the marriage may have also been strained.

Although he excelled at portraiture, Gainsborough often chafed at what he called the 'curs'd Face Business',[17] and much preferred to paint landscapes. 'If people with their damnd faces would but let me alone a little,' he exclaimed to James Unwin.[18] And to his friend William Jackson he famously complained:

I'm sick of Portraits and wish very much to take my Viol da Gam and walk off to some sweet village where I can paint Landskips and enjoy the fag End of Life in quietness & ease.

But these fine Ladies & their 'D̶_̶m̶n̶d̶' Tea drinkings, Dancings, Husband huntings, &c.&c.&c. will fob me out of the last ten years, & I fear miss getting Husbands too – But we can say nothing to these things you know Jackson, we must Jogg on and be content with the jingling of the Bel[l]s, only d-mn it I hate a dust and the kicking up a dust; and being confined in Harn[ess] to follow the track, whilst others ride in the Waggon, under cover stretching their Legs in the straw at Ease, and gazing at Green Trees & Blue Skies without half my Taste. That's d-mn'd hard.[19]

The wagon, a familiar image in his landscapes, constitutes here a sign for the passage of life.[20] This intimation of mortality is provoked by what he sees as the vain pursuits of his daughters, now 'fine ladies', and his need to paint portraits in order to support them financially.

Molly and the Captain

Long before they became fine young ladies, Mary and Margaret were the apples of their father's eye and, next to landscape, among his favourite

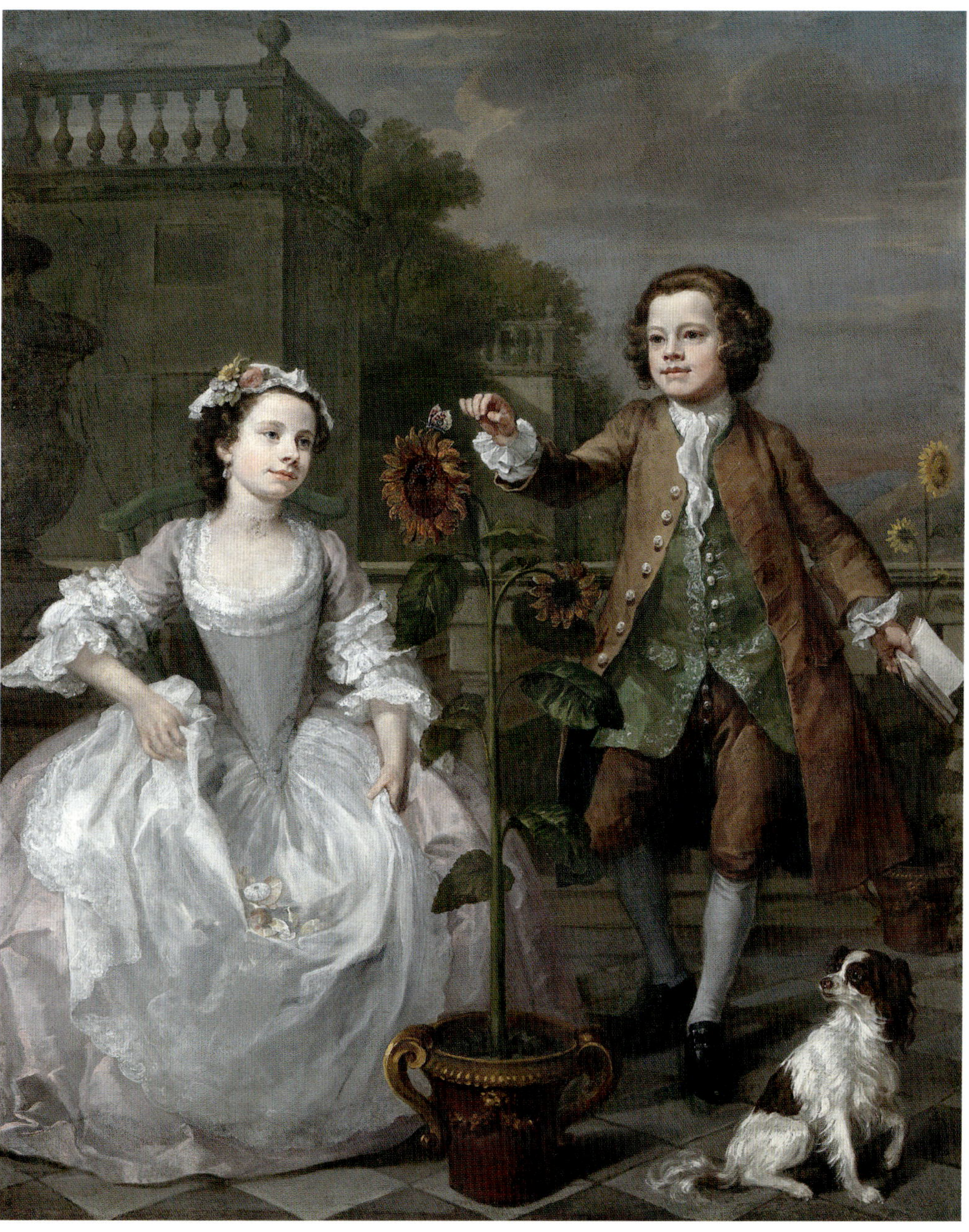

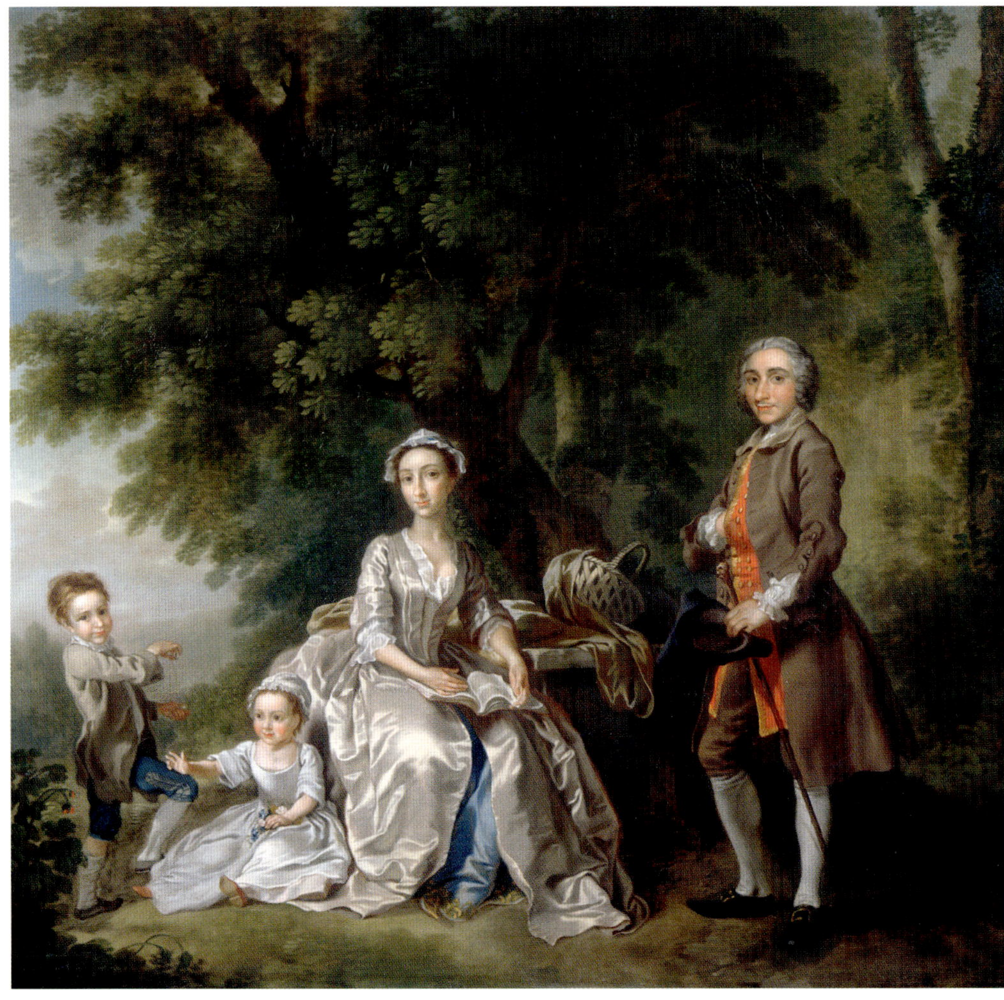

subjects. To their father, Mary was affectionately known as 'Molly', while
Margaret was 'the Captain' – a reference perhaps to a bossy disposition.
Although the art historical literature has often confused the two girls and their
portraits,[21] their appearances are, in fact, quite distinct. Mary inherited the
small nose and rounded face of her mother, while Margaret's long face and
nose, prominent lower lip and eyebrows, and her heavy-lidded, sloping eyes
recall something of her father. The earliest surviving portrait of the two girls
was painted in Ipswich (cat. 9), where the Gainsboroughs moved in either late
1751 or early 1752. Judging from the fact that Mary looks to be about six and
Margaret about four or five, the work probably dates to 1756 or thereabouts.
It shows the pair in a landscape, where Mary is restraining her younger sister
from chasing a butterfly that is about to land on a thistle. The painting is life-
sized and, like most of Gainsborough's double portraits of his daughters, is
unfinished. As David Solkin has argued (see page 20), the unfinished state of
most of Gainsborough's portraits of his family members would have been one
way of signalling their personal and non-commercial nature.

The authority, freshness and directness of *The Artist's Daughters Chasing a
Butterfly* form a stark contrast with what we find in Gainsborough's finished
Ipswich-period portraits. Closer parallels can be found in the works of his

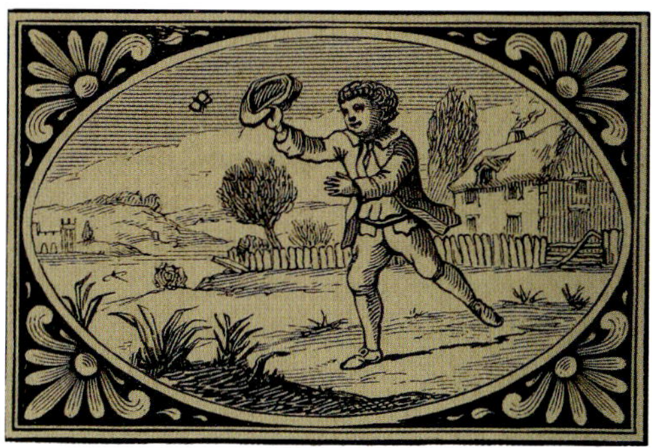

Anon.
Of the Boy and Butterfly
Illustration from *Divine
Emblems: or, temporal
things spiritualized.*,
John Bunyan,
London, 1757
Library of Congress,
Washington

older contemporaries: Margaret's gesture echoes one in William Hogarth's *Mackinnon Children* (fig. 17), as well as in Francis Hayman's conversation piece of *The Grant Family* (fig. 18), where the youngest child is depicted reaching out towards a dragonfly.[22] As the art historian Michael Levey has pointed out, the childish action of trying to grasp a dazzling winged insect has its origins in John Bunyan's *Divine Emblems* (*c*.1686), arguably the first book of poetry ever published specifically for children. The emblem in question (fig. 19) signifies a pursuit of worldly delights that is foolish and ultimately futile.[23] But Gainsborough's portrait gives this symbolic gesture a slightly different emphasis, suggesting that the danger faced by his young daughters is not vain pleasure, but the sharp thistles that will prick Margaret's hand if she touches the butterfly. Her unthinking action demands, in the figure of Mary, the need for constant vigilance. As luminous and exuberant as the portrait is, one cannot help but sense in it Gainsborough's unease, no doubt sharpened by the death of his first-born, about the dangers and vulnerabilities attending the state of childhood. This remarkable work was given to (or possibly bought by) the Reverend Robert Hingeston, an Ipswich friend and neighbour, when Gainsborough moved to Bath. As his letters reveal, the artist cultivated intense male friendships throughout his life, and Hingeston's appears to have been one of these.[24] The fact that Gainsborough could leave this work with him indicates the depth of their connection; in addition, it suggests that as much as he saw the painting as a portrait of his daughters, he also saw it as conveying a moral lesson, and therefore as a suitable adornment for a clergyman's house.[25]

What may well be the next double portrait Gainsborough painted of his daughters shows Mary adjusting Margaret's hair, perhaps trying to fasten a bow in it to match the one in her own (cat. 15 and fig. 33).[26] The girls are dressed in similar clothing and look almost like mirror reflections of each other.[27] Painted shortly after the family's move to Bath, when Mary was around ten years old and Margaret about eight or nine, the portrait reveals Gainsborough experimenting with his paint-handling, in the long feathery brushstrokes on the girls' faces and the loose, bravura treatment of the landscape background. A comparably bold handling can be found in the third double portrait, probably also from around 1760, in which a cat hisses and scrambles to escape Margaret's lap as Mary, in a presumptive affectionate embrace of her sister, slyly pulls the animal's tail (cat. 16). The sisters' expressions remain oddly impassive, despite the cat's flattened ears and bared teeth. The portrait reveals Gainsborough's practice of sketching the composition directly onto a primed, toned canvas, presumably without the use of preparatory drawings.[28] Both of these works display Gainsborough's adaptation of the brushwork of Rubens and Van Dyck, and manifest a facility of handling and freedom of touch that would soon come to characterise his society portraits as well. This would suggest that in addition to serving as tokens of affection, the early portraits of the girls also functioned as important experiments in style.

At some point during the early 1760s, Gainsborough also posed Mary

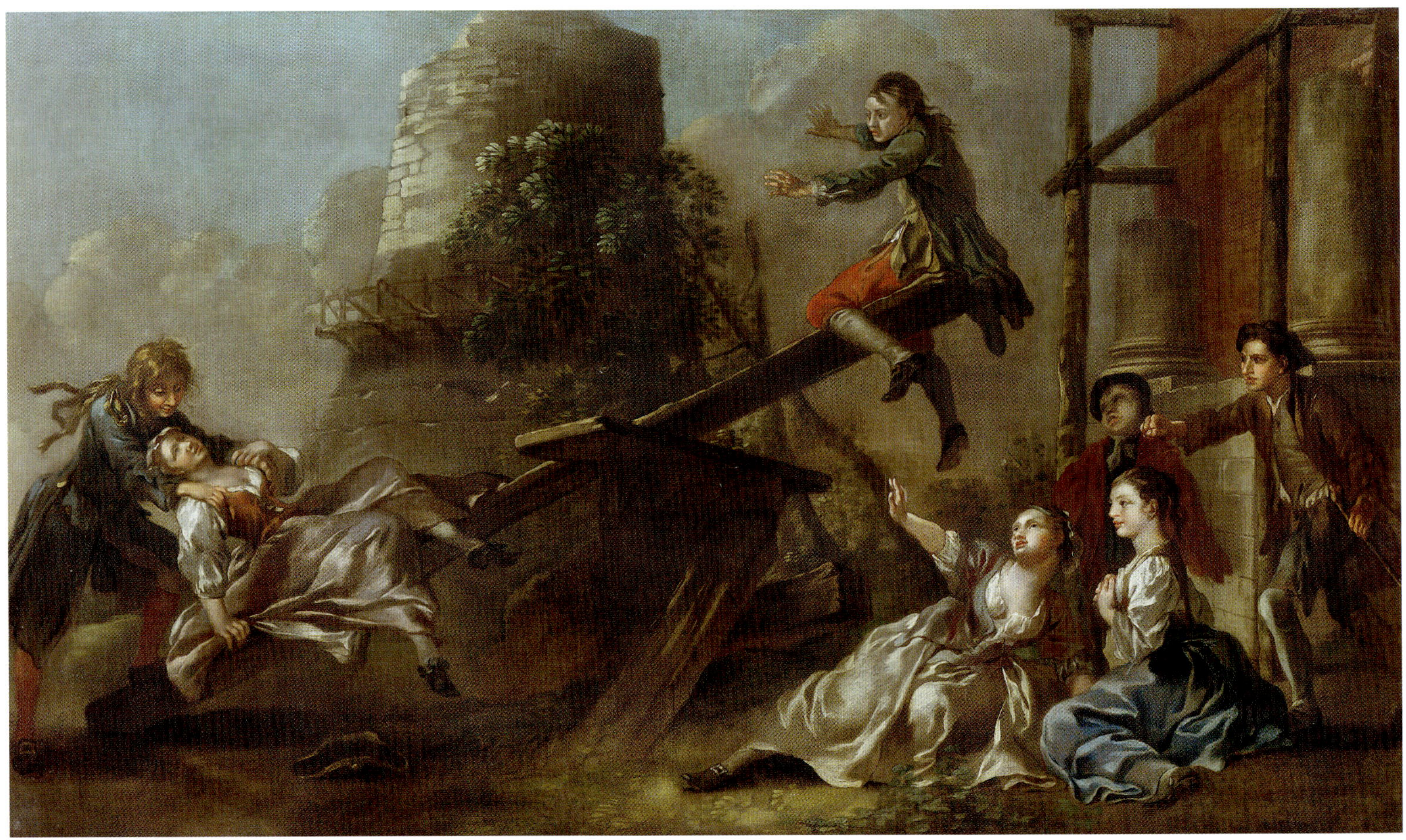

and Margaret as gleaners in a cornfield. Like the double portrait of Mary fastening a bow in her sister's hair, this unfinished painting was also cut in two, probably in the mid nineteenth century, but in this case only one half of the original canvas has survived (cat. 17).[29] This fragment shows Margaret, though her features look to be somewhat more generalised than in her other likenesses. To a greater extent than any of the pictures we have looked at thus far, this painting moves away from portraiture into the territory of the 'fancy picture', a genre of imagery that Gainsborough would take up seriously in his later London period (fig. 27).

'Fancy picture' is an eighteenth-century term that refers to paintings of anonymous social types, typically depicted life-size and at half-length; a particularly popular subcategory was devoted to the representation of children masquerading as historical or literary characters, or posed as ragged urchins or cottagers in fantasy scenarios. Originating in the Low Countries in the seventeenth century, the genre found a home in Britain during the 1730s and 1740s, thanks mainly to the efforts of the Berlin-born French artist Philip Mercier.[30] Gainsborough's earliest teachers, Hubert-François Gravelot and Francis Hayman engaged in fancy painting. Indeed, Hayman, with assistance from Gravelot and the young Gainsborough, decorated the supper boxes at Vauxhall Gardens with fancy pictures in the early 1740s (fig. 20).[31]

Given its mutilated state, it is difficult to determine with certainty if

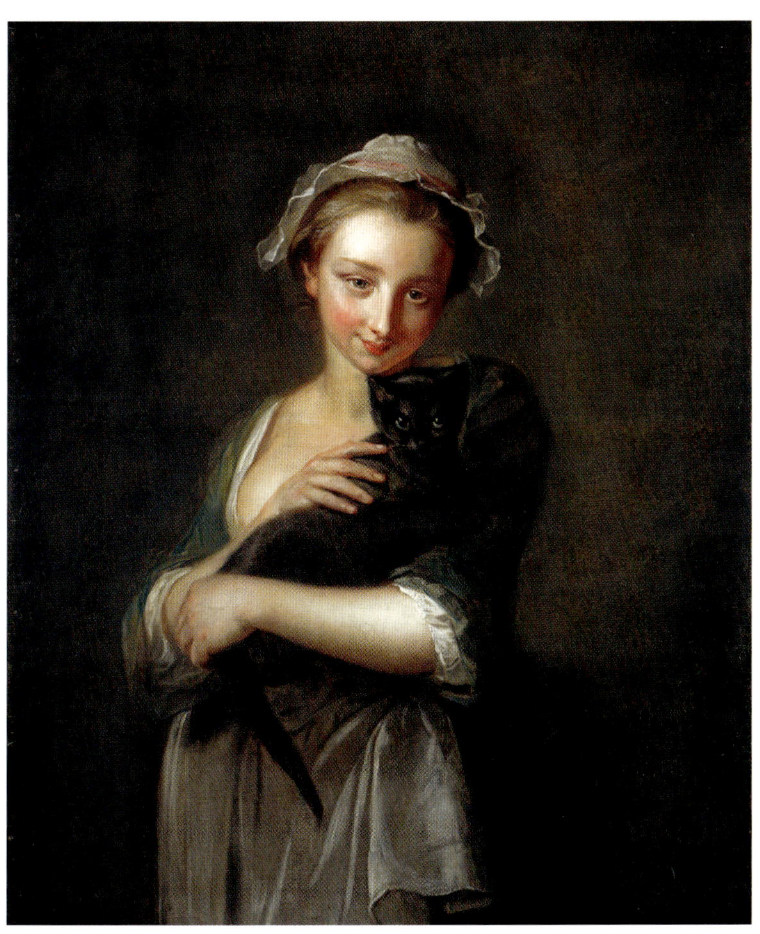

the painting of the girls as gleaners is a portrait or a fancy picture. My belief, based on the generalisation of Margaret's features and the unusual subject of rural labour, is that it is probably a fancy picture, though one with elements of portraiture, just as the other three early images of Mary and Margaret are portraits with elements of fancy painting. For example, Gainsborough's picture of Mary and Margaret holding a cat echoes Mercier's painting of a *Girl Holding a Cat*, (fig. 21), and also perhaps the sentiments found in his *The Sense of Touch* (fig. 22), which illustrates the Dutch saying that 'whoever plays with a little cat will be scratched'.[32] As in the painting of the girls chasing a butterfly, the portrait of them holding a cat hints at moral and physical dangers. These early portraits show Gainsborough using fancy painting to push beyond the conventions of portraiture.

Gainsborough depicts Mary and Margaret in imaginary situations doing imaginary things – chasing butterflies, adjusting bows, teasing cats – being more active than any of the children who appear in their father's commissioned portraits from this or any other period in his career.[33] It takes only a glance at works such as *Heneage Lloyd and His Sister, Lucy* (fig. 23) or *Robert and Susannah Charleton* (Museum of Fine Arts, Virginia) to appreciate the difference. Instead the animation of Mary and Margaret far more closely recalls that of the children found in Hogarth's portraits of the early 1740s, like *The Mackinnon Children* (fig. 17) or *The Graham Children* (The National Gallery, London), where action is mixed with moralising themes. They also echo Gainsborough's teacher Francis Hayman's portraits where, as art historian Brian Allen points out, the subject matter of the Vauxhall fancy pictures spills over into his outdoor conversation pieces.[34]

One consequence of the eighteenth century's embrace of childhood as a distinct stage in human development, when character was yet to be formed, was that children were especially subject to allegorical, proverbial and emblematic treatment by portraitists.[35] Thanks to the elements of fancy painting in Gainsborough's early depictions of Mary and Margaret, there is a palpable tension between what might have been personal to Gainsborough and his daughters on the one hand, and what was conventional or related to the moralising thrust of fancy pictures on the other. For instance, if the butterfly portrait of Mary and Margaret suggests a parent's fear of loss as well as the moralising of John Bunyan, the two other portraits can be read as reflections on Mary's domination of her younger sister, but also as commonplaces about little girls, warning of their incipient vanity and their sly cruelty.[36]

The portraits of Mary and Margaret seem at once intimately sentimental and ferociously ambitious. They push the limits of Gainsborough's art in size,

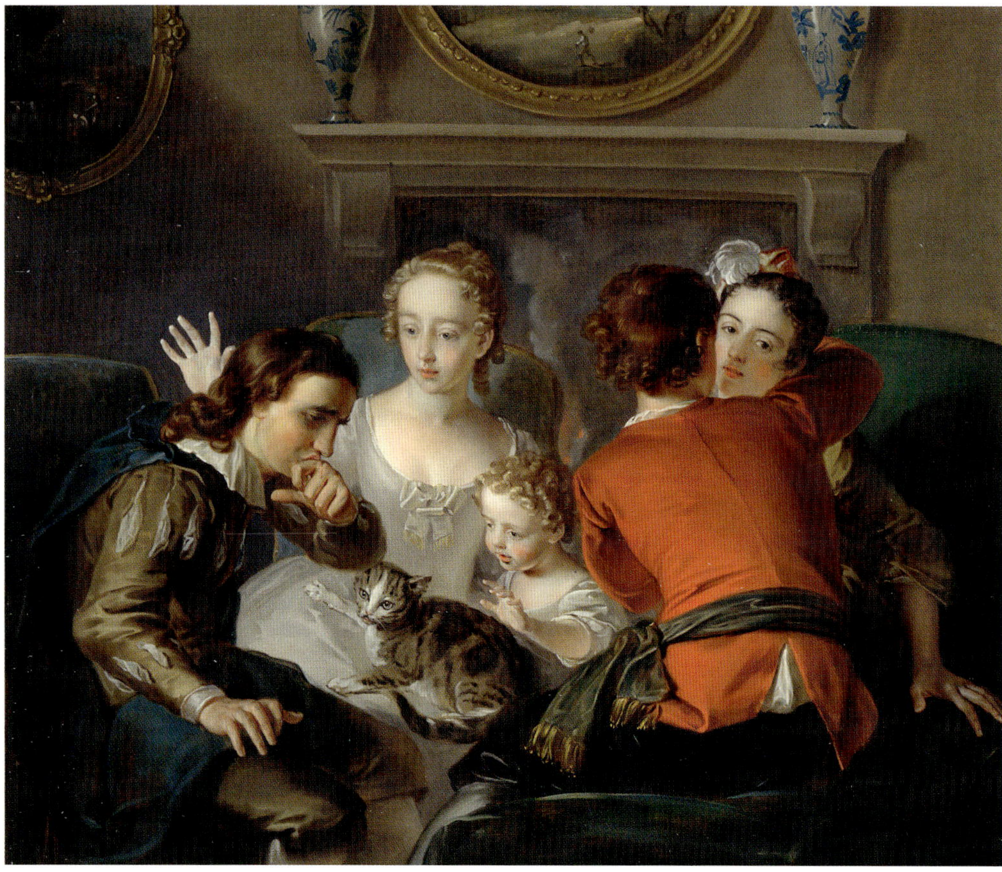

composition, brush handling, stylistic innovation and subject matter, and they display his experimentation with fancy painting and the emblematic tradition. Indeed, they tell us more about Gainsborough as an artist and a father than they do about Mary and Margaret. They reveal his concerns for his girls' moral development and his observation that Mary, the older, was the more active and dominant. But when looking at these pictures, we have to keep in mind that what they represent is a father's perceptions and not necessarily the truth about his daughters.

During the years that followed, Gainsborough went to great efforts to establish himself as the leading portraitist in Bath. While never robust, in September of 1763 he suffered a complete collapse of his health and his life was despaired of. He told his friend James Unwin that he had succumbed to a 'Nervous Fever', and hinted that in addition to overwork, his illness had been brought on by a recent trip to London, during which he had overindulged in the sexual pleasures of the capital.[37] One consequence of this crisis was that he moved his family out of the centre of Bath to a more rural location on the Lansdown Road. To recover his health he also took up riding in the countryside, a practice he would continue for the rest of his time in Bath.[38] It was during this period of recuperation that Gainsborough painted the extraordinary picture of Mary and Margaret now in the Worcester Art Museum (cat. 19). In it, we see Mary seated holding a portfolio of drawings and a porte-crayon, while Margaret stands by her side grasping a drawing

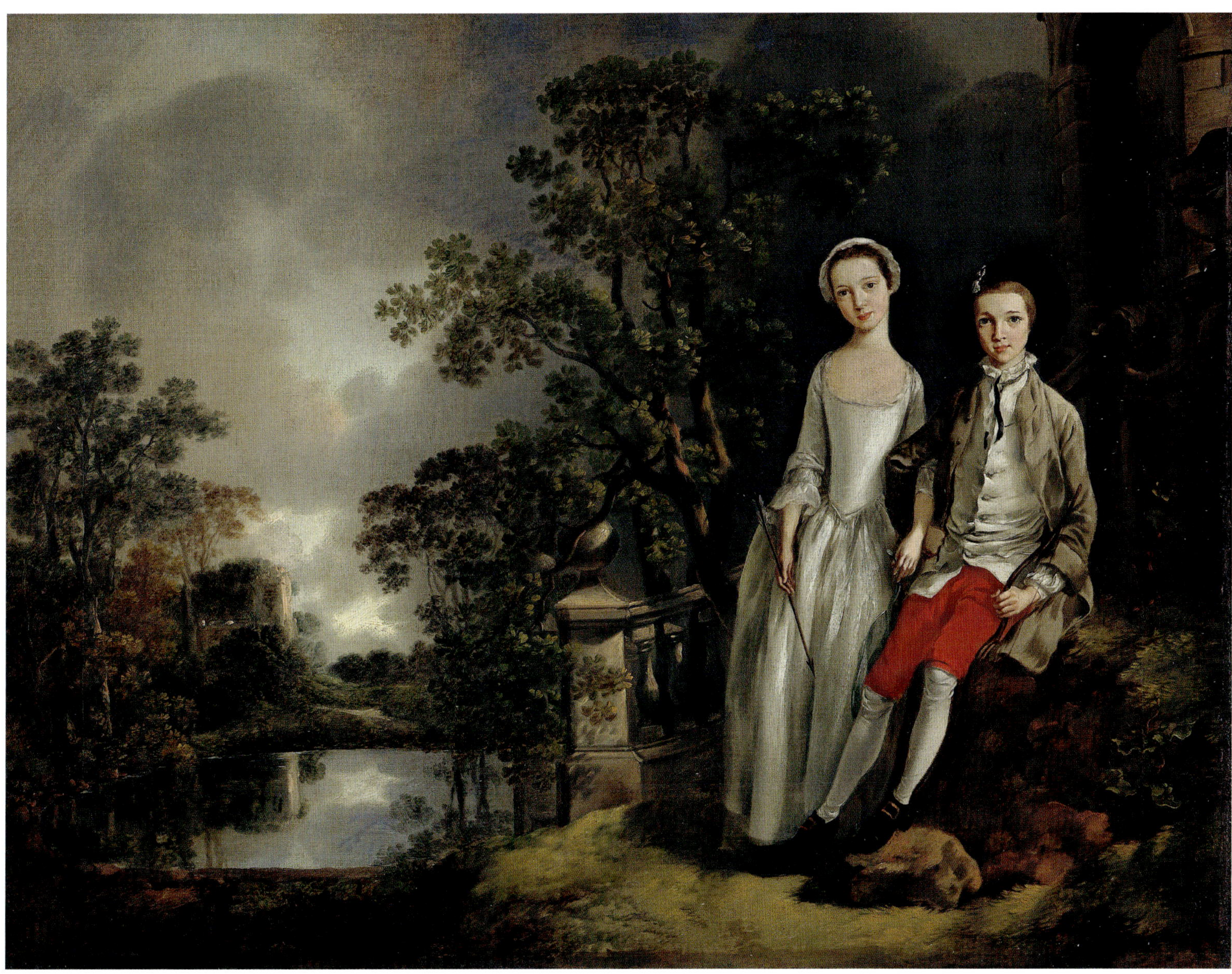

or canvas and gazing at a reduced plaster cast of the antique statue of the Farnese Flora. A second classical sculpture of an unidentified female figure appears below the first. These props and the edge of a gold picture frame conjure up an artistic environment, quite possibly that of Gainsborough's painting room.[39] The girls look to be in their early teens, on the threshold of womanhood – a fact emblematically reinforced by the presence of Flora, the goddess of springtime.

A faint but visible pentimento in the upper left portion of the canvas shows that originally Gainsborough had positioned Margaret in profile standing facing her older sister.[40] He then changed his mind, pausing to rework the composition on paper in a chalk drawing that still survives (cat. 18).[41] Combined with the fact that the final painting is relatively finished, this reworking of the composition reveals how significant the painting was for Gainsborough. The change in the composition results in a stable pyramidal structure for the girls, which is echoed on the left by the placement of the statuary. Just as important, the revised composition creates a note of sisterly affection.

The composition recalls the fancy-picture motif of the 'young artist', while the statue of Flora harkens back to the emblematic strategies of the earlier portraits. However, it can be argued that there is a significant difference between them and this work – attributable to the fact that at the time it was painted Gainsborough had begun mapping out his daughters' futures. In an exceptionally revealing letter again to James Unwin, written in the spring of 1764, Gainsborough talks frankly of his plans for the girls.[42] Unwin seems to have made some kind of suggestion regarding Mary's education, to which the artist responded:

> You have my sincerest thanks for your kind offer and intention in regard to Molly; but you must know I'm upon a scheme of learning them both to paint Landscape; and that somewhat above the common Fan-mount style. I think them capable of it, if taken in time, and with proper pains bestow'd. I don't mean to make them only Miss Fords in the Art, to be partly admired & partly laugh'd at at every Tea Table; but in case of an Accident that they may do something for Bread. You know it will be an Employment not so apt to lay snares in their way as Portrait or Miniature Painting, because they may be retired. I think (and indeed always did myself) that I had better do this than make fine trumpery of them, and let them be led away with Vanity, and ever subject to disappointment in the wild Goose chace. I've mark'd the end of it sufficiently. I'm in earnest and shall set about it in good earnest.

In this suggestive letter Gainsborough is proposing to teach his daughters to become accomplished painters of landscape – painters above the polite amateur level of what he calls the 'Fan-mount style' – so that, if necessary, they will be able to use their skills to make a decent living. When their father says that he doesn't 'mean to make them only Miss Fords in the Art', he is probably referring to Ann Ford, a singer and accomplished player on the English guitar, the viola da gamba and the glass harmonica, who performed publicly in London at subscription concerts. Before her marriage to Gainsborough's friend Philip Thicknesse, Ann Ford had become something of a sensation as a musician, earning, as art historian Michael Rosenthal has noted, £1,500 from one concert alone.[43] Her beauty and talent attracted the attention of the ancient Earl of Jersey, who offered her £800 a year to be his mistress; Ford's rejection of this offer became the subject of gossip and even a pamphlet war. This unfortunate episode highlighted the fact that respectable women (a category that excluded professional actresses and musicians) were welcome to perform in private, but by going on a public stage ran the risk of scandal and ignominy. In this context, Gainsborough's comment about portraiture's 'snares' is suggestive, evoking the possibility that the intimate art of taking a likeness could lead to improper entanglements between artist and sitter; that is to say, like the public performance of music, portraiture could endanger his daughters'

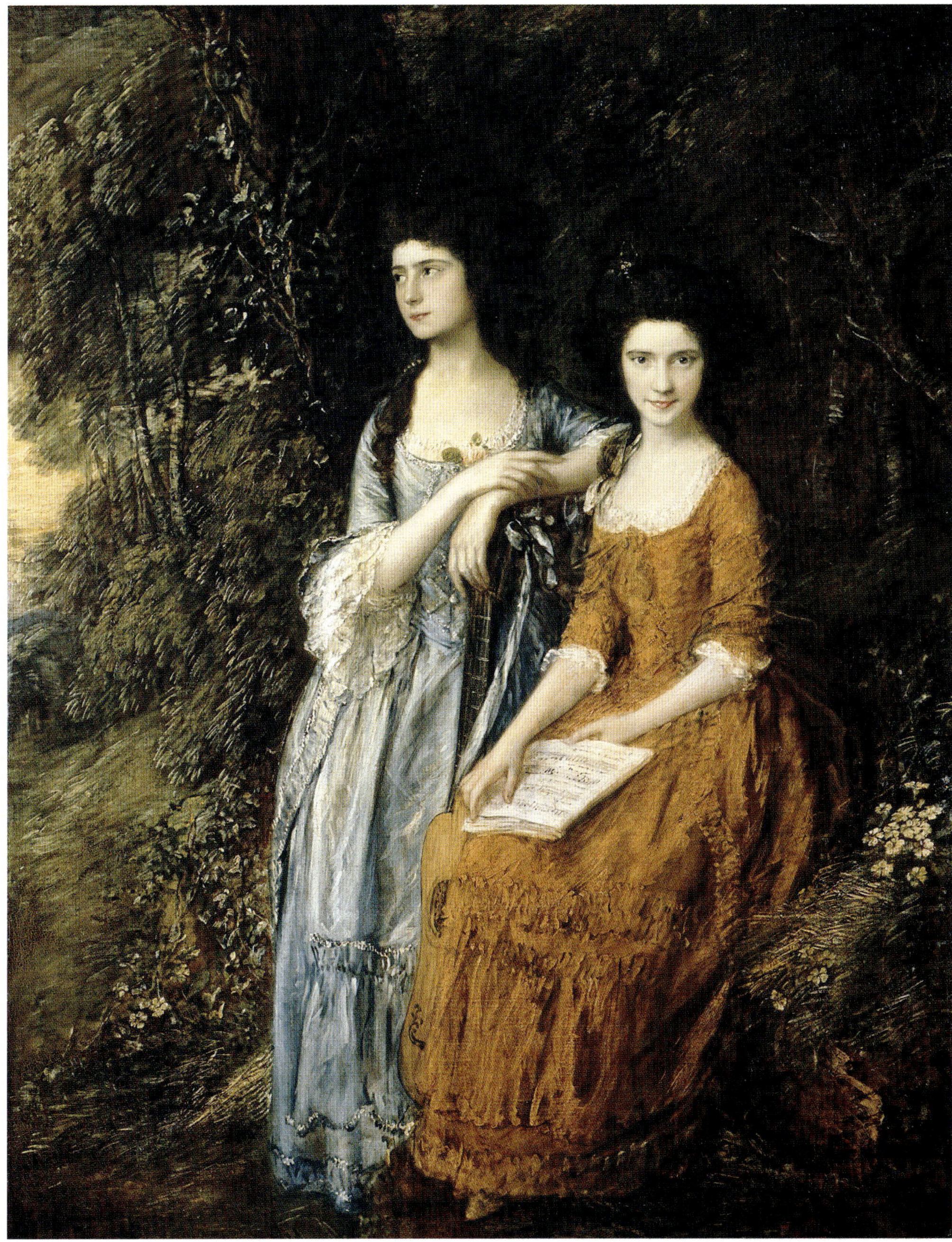

reputations. Landscape painting had the advantage of being a private or, as Gainsborough put it, a 'retired' occupation.

If his daughters could support themselves by producing landscapes, they would also have the option of remaining unmarried. As the resident of a spa town where families brought daughters to find husbands, Gainsborough had had ample opportunity to see at first hand how often this led to bitter disappointment, hence his remarks about the 'wild Goose chace'. Teaching Mary and Margaret how to paint landscapes was his alternative to making a 'trumpery' of them by parading them at public balls and assemblies in search of husbands. His letter reveals a fear that they might be unable to resist the vanities of Bath and the lures of men. In his mind, landscape painting promised to serve as a kind of insurance policy to protect them from penury, scandal and heartbreak.

By the time Gainsborough wrote to Unwin, the girls' lessons in art had already begun. About a year later, in 1765, he enrolled them in Blacklands School in Chelsea, London, where among other things they were taught how to draw. Margaret later recalled that while they were at Blacklands, Gainsborough sent her and Mary numerous letters containing detailed instructions for drawing. Unfortunately, she reported, all those letters had since been lost.[44]

Given Gainsborough's anxiety about his daughters' financial security and independence, it is curious that he chose to train them as landscape painters, since his own experience had taught him that landscape was neither a lucrative branch of art, nor a reliable source of income. Despite all the good notices that his landscapes received from reviewers of the annual exhibitions, he found these works extraordinarily difficult to sell. Indeed, after his death the artist William Beechey recalled seeing landscapes stacked in long lines along the hallway to Gainsborough's painting room in his London house, where they remained unwanted and unsold.[45]

Thus, at the moment of the Worcester portrait, Gainsborough tried to imagine the best for his children – an independent, financially secure future, free of husbands and out of the public eye. Molly and the Captain would not have to parade themselves in the marriage market because they would always have a polite and respectable means of supporting themselves. Except, of course, they wouldn't. What are we to make of Gainsborough's wilfully blind and wildly unrealistic plans for his daughters? How could he, of all people, have equated landscape painting with financial security?

The answer could perhaps lie in Gbenga Adesina's sentiment expressed in the epigraph to this chapter: a man called to paint a girl reveals 'all of himself'. Unlike the earlier double portraits in which Mary and Margaret embody moralising statements and generic truisms that might apply to any young girls, their portrayal as budding artists shows them as vehicles for their father's most personal and fervent desires. Landscape represented for Gainsborough both his own modest financial independence – recall that he kept as his personal allowance the money he made from landscapes – and freedom from what he saw as the drudgery of portraiture, of having to 'Jogg on … in Har[ness], whilst others ride in the Waggon'.[46] That is to say, landscape meant freedom from having to paint subjects that did not interest him and to flatter people who annoyed him.[47] Moreover, landscape further represented freedom from the confines of marriage and family – the desire, as he expressed it to his friend Jackson, 'to take [his] Viol da Gam and walk off to some sweet Village' where he could 'paint Landskips and enjoy the fag End of Life in quietness & ease'.[48] In short, even as the Worcester painting serves as a likeness of Mary and Margaret, it is also an image of all that Gainsborough desired for himself as an artist and a man projected on to his daughters.

The difference between this deeply felt image and the last double portrait of Gainsborough's daughters (cat. 30) is profound. Painted around 1774, when the family left Bath for London, Mary and Margaret, now in their early twenties, appear as elegant society women.[49] The painting fits a generic full-length portrait type so closely that it is difficult to distinguish this presentation of his daughters from Gainsborough's ordinary commissioned likenesses. His roughly contemporary full-length of the Linley sisters (fig. 24) offers a particularly close comparison, both compositionally and stylistically. Also, for the first and only time in his life, Gainsborough finally brought a portrait of his two daughters to completion. It is probably not a coincidence that, like the only pair of portraits he ever completed of himself and his wife (cats 12, 13), this work was painted when the family moved to a new location.[50] As much as it may have been intended to introduce his daughters to London society, it may also have been designed, perhaps like other double portraits of the girls, to demonstrate Gainsborough's prowess in portraiture to a new group of clients.

When compared to its predecessors, the double full-length appears at first glance to be evacuated of meaning and sentiment. If the painting of the sisters as young artists represents Gainsborough's desires for his daughters, this later and last of the double portraits, painted when Mary and Margaret had become young women, likely reveals something of his daughters' desires for themselves. Through the social mask of impassive politeness we spy sisterly affection, and a taste, inherited no doubt from their mother, for elegant clothes. What exceeds this rather ordinary presentation is the presence of the dog, a traditional iconographic reference to fidelity usually reserved for a marriage portrait such as Gainsborough's own (cat. 2) or his double full-length of the newlyweds William and Elizabeth Hallett known as *The Morning Walk* (National Gallery, London). Its deployment in a portrait of sisters is unusual, and would seem to be intended to emphasise the strength of their love and devotion to each other. This unusual bit of artistic licence conforms to Gainsborough's hope, expressed years earlier to James Unwin, that Mary and Margaret would not have to marry and presumably would remain companions for life. Knowing what we do about Gainsborough's desires for his daughters, this emblematic use of the dog makes it difficult to dismiss this painting as simply bowing to the conventions of society portraiture. The Gainsborough who feared for his children's moral development and planned for their adult futures lingers alongside the artist charged with depicting the 'fine ladies' his young girls have become.

Fine Ladies

As it turned out, Gainsborough's daughters never had to paint landscapes for money. Rather than exert themselves as professional artists, Mary and Margaret relied on their mother's thrift, their father's investments, and on the proceeds from the sales of his work that took place after his death.[51] In his final days Gainsborough was relieved to hear his wife confess that she had put by money over the years and now had a tidy sum.[52] While the posthumous sales of his works yielded disappointing returns, the funds realised – combined with his daughters' bank annuities and Mrs Gainsborough's savings – meant that Mary and Margaret could live securely and respectably for the rest of their days. At her death in 1798, Mrs Gainsborough's estate was estimated

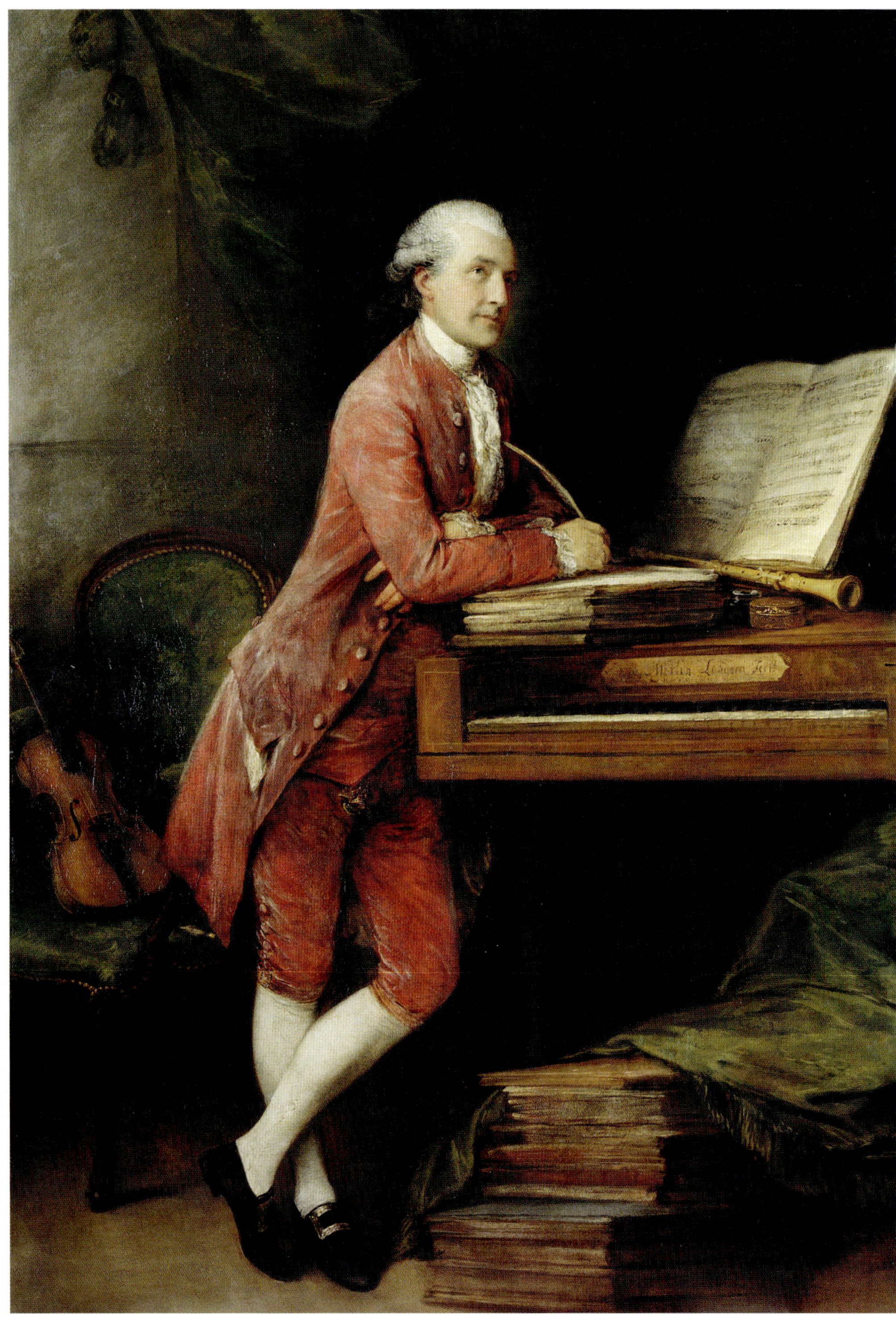

at £10,000 – just £2,000 more than the value of Margaret's estate when she passed away twenty-two years later.[53]

The story of Mary and Margaret after the family's move to London and their parents' deaths is a tragic one. Neither path mapped out for them in their last two double portraits, as artists or as society ladies, was travelled. Gainsborough's efforts to protect his daughters from vanity and the wild goose chase of husband hunting had been disappointed in 1780, when, against her father's wishes, Mary had married the musician Johann Christian Fischer (fig. 25). The situation was further complicated by the fact that Margaret had believed Fischer to be in love with her, so his marriage to her older sister caused unhappiness between the girls. To make matters even worse, before a year had passed the newly married couple found themselves in severe financial straits. Gainsborough discovered to his great dismay that to relieve the strain Mary had ordered expensive fabric from two London shops, only to try selling it immediately through a third, with the (illegal) proceeds going to herself and her husband. Believing the scheme to be Fischer's idea, Gainsborough wrote to his sister, 'She has convinced me that she would go to the Gallows to serve this Man'.[54]

Despite Mary's devotion to Fischer, the marriage did not last and the couple separated after a few years. In his will Gainsborough left his property to his wife and Margaret, with instructions that they should 'pay such sums as they thought proper to Mrs. Fischer, at such times as they thought fit'.[55] This instruction was clearly an attempt to secure for Mary an inheritance free from any claims Fischer might make as her undivorced husband.

Sly and headstrong but also impulsive and unstable, Mary, when still a young woman, had started manifesting the signs of mental illness that would mar the rest of her life. In the autumn of 1771, the theatre manager John Palmer reported to the eminent actor David Garrick that Mary had been suffering from a 'delirious fever', and that the family doctor had given up on her, 'declaring that it was a family complaint and he did not suppose she would ever recover her senses again'.[56] The fact that Gainsborough himself had been felled by a similar illness in 1763 may account for its diagnosis as a 'family complaint'. To save Mary, Gainsborough was obliged to call in two further doctors, who cured her, at least for the moment.

After the death of Mrs Gainsborough in 1798, Margaret, who was herself subject to bouts of eccentricity in later life, became the caretaker of her older sister, who now needed constant attendance. Their mother stipulated in her will that, 'If my daughter Mary Fisher [sic] should outlive my daughter Margaret Gainsborough … it is my will and earnest desire that [she shall] board and lodge with one of her cousins … who I know will be very kind to her and see that an honest, cleanly, good tempered servant do attend upon her.'[57] In 1818 an Ipswich friend, Mrs Dupuis, described Margaret as 'odd' and Mary as 'quite deranged'.[58] The form their delusions took seems directly attributable to their mother's paternity. Both girls seem to have suffered from grandiosity, and Gainsborough's increasing irritation with their 'airs' emerges in his later letters. To his sister Mary Gibbon, he complained that while the world showered him with every acknowledgement, at home he was 'counteracted with disobedience Pride and insolence, and eternal Obraidings & reflections'.[59] In another letter to his sister, he reveals that his daughter Margaret was particularly insolent and proud in her behaviour towards him.[60]

And not just towards him, apparently: her cousin Sophia Lane would later report the family story that on one occasion Margaret had haughtily refused a request from no less a personage than Queen Charlotte to demonstrate her

skills on the harpsichord.[61] By the
end of her life, Mary's delusions of
grandeur had gone to even greater
extremes. In 1824, the writer and
artist, W.H. Pyne observed that
she 'has long survived her mental
faculties, and is now doomed, to all
speculation, to waste the remainder
of life in the vain pomp and self-
complacency of fancied royalty'.[62]
Another source tells us that later in
life Mary gave out 'that she would
receive no untitled visitors, so that
those who had business with her
were obliged to invent patents of
nobility for themselves'.[63]

Such anecdotes suggest that
Gainsborough's 'fine ladies' came to
believe, and act, as if they were very
grand and certainly born above their
father's station. Clearly, Margaret
Gainsborough had shared with her daughters her knowledge about her
natural father – and this sense of social privilege, more than Gainsborough's
reputation as one of the greatest artists of his generation, was what they clung
to. Thus their mother's paternity became for both girls a defining feature in
their own self-images.[64]

In 1806 Mary and Margaret moved to Acton, at that time a small village
to the west of London.[65] There they fell back on their inheritance, living the
socially constrained lives of genteel ladies of modest means in a quiet rural
backwater. Mary's illness, as well as their need to save money after they failed
to secure their mother's annuity following her death, may well have made
the sisters' withdrawal from London a necessity. While their life together was
not remotely like the one imagined for them by their father, it was certainly
defined by Margaret's, if not Mary's, sisterly devotion.[66]

Ironically, while the girls' oddities and mental instabilities resulted in their
retirement from the public eye, these same failings inscribed them forever
into the public register of art history. For even while they lived a retired life
in Acton, their reputations, along with their mother's, were openly dissected
in the accounts of Gainsborough that began appearing after his death.
Thicknesse's was the first. He went to great lengths in his 1788 *Sketch* of
the artist to accuse Mrs Gainsborough, a 'pretty Scots girl of low birth', of
extreme miserliness.[67] Pyne relayed the fact of Mary's insanity and her dreams
of royalty in the *Somerset House Gazette* two years before her death. And
finally, George Fulcher, in the first full biographical account of Gainsborough
(1856), reported, on the basis of the interviews he did with surviving friends
and family members, that both girls had their 'idiosyncrasies', citing as

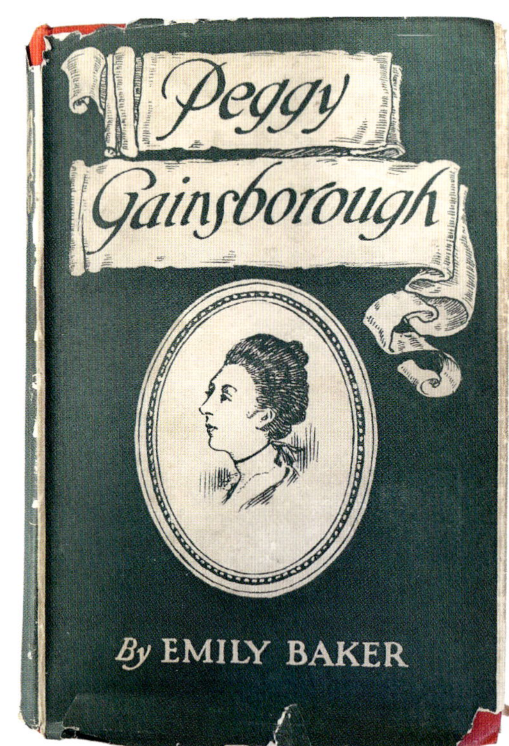

examples Mary's delusions about the Prince of Wales's love for her, and Margaret's refusal to play for the queen.[68]

Around half a century later, Mary and Margaret reappeared in semi-fictionalised form in Emily Baker's 1909 novel entitled *Peggy Gainsborough, the Great Painter's Daughter*, which imagines the life of Margaret in Bath and London, and the famous and infamous people she met in her father's studio (fig. 26). Here Mary's marriage to Fischer and her eventual madness are attributed to the musician's satanic powers of hypnotism. In this vein, the photographer Cecil Beaton wrote his one and only play, *The Gainsborough Girls* (1950), which flopped in previews and was renamed, interestingly, *Figures in a Landscape* when it was performed at the Olympia Theatre, Dublin, in 1959.[69]

As it happens, tradition has it that Gainsborough's daughters do appear as figures in one of their father's most famous landscapes, *The Harvest Wagon* (1767, fig. 16 and cat. 20), where Margaret is shown climbing in and Mary is already seated.[70] As in his fancy picture of the pair as gleaners, here Gainsborough imagines his girls as living the life of simple country folk, a life that he himself had come to envy. If the figures in *The Harvest Wagon* are indeed Mary and Margaret, this offers us our final glimpse of Molly and the Captain before they became 'fine ladies'. Here portraiture and landscape make common cause; in the soft evening light birds fly home to roost, the view is filled with green trees and blue skies, and the passage of life for fathers and daughters is easy and natural. Ushered into the rural idyll of *The Harvest Wagon*, Mary and Margaret are welcomed for the last time into the fantasy world of their father and invited to share its joys. Perhaps it was an invitation they never understood, or one that, having understood, they found impossible to accept.

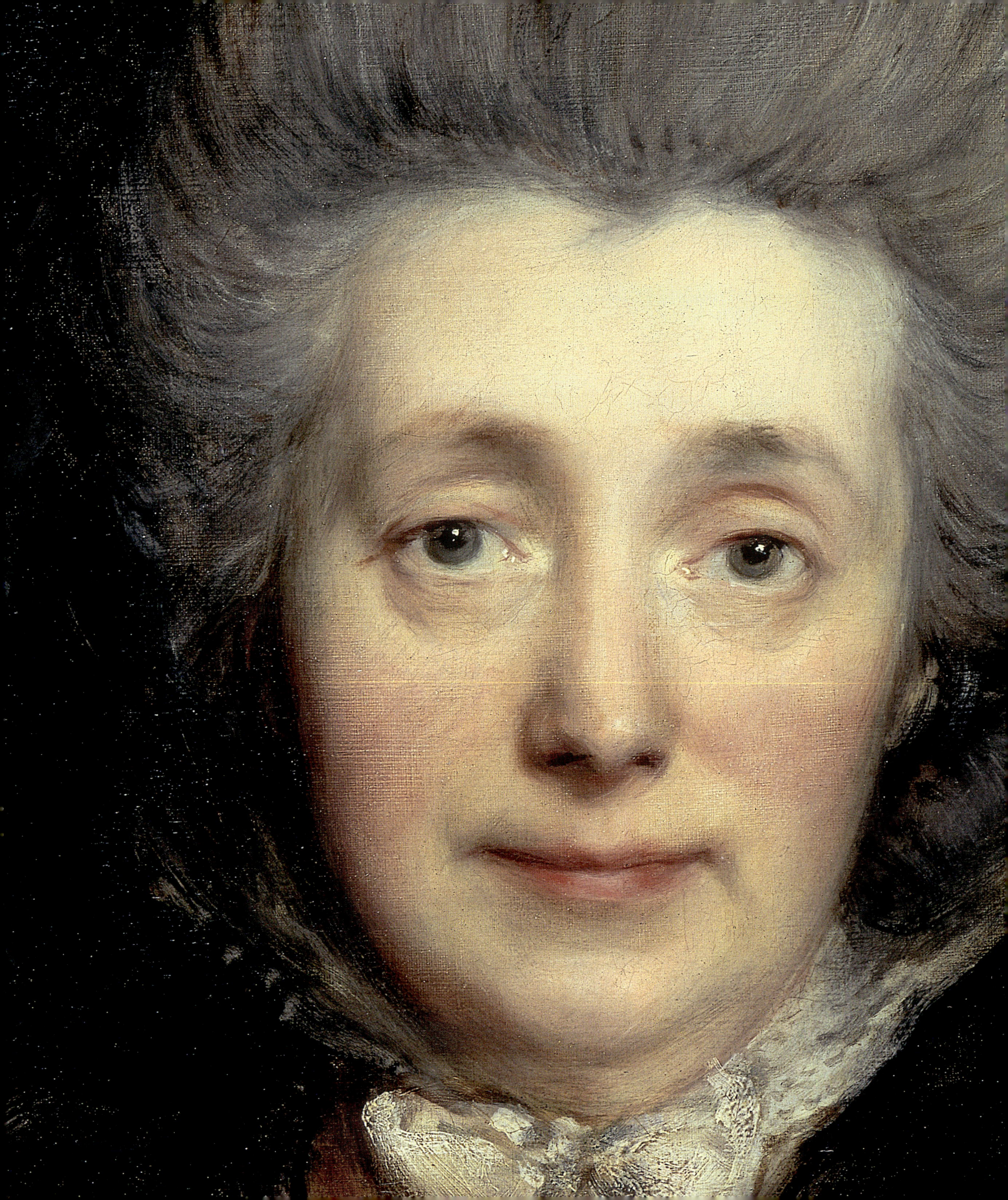

WOMEN OF CONSEQUENCE

Susan Sloman

WOMEN OF CONSEQUENCE: MRS GAINSBOROUGH AND MRS GIBBON

Susan Sloman

'No man is an island, entire of itself' – although this claim may have become something of a platitude since it first appeared in John Donne's *Meditations* in 1624, the poet's words still hold a fundamental truth undiminished by the passage of time. Yet when it comes to thinking about male artists, how often do we acknowledge the extent of their dependence on the people closest to them, and in particular on the women in their lives? As so little of the evidence has been deemed worth preserving, the task of assessing the importance of the contributions made by mothers, wives, sisters, daughters or other female relations to a painter's or sculptor's achievements may present enormous challenges. But surely the attempt must be made if there is to be any hope of correcting the gross imbalance of an historical record largely created by, and in the interests of, one half of humankind. A history of eighteenth-century British art that seeks to do full justice to the roles played by women should not restrict itself – as has mainly been the case up until now – to considering occasional acts of patronage, or the relatively small cohort of recorded practitioners, both professional and (mainly) amateur, whose works can be identified. Instead it might begin with the recognition that the artist's occupation in this period almost invariably had its roots in a family business, and that, in the vast majority of instances, the men whose names now dominate the canon of 'great masters' relied on women of consequence to help them build and sustain the foundations of a successful career.

We know that William Hogarth, for example, lived and worked within a predominantly female household.[1] The same holds true for Thomas Gainsborough, and in both families several of these women were milliners. Outside the home, in the conduct of his professional life, Gainsborough was also acquainted with notable craftswomen and female musicians. Elizabeth Buteux (later Elizabeth Godfrey), a silversmith who supplied London's aristocracy and royalty, was the mother of Panton Betew, Gainsborough's picture dealer. Betew's standing in the commercial world, which in turn gave credence to the painter's early landscapes and drawings, was dependent on his mother's formidable reputation. This family may have been the one with whom Gainsborough lodged on moving to London to begin his artistic career at the age of twelve or thirteen in 1740 or 1741.[2] In 1746 he married Margaret Burr, a young woman with a substantial income.[3] The financial settlement that came Gainsborough's way via his marriage gave him a degree of freedom undreamt of by most aspiring painters of his generation. Without it, he might not have been able to devote time to painting landscapes and fancy pictures, the works that gave him the deepest sense of fulfilment. By the early 1750s, when he was living as a young married man in Ipswich, Gainsborough's eldest sister Mary Gibbon was in charge of a busy millinery and taking apprentices in her own name in nearby Colchester.[4] She was the artist's confidante and adviser on matters professional and personal. Without her support, and that of his wife Margaret, Thomas Gainsborough's fortunes, as a man and as an artist, might have been very different indeed.

One way of gauging their impact on his personal behaviour is by considering his conduct as the father of two girls. The example of both women must have been a key factor in the thinking process that prompted Gainsborough to inculcate a sense of self-sufficiency in his daughters. His intention was that they should learn to paint landscape so that 'in case of an Accident … they may do something for Bread'.[5] He wrote them long letters about drawing when they were away at school, and when they were at home, he painted them as artists (cat. 19). Of course, as Ann Bermingham observes (see page 54), landscape painting was not a particularly good way of earning a living, and there is no evidence that either daughter had the application or ability to make anything of their father's teaching. Their aunt Mary Gibbon did, however, provide a model for what strong-willed women could do 'for Bread' at this date. She was unusual in that she became an independent retailer while her husband, a clergyman, was still alive.[6] More commonly, women were unnamed participants in family enterprises. Often it was only after the death of a businessman that the scale of involvement by his wife, sister or daughter became apparent. In Birmingham, for example, Sarah Baskerville continued to run her husband's type foundry after he died in 1775, adapting the company to her own abilities. She gave up his printing press, but maintained the business of glazing paper for London booksellers, and jealously guarded the secret of her process.[7] There are also records of female ironmongers, grocers, cheesemongers and even a female manufacturer of fireworks and rockets in England in the eighteenth century, but the insured trades with the largest numbers of women policyholders were millinery and mantua-making (dressmaking).[8] Mrs Gibbon was both milliner and mantua-maker. A significant number of women, like Mrs Baskerville, were involved in publishing and printing, and after Gainsborough died, his wife joined forces with John Boydell, London's leading print publisher, in an attempt to market her husband's landscape etchings.

Mrs Margaret Gainsborough was reputed to be a great beauty in her youth. The Courtauld Institute portrait of her from the later 1770s (cat. 34) shows that her good looks continued into middle age. This, perhaps the greatest of the family pictures, was painted around the time of her fiftieth birthday and may have been intended to mark that milestone. It is important

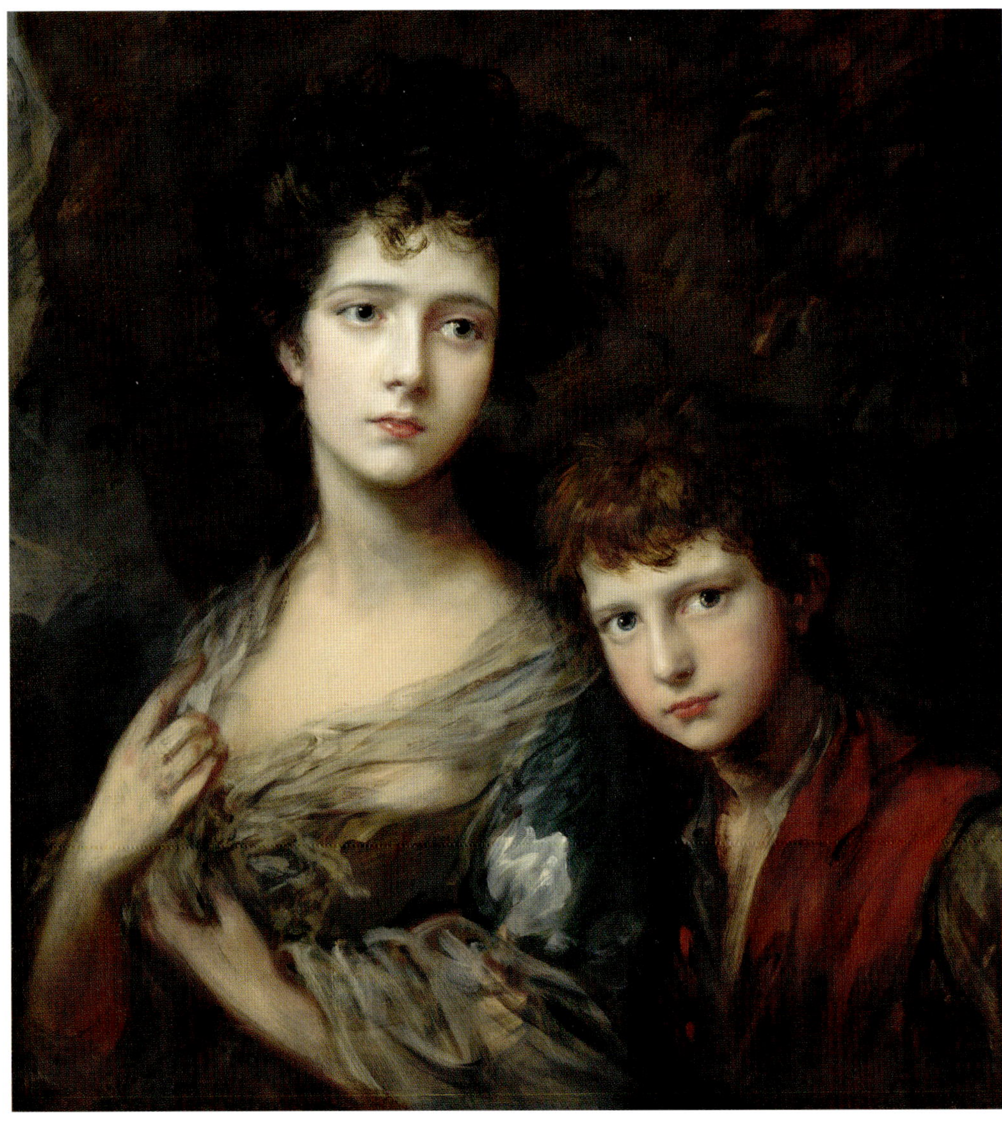

to consider this portrait at the outset, not just on account of its extraordinary quality as a painting, but because of what it tells us about the relationship between husband and wife. Mrs Gainsborough often gets a bad press. Some uncomfortable home truths are revealed in family correspondence, but it should also be noted that the author of an early memoir of the painter, Philip Thicknesse, disliked her, and that this influenced the subsequent literature. The portrait tells its own story. The composition Gainsborough devised for it is the same as the one he used for another beautiful woman, Elizabeth Linley, when he adapted an unfinished double portrait of her and her brother Tom Linley from 1768, changing it into a fancy picture in 1784 for the Duke of Dorset (fig. 27).[9] The black satin, lace-trimmed shawl (cat. 34) that frames Margaret Gainsborough's face and sets off her complexion was probably a studio 'prop' or something borrowed from Mary Gibbon: Isabella, Viscountess Molyneux is wrapped in what appears to be the same garment in the full-length that was Gainsborough's star female portrait in the first Royal Academy exhibition in 1769 (now in the Walker Art Gallery, Liverpool).[10] Margaret Gainsborough's hair is carefully dressed in the elevated style that characterised the 1770s, and held by a white cap, of which only the bow that secures it under her chin is visible. The painting is strictly limited in colour. Warm flesh, hints of a gold gown and a thinly painted brown background are contrasted with shades of black, white and grey. Above all, the picture is a demonstration of Gainsborough's debt to Van Dyck, the master painter of black fabrics, and one of the most sensitive portrayers of human vulnerability in the history of portrait painting. Mrs Gainsborough certainly did have delusions of grandeur and tendencies to parsimony and bossiness, but the portrait speaks of tenderness and respect.[11] She looks the painter steadily in the eye, much as Gainsborough Dupont does in *The Blue Boy* (fig. 12) (if we accept that identification of the sitter). Sophia Lane, the artist's niece who at one time lived with the family, and who helped care for Gainsborough in his final illness, called Mrs Gainsborough 'a remarkably mild and sweet-tempered woman' who generally let her husband do things his own way.[12] As he approached death, Gainsborough made his wife his executrix and ensured that Samuel Kilderbee, one of his oldest friends, would help her to administer his estate.[13] When facing her own death, Margaret Gainsborough requested that she be buried 'in the same vault with my late dear husband at Kew Burial Ground'.[14]

Without Margaret Gainsborough in the background, the painter's portrait practice would have run less smoothly than it did. Gainsborough did not accumulate in his studio nearly as many unfinished or undelivered portraits as, for example, George Romney or Sir Thomas Lawrence. Dupont must take much of the credit for this, but Mrs Gainsborough played her part. Glimpses of her management of the business can be picked up from Gainsborough's letters. On 2 October 1767 the artist wrote apologetically to a client about the delivery of a portrait. The letter ends with a postscript: 'Packing Case cost me 7 Shillings which My Wife desires me always to remember and I often forget Voluntarily because I am ashamed to mention it.'[15] There were grounds for her interventions, as he himself admitted. Writing reflectively to Mary Gibbon a decade later, Gainsborough had no doubt that had he always handled things his own way, he would have 'wasted many thousands'.[16]

Margaret Gainsborough's £200 annuity, which was paid until the end of her life, came from the Dukes of Beaufort.[17] She was an illegitimate daughter of the 3rd Duke, perhaps best remembered for having commissioned the famous Badminton Cabinet (one of the great masterpieces of eighteenth-century Florentine decorative arts, now in the Princely Collections, Lichtenstein), who died young in 1745. Her mother's identity has proved elusive, but thanks to the work of John Bensusan-Butt and David Tyler, we know that Margaret Gainsborough descended from the Aikman family of Edinburgh, through whom she was connected to the world of international trade and commerce. Her will identifies a nephew, James Burr of Bells Mills, Edinburgh, and a niece, Mary Burr of Panton Street, Haymarket, London.[18] From this it can be shown that Margaret Burr must have been a half-sister of Isaak Burr and Alexander Burr, and daughter of Margaret Burr, née Aikman. There is no indication of how the Duke of Beaufort came into contact with

Mrs Burr, the only clue being the fact that he had his Grand Tour purchases shipped home by Messrs Winder & Aikman of Edinburgh and Leghorn [Livorno].[19] Mrs Gainsborough's niece Mary, the daughter of Alexander Burr, married a James Scott; the couple named their second daughter Margaret, and their second son 'Gainsborgh'.[20] In 1821 the same Mary was responsible for the disposal of the belongings of the recently deceased Miss Margaret Gainsborough, the painter's daughter.[21]

Mrs Gainsborough took charge of her husband's income from portraiture.[22] Like other portrait painters, Gainsborough worked to standard canvas sizes and standard fees, so it was relatively easy to keep track of commissions. Half-payments were often taken in advance, with the balance due on completion. Framing, packing and delivery arrangements were the only variables, and it was in these areas that accounting mistakes and omissions could easily be made. If she did grow up with some knowledge of the Aikman shipping and packing business, this would certainly have proved useful when the portrait practice expanded on the family's move to Bath in 1759. There the artist packed pictures at home, and relied on his friend Walter Wiltshire's 'Flying Waggon' to deliver them.[23] After his move from Bath to London in 1774 we do not know which carrier he used, but it appears that packing was still organised at home. In 1782, when a portrait of the Prince of Wales was to be sent to the prince's brother Frederick Augustus in Hanover, the prince himself wrote to Frederick, 'I intend sending you among other things by ye next messenger a portrait of me painted by Gainsborough & reckoned by everybody to be a remarkable strong likeness. He is to pack it up himself. It will be rol'd & sent in a tin case. You will therefore make yr. servants take care how they unpack it.'[24]

We can be pretty sure that Gainsborough did not personally roll the picture or commission the waterproof case: these tasks must have been shared between Dupont and servants, with Margaret Gainsborough overseeing proceedings. In this instance, she did not manage to extract payment for the picture. A significant number of artists and craftsmen suffered from the prince's over-expenditure on Carlton House and other extravagances (his debts by 1784 amounted to £150,000) but Gainsborough declined to join the official list of creditors on the grounds that the prince 'had always behaved in a gentlemanly manner to him'.[25] At the time, Mrs Gainsborough evidently bowed to her husband's wishes, but after his death she submitted an account for the £1,228.10s that was then owed for a grand total of fourteen canvases. She received payment in two instalments in 1793.[26]

The only income that the painter managed to keep from his wife was that generated by the sale of his landscapes.[27] These were not priced by size, although many of them are painted on standard portrait canvases, and any sales that did take place were privately negotiated between artist and buyer. When he exhibited landscapes at the Royal Academy, Gainsborough maintained the pretence that they were not for sale.[28] This was partly a matter of personal pride – the implication being that he did not *need* to sell them – and partly a way of keeping their value to himself.

While she was able to keep her eye on the portrait business, Margaret Gainsborough had no control over her husband's use of her annuity. This was paid to him after their marriage, and documents show that in the 1750s he used it as security for loans.[29] Later on, it helped to pay for stylish premises. There is an intriguing parallel between Gainsborough's personal and financial circumstances and those of fellow portrait-painter Nathaniel Hone. In the early part of his life, Hone also benefited from an annuity paid to his wife. In his *Memorandum Book* of 1753 he wrote that he received 'from Annuity' a figure of £125 in January of that year; in the previous year there is a record of him receiving the same sum in July.[30] By the time his first wife died in 1769, Hone's career was well established and he, like Gainsborough, had developed a predilection for smart addresses.[31] When Gainsborough and his family made the move from Ipswich to Bath, Thicknesse tells us that Mrs Gainsborough was alarmed by the artist's plan to rent a prime town-centre property, 'fearing it [the cost] must all come out of her annuity'.[32] The Beaufort annuity could, indeed, have paid for Gainsborough's Abbey Street house, even though, at a rent of £150 a year, it was one of the most expensive in Bath.[33]

Gainsborough and Hone used their wives' annuities to similar effect. Both invested in property that boosted their status as portrait painters, and both felt free to take risks with their careers. They explored subjects outside the safe bounds of portraiture and refused to kowtow to authority. Both adopted an independent line over the exhibition of their work. While Gainsborough took pleasure in landscape, Hone enjoyed painting fancy pictures, and both portrayed members of their own families in fancy mode. Hone's *Brickdust Man*, exhibited at the Society of Artists' (SA) exhibition in 1760, is a landmark in the history of British fancy painting.[34] He followed this up with *A Boy Deliberating on his Drawing* (fig. 28; SA, 1766), *The Piping Boy*, shown at the inaugural Royal Academy exhibition in 1769 and *The Spartan Boy* in 1775, in each case a likeness of his son, Camillus. All these precede Gainsborough's concentrated period of fancy painting, which began in 1781, but Gainsborough's double portrait of his daughters as gleaners (cat. 17) predates Hone's experiments. Hone's *Piping Boy* and *Spartan Boy* engage with the tradition of history painting, and are different in this respect from Gainsborough's portraits of his children, but it is worth noting that the iconography of two of the paintings of Mary and Margaret Gainsborough may be more complex than is usually thought. The thistle in *The Artist's Daughters, Chasing a Butterfly* (cat. 9), for instance, may allude to the children's Scottish heritage, and the admonitory notion of 'whoever plays with a cat will be scratched' is incorporated into *the Artist's Daughters, Playing with a Cat* (cat. 16) as Ann Bermingham explains (see page 49). There are parallels to be drawn between Hone's *Boy Deliberating on his Drawing* and Gainsborough's double portrait of his daughters as young artists (cat. 19). Both belong to an established Continental tradition that was familiar to English artists through prints such as John Faber's mezzotint of a youth with a portfolio and porte-crayon after Jean-Baptiste-Siméon Chardin, published in London in 1740.[35] Between 1774 and 1780 Hone and Gainsborough were

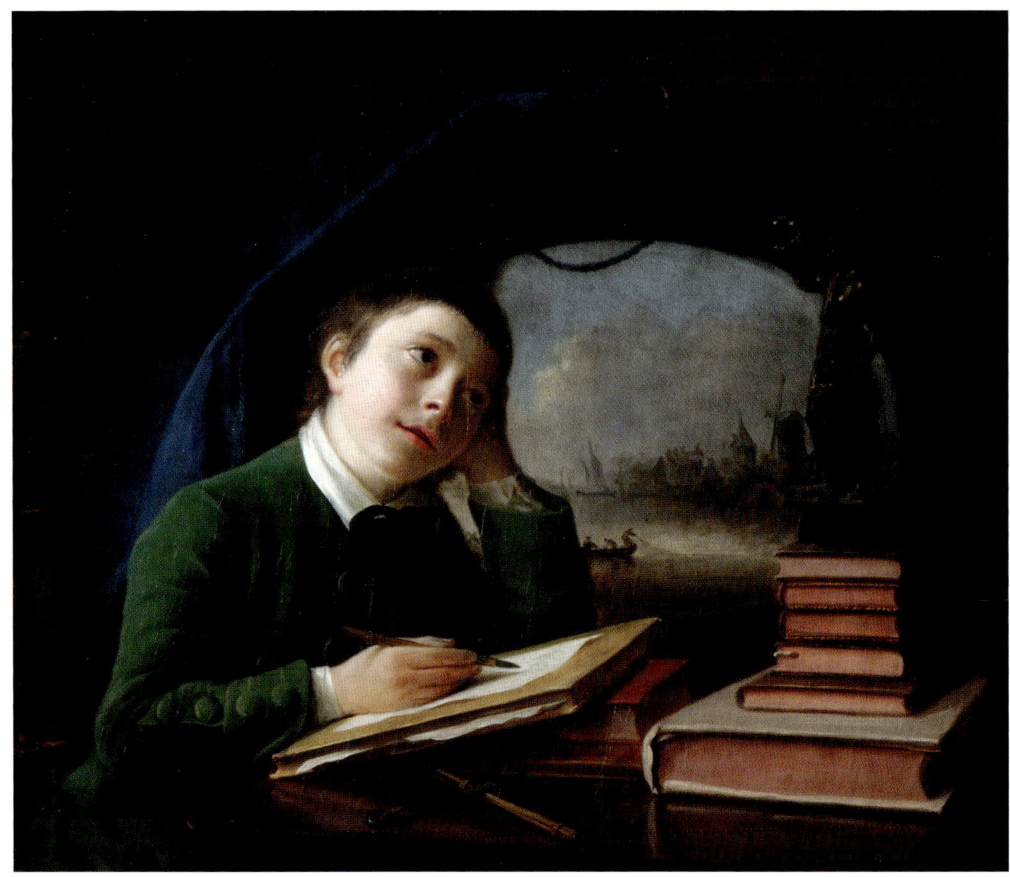

near neighbours in Pall Mall, central London, and both fell foul of the Royal Academy on more than one occasion. Hone's *The Conjuror* (now in the National Gallery of Ireland, Dublin), which he had the temerity to send to the Academy in 1775, insulted its president, Sir Joshua Reynolds, by implying that he, 'The Conjuror', was a plagiarist.[36] Gainsborough made impossible demands of the Academy's Committee of Arrangement and eventually withdrew altogether from the annual exhibitions. We can only speculate as to how far the two men's seemingly arrogant behaviour was bolstered by the financial security that stemmed from their annuities.

For Gainsborough, his investment in the Duke of Kingston's Abbey Street town house in Bath reaped rewards for him and his extended family. That same year (1760) Mrs Gibbon's husband died, and in 1761–2 she wound up her business in Colchester. In fact, Mary Gibbon's spirit lived on in the Essex town, since the millinery that cornered the market there for the next twenty years was run by members of the Reeve and Wood families, three of whom were closely linked with her.[37] Hannah Reeve had been a witness to the Reverend Christopher Gibbon's will in 1759, and two of the Woods were Mrs Gibbon's apprentices.[38] The most successful milliners of this period had the ability to cross class and professional boundaries, as a recent study has pointed out.[39] In 1763 the younger Hannah Reeve married Frederick Charles Reinhold, a musician with a distinguished pedigree, whose portrait was painted by Johann Zoffany.[40] In March or April 1762 Mrs Gibbon moved from Colchester to Bath to share the Abbey Street property.[41] It was only a month later that Gainsborough opened a London bank account with Hoare's of Fleet Street, quite possibly on his sister's advice.[42] The trust and companionship that existed between Gainsborough and Mary Gibbon is clear from the artist's correspondence, but there does not appear to be any portrait of her.[43] Perhaps she had no inclination to be painted. In 1779 he commented to a friend that he would like to give her one of his landscape paintings, but she 'delights not in Worldly prospects'.[44] Always a devout woman, Mary Gibbon may have been married to a Church of England cleric, but she was increasingly attracted to Methodism, a branch of non-conformity that was promoted in Bath by the Countess of Huntingdon and other high-profile adherents. When she stayed with her brother in London in the 1770s, he complained of the difficulty of finding 'new Methodist Chapels enough for Her'.[45] Mrs Gibbon's piety did nothing to dampen her enthusiasm for business, and although Gainsborough joked about her praying 'double Sides', it never caused a rift between brother and sister.[46] It also never prevented him from sharing confidences with her. In 1777 he appealed to her for a loan of £20 to help a 'poor wench', a prostitute he had known in Bath, who was in urgent need of medical attention.[47] He explains that he has a commission for two landscapes, but these are not yet delivered, so he has no cash that can be used without his wife's knowledge.

Gainsborough himself called Mrs Gibbon 'a Woman of Corage'.[48] In order to operate independently in a man's world, as she did, women had to be steely in temperament. The famous wax-modeller Patience Wright, who had rooms in Pall Mall when Gainsborough was there in the 1770s, was said to have possessed 'a strong and masculine understanding'.[49] From what we know about Mary Gibbon, it appears that she had an equally 'masculine' grasp of commerce. In Colchester, between 1753 and 1761, she took on nine or ten apprentices; in Bath, over the decade 1763–73, she took on ten more.[50] When she settled there in 1762, the corner shop in Gainsborough's house was arguably the finest retail site in the town (fig. 7). It had northerly windows facing Abbey Churchyard, the paved open space in front of Bath Abbey, and east-facing windows on Abbey Street, the thoroughfare down which everyone had to walk to reach the Assembly Rooms. She used the situation to launch a second and probably even more lucrative career as a lodging-house keeper. Having his sister on site meant that Gainsborough acquired a millinery that perfectly complemented his portrait practice, and a loyal supporter and adviser.

When Gainsborough moved to 17 Circus in the newly developed upper town in 1766, Mrs Gibbon followed suit, renting 15 Circus, two doors away. She took responsibility for the whole of the Abbey Street house and over the next twenty-four years she managed nine or ten properties in Bath, offering full board as well as lodgings at two of them.[51] The investment in furnishings alone must have been enormous. These were substantial houses, four storeys or more high, with basements and sub-basements, the main floors having high ceilings and large windows. But the earning potential was equally impressive, and, in due course, a procession of other family members arrived in Bath to

join the lodging-house and millinery businesses, including Gainsborough's
sister Susanna Gardiner (cat. 42), two of the Gardiner daughters and one
son, Gainsborough's nephew Edward Gainsborough and a great-nephew
also called Edward Gainsborough.[52] The two Edwards were especially close
to Mrs Gibbon and both are mentioned in her will, possibly because they
associated with the Methodists. The younger Edward Gainsborough and his
bookseller partner Campbell printed the Reverend John William Fletcher's
history of the Methodists and published a mezzotint portrait of John Wesley
by John Jones after Lewis Vaslet.[53] Campbell and Gainsborough's trade card
advertises books of history, philosophy, poetry and divinity.[54] It would appear
that the elder Edward was an illegitimate son of Gainsborough's brother John
'Scheming Jack' (cat. 29), a fact that might also account for Mrs Gibbon's
motherly concern for this branch of the family.[55]

For twenty years, between 1753 and 1774, Mary Gibbon's and
Gainsborough's careers ran in parallel. In the 1750s the painter's stay in
Ipswich matched hers in Colchester; in the 1760s and early 1770s both were in
Bath. When Gainsborough settled in Pall Mall in 1774, they remained in touch
by letter and in person. In June 1779 he refers to his sister's visits to London,
where she evidently stayed with him at Schomberg House.[56] He was in Bath for
most of the month of July 1779, and was there again in January 1786.[57] It may
have been very early on in their professional lives that Gainsborough and Mary
Gibbon decided that inter-connected careers, rather like the ones that existed
in Hogarth's family, could be mutually beneficial. The advantages are obvious.
Sitters could browse in the shop while they waited for their appointment and
get wind of the latest fashions. Since it was normal practice for clients to leave
clothes behind in the studio to be painted from lay figures or models, some of
Gainsborough's sitters may have commissioned or hired clothes and accessories
from Mrs Gibbon that could afterwards be recycled. It should be said that
although she is generally called a milliner, half of her Colchester apprentices
were dressmakers, so her shop dealt with a diverse range of goods, and not just
hats, trimmings and accessories.

As Gainsborough's reputation grew, he himself probably had some say in
his sitters' choice of costume. There is documentary evidence to show that
on occasion Reynolds and Romney persuaded their subjects to wear specially
made clothes they did not even like.[58] Romney's sitter Lady Newdegate told
her husband, 'he insists on my having a rich white sattin with a long train
made by Tuesday & have it left with him all summer. It is ye oddest thing I
ever saw.'[59] Yet for all their skills, neither Romney nor Reynolds portrayed
costume with the same flair and sensitivity as Gainsborough. In 1777 one
newspaper critic observed that the portrait of the Hon. Mrs Graham (fig.
29) proved Gainsborough to be superior to all his rivals in the painting
of drapery.[60] He was less inclined than Reynolds and Romney to paint
women in generalised, vaguely classical dress, and was particularly good at
distinguishing between the different weights and surfaces of cottons, silks,
satins and furs. He knew how fabrics were quilted and layered, and how
garments were constructed. Similarly, he would have been familiar with

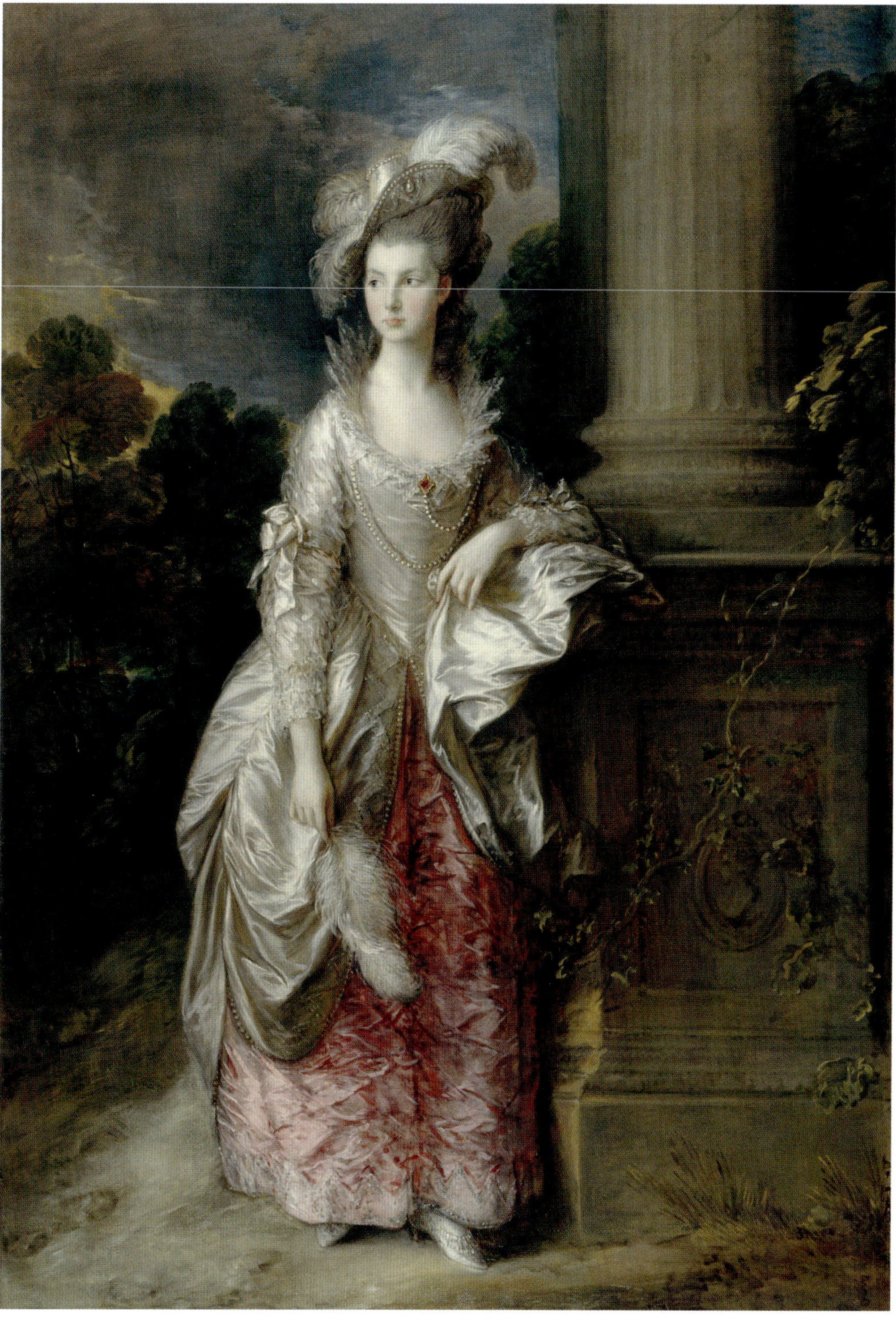

the materials of the milliner's trade, some which were also used by artists: isinglass, for example, was a means of stiffening gauze and ribbons, but also a fixative for works on paper. With reference to the brilliant full-length double portrait of Gainsborough's daughters (cat. 30), the dress historian Aileen Ribeiro points to the way in which the artist superimposes historical details on to a fashionable modern outline, merging fact and fantasy. In her words, 'Mary's gown of dusky pink has short scalloped sleeves in the Lely style, a

bodice front that suggests the 1670s design of
sloping sides with a triangular underbodice,
forming a point at the centre of the neckline,
and – for good measure – a fringed sash in
oriental style.'[61] Ribeiro has recently reached
the conclusion that Mrs Graham's dress is
not a real masquerade costume, as she once
thought, but a work of Gainsborough's
imagination.[62] If this is true, it underlines the
thoroughness of his understanding of fabrics
and of dress, and the significance of Mrs
Gibbon's behind-the-scenes presence in his life.

Brother and sister were no longer in daily
contact after the artist's move to London,
but in 1784 Gainsborough acquired a new
milliner neighbour in Pall Mall. The company of
Hartshorn & Dyde moved into the east wing of
Schomberg House (then numbered 89 Pall Mall),
taking the shop and rear warehouse premises that
mirrored Gainsborough's professional rooms in
number 87, the west wing.[63] Mrs Dyde, styling
herself 'a Milliner of character, and in the first
line of business', sought apprentices for the new
shop in November 1784.[64] Since 1781 this firm
had also had a shop in the Circus at Bath, where
Mary Gibbon still lived, and where she managed
numbers 15, 17 and 28 as lodgings.[65] Hartshorn
& Dyde's in Bath was a large property at the
corner of the Circus and Bennet Street, numbered
19, two doors from Gainsborough's former
house.[66] The new Assembly rooms were only a
few yards away in Bennet Street, so Hartshorn & Dyde was as strategically
placed as Mrs Gibbon's Abbey Street millinery had been in the 1760s. In 1786
the Hartshorn & Dyde premises passed to Robert Minchin and his daughter:
their name board can be seen on the façade of 19 Circus in their trade card
(fig. 30).[67] Minchin's was taken over by Gainsborough's nieces, the Misses
Gardiner, in 1800.[68]

It is hard to believe that Hartshorn & Dyde's appearance at Schomberg
House in 1784 was purely coincidental. They would have known Mrs Gibbon
and must have been aware of the historic link between Gainsborough's portrait
practice and Mrs Gibbon's millinery. The Abbey Street property, where
brother and sister had flourished under the same roof, was still referred to
as 'Gainsboroughs' in 1785.[69] Hartshorn & Dyde's relocation of the London
arm of their firm from Wigmore Street to Pall Mall was a progressive step into
upmarket St James's, as is made clear by their advertisements. It also brought
them within the orbit of one of London's most famous portrait painters. For

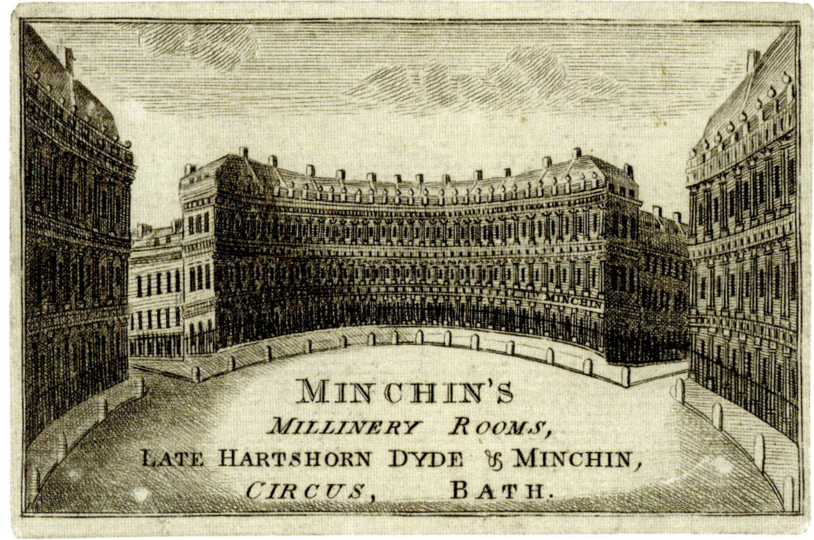

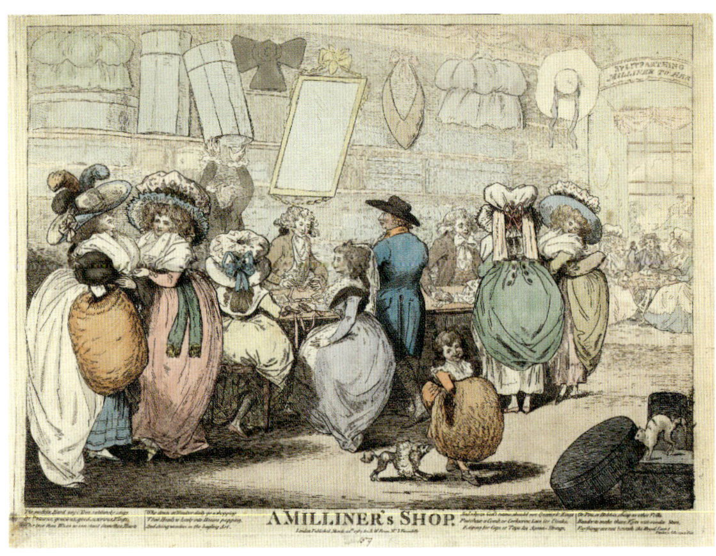

FIG. 30
*Trade card for Minchin's
Millinery Rooms, Bath*,
1786–99
Etching
62 x 94mm

British Museum, London.
Banks Trade Card Collection

FIG. 31
A Milliner's Shop,
published by S.W. Fores,
1787
Etching, hand-coloured
389 x 505mm

Yale Center for British Art,
Paul Mellon Collection,
New Haven CT

Gainsborough, Mrs Dyde effectively became the new Mrs Gibbon, handily placed to provide his clients with clothing and accessories that they could try on in rooms that she says are 'particularly warm'.[70] There is no known record of the internal appearance of Mrs Gibbon's or Mrs Dyde's shops, but an anonymous print of 1787 gives a good impression of one such shop at a time when outsized hats and fur muffs were all the rage (fig. 31). Two of Gainsborough's late portraits of his wife (cats 44, 45) show her wearing a mob-cap with a very large puffed crown, a style that reflects the form of the 'balloon' hat that came into vogue in London in 1784/5.[71] An awareness of fashion was part and parcel of life within the Gainsborough family; it was evidently something that stayed with the artist's wife into her old age.

On Gainsborough's death in 1788, his studio effects passed to Dupont. Along with painting materials, there was an array of plaster casts of limbs, hands and feet, items that were to be found in every portrait painter's premises.[72] There were also copper plates dating from the 1770s and 1780s, when Gainsborough had experimented with printmaking. His attention was caught by technical developments that allowed prints to imitate drawings in a fresh and convincing manner. Before 1770, British artists used various combinations of etching, mezzotint and woodblock printing to copy the effects of pen and ink, chalk, watercolour and ink wash. Now, with the advent of aquatint and soft ground etching, fluid tonal effects and chalk marks could be reproduced with remarkable veracity, and Gainsborough was one of the first to try out the new media. His landscape prints were never published in his or Dupont's lifetimes, but after Dupont's premature death in January 1797, Mrs Gainsborough retrieved the plates and entrusted them to John and Josiah Boydell.[73] An announcement appeared in the *Morning Post* on 17 August 1797:

> This day are published,
> For Mrs. GAINSBOROUGH, by J. and J. BOYDELL, No. 90, Cheapside,
> and at the Shakespeare Gallery, Pall Mall,
> TWELVE PRINTS OF LANDSCAPE SCENERY, with Cattle and
> Figures, from Plates executed by the hand of the late Mr. THOMAS
> GAINSBOROUGH …

A number of artists' widows sought to earn a continuing income by marketing prints. William Hogarth's will ensured that his widow and his sister Ann remained in possession of engraved plates after his work and stipulated that the plates should not be disposed of without the consent of both parties.[74] Mary Worlidge, the widow of Thomas Worlidge, an artist who regularly worked in Bath, issued sets of his prints of antique gems on a monthly basis, completing a process he had begun several years earlier. She maintained her late husband's London house in Great Queen Street, Lincoln's Inn Fields, and accommodated his pupil George Powle, who continued Worlidge's practice of painting portraits in oils and in watercolours.[75] After Gainsborough's death, Dupont had similarly stayed on at Schomberg House, but, left to his own devices, he had no real prospect of supporting so large a property.

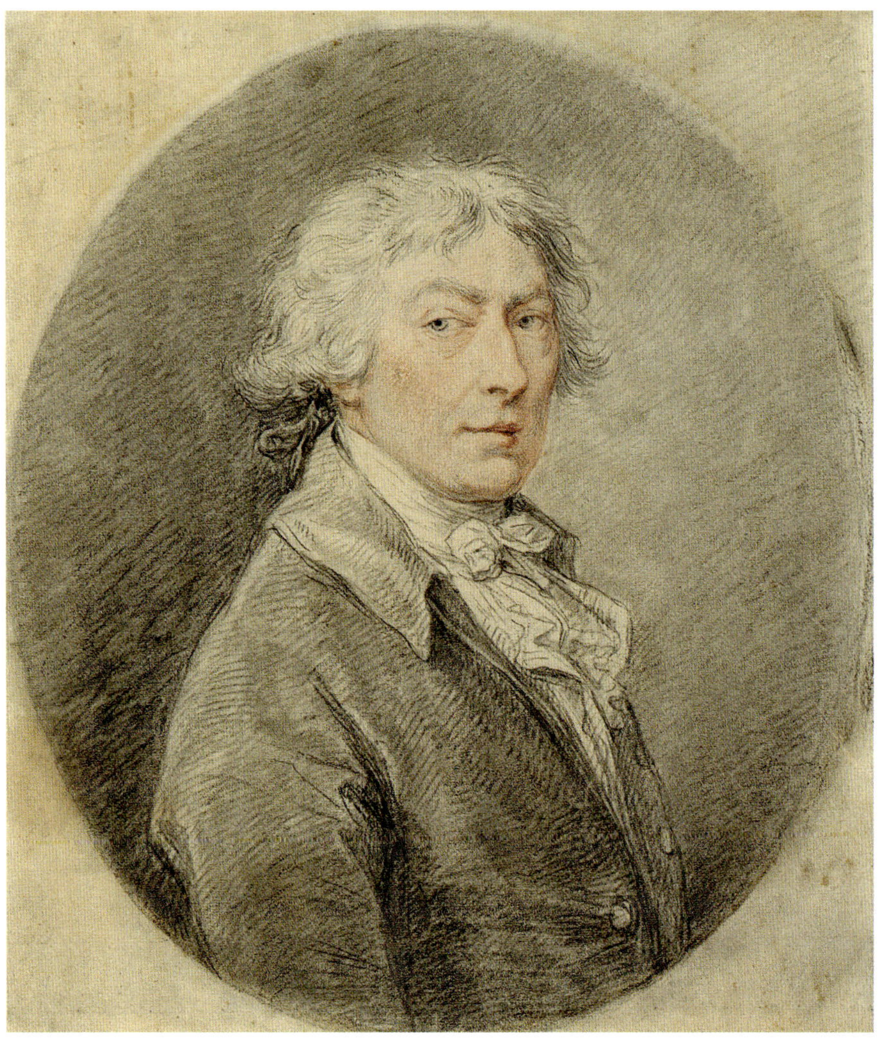

Consequently, when the lease came up for renewal in 1792, he took more modest professional rooms in a new house near Fitzroy Square, and the female members of the family moved to Sloane Street. Mrs Gainsborough must have entertained high hopes of selling Gainsborough's landscape etchings in 1797. Boydell's Shakespeare Gallery stood almost directly opposite Schomberg House, which would have struck a chord with the late artist's long-term admirers; people were interested in Gainsborough's drawings, and at 3 guineas for the set of twelve, the price was not excessive. Despite this, the relatively small number of impressions of these prints that are known today suggests that sales were limited. In London, generally, there was a steep downturn in the market in the wake of the French Revolution, and Boydell's edition of Gainsborough's landscapes was not the only failed printing project. William Dickinson, Robert Pollard and Thomas Gaugain are just three of the London printmakers and printsellers whose businesses collapsed in the mid 1790s.[76]

Later on, in 1797, young Margaret, who had never married, assumed responsibility for her father's artistic legacy. The painter had left instructions that no death mask or portrait should be taken.[77] If some memorial likeness was required, he consented to the production of a print after the self-portrait he had painted for Carl Friedrich Abel, his closest friend (cat. 47). He recommended the engraver William Sharp who had just executed a fine print of the Scottish surgeon John Hunter, one of the medical men then attending him.[78] Eventually it was not Sharp but Francesco Bartolozzi who made the print that was published on 1 January 1798, nearly a decade after Gainsborough's death (fig. 40). Miss Margaret Gainsborough was not convinced that the portrait intended for Abel was the best likeness of her father, and sent Bartolozzi an additional painting for reference. She outlined her reasons in a polite accompanying letter:

> Miss Gainsborough presents her compliments to Mr Bartolozzi, and has taken the liberty of sending another picture of her father – just for him to look at – for she is sure that so great an artist as Mr. B. will see what she means respecting the nose, etc., as she thinks the picture more like her father than the other; but as it was his particular desire to have a print from the picture Mr. Bartolozzi has, it was sent to him in preference to the one now sent. She hopes she has not taken too great a liberty.[79]

Whether the extra picture was one of those exhibited here (cats 12, 46, or possibly the Zoffany, cat. 49) we cannot tell, but Bartolozzi's intermediary drawing (fig. 32) shows that he honoured his old friend's commands, and followed the portrait painted for Abel.

Miss Gainsborough was demonstrably protective of her father's memory. At the same time, she inherited some pragmatism from her mother and her aunt. In 1801 Dr Thomas Monro purchased from her about eighty of Gainsborough's drawings for 160 guineas. On reflection, she decided this was not enough, and Monro was obliged to pay another 20 guineas.[80] After her mother's death she was sufficiently relaxed about her circumstances to buy a 'chariot', a vehicle that was at that time a sporty two-seater conveyance designed for the wealthy.[81]

Gainsborough's obituaries suggest that the artist's impulsive generosity deprived members of his immediate family of rewards that should have been theirs.[82] This is not borne out by the evidence, however, and it is a reminder that even friends such as Henry Bate, who spread this idea abroad, knew relatively little about the painter's home life. With the advantage of hindsight, and of being able to pore over some of Gainsborough's intensely private correspondence (as well as his bank accounts), we can better appreciate than many of his contemporaries how, when it came to managing his financial affairs, this brilliant but rather undisciplined artist relied on the supportive yet restraining influence of his wife, and of his sister Mary Gibbon. The force of their example looks in turn to have informed the care with which Thomas's daughter Margaret managed those of her father's pictures that passed down to her and her sister. Among these, of course, were a high proportion of the contents of Gainsborough's 'family album' – images that today provide such important keys to our understanding and appreciation of this endlessly fascinating artist.

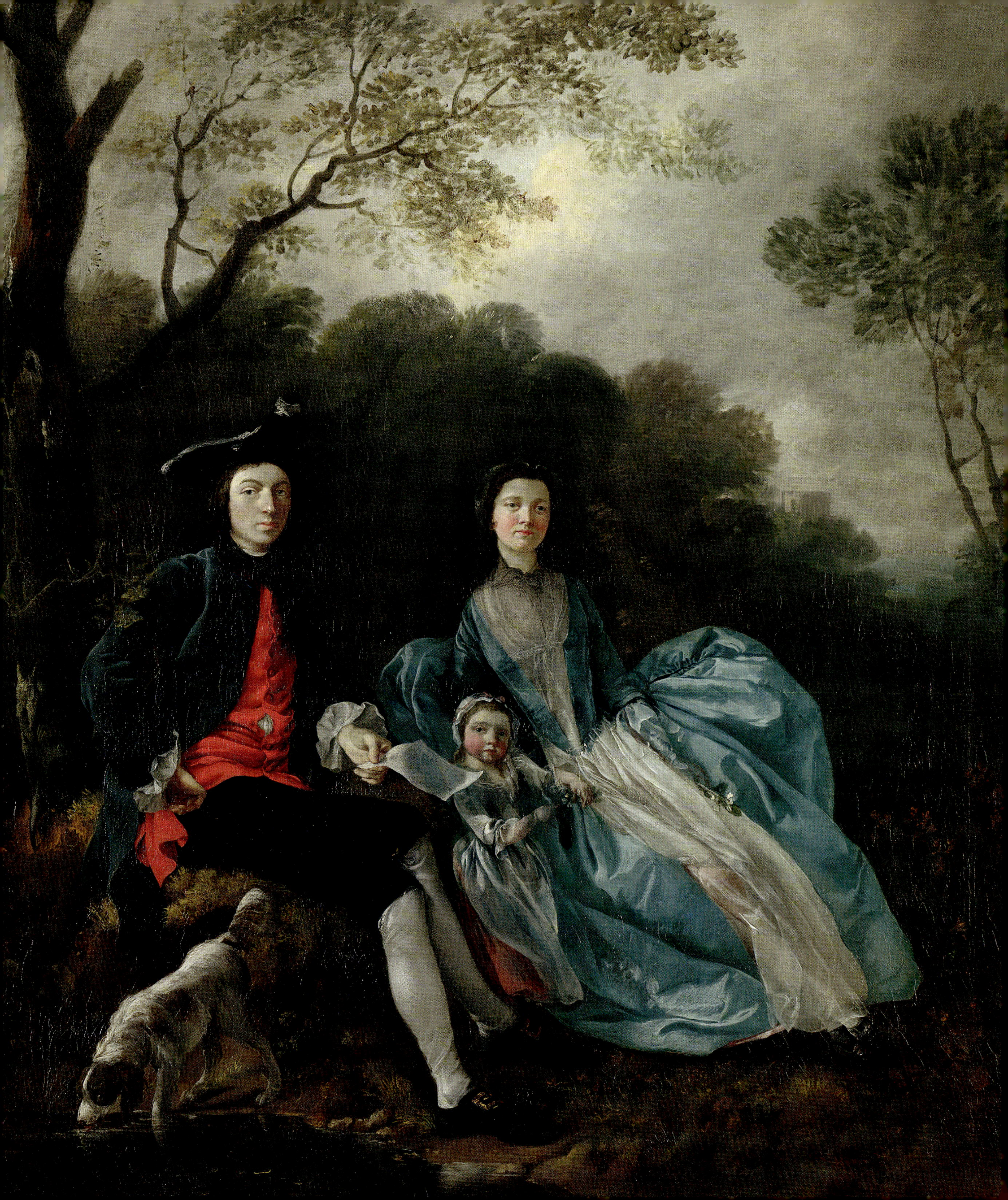

LONDON & SUFFOLK

1727–1758/9

Thomas Gainsborough grew up in Sudbury in Suffolk, but left for London in his early teens to be apprenticed to Hubert-François Gravelot, a French engraver, illustrator and designer. Gravelot introduced his young pupil to the circle of artists, including William Hogarth and Francis Hayman, who formed the core of the St Martin's Lane Academy. By 1743–4, when he was still only about sixteen, Gainsborough had set up an independent studio in Hatton Garden, and in 1746 he married Margaret Burr. Their first child, Mary, was born soon afterwards, but died less than two years later, after which the artist moved back with his wife to Sudbury; this is where their daughters Mary and Margaret were born.

Although work continued to demand Gainsborough's occasional presence in London, throughout the next decade he devoted most of his time to establishing a portrait practice in Suffolk – initially in Sudbury and, from 1752 onwards, in the larger market town of Ipswich. Here he made the transition from conversation pieces — small-scale likenesses of full-length figures, depicted individually or in small groups – to portraiture on the scale of life. Landscape painting, too, became a major preoccupation, but one that he found he had no choice but to pursue for love rather than money. In the most ambitious canvas from his Suffolk period, showing his daughters chasing a butterfly, Gainsborough experimented with a dynamic combination of large-scale portraiture and landscape; yet if this was an option that he offered to his paying customers, it was one they declined to accept. With conservative images like that of his cousin the Reverend Henry Burrough, the young painter stood on far safer ground.

1

John Gainsborough, the Artist's Father

*c.*1746–8
Oil on canvas, 613 x 511mm

Corcoran Collection (Edward C. and Mary Walker Collection)

If this picture was painted before the sitter's death in 1748, as seems most likely, then it is one of Gainsborough's earliest known head-and-shoulders portraits. Here he has depicted his father John, who had been employed as Sudbury's postmaster since the failure of his clothing business in the mid 1730s. He is dressed in a plain, three-piece woollen suit and wearing a slightly ill-fitting long bob-wig; whilst his appearance may be perfectly respectable, it is anything but fashionable. The close attention paid to the different tints of John Gainsborough's craggy face, as seen under a harsh and rather unforgiving light, locates this image in the same tradition of Dutch naturalism that the young artist was exploring in his 1740s landscapes, and sets it apart from the more polished manner adopted by his former teacher Francis Hayman and other contemporary London portraitists. Gainsborough would have had to devise an approach of considerably greater refinement to succeed with paying sitters from the higher ranks of society.

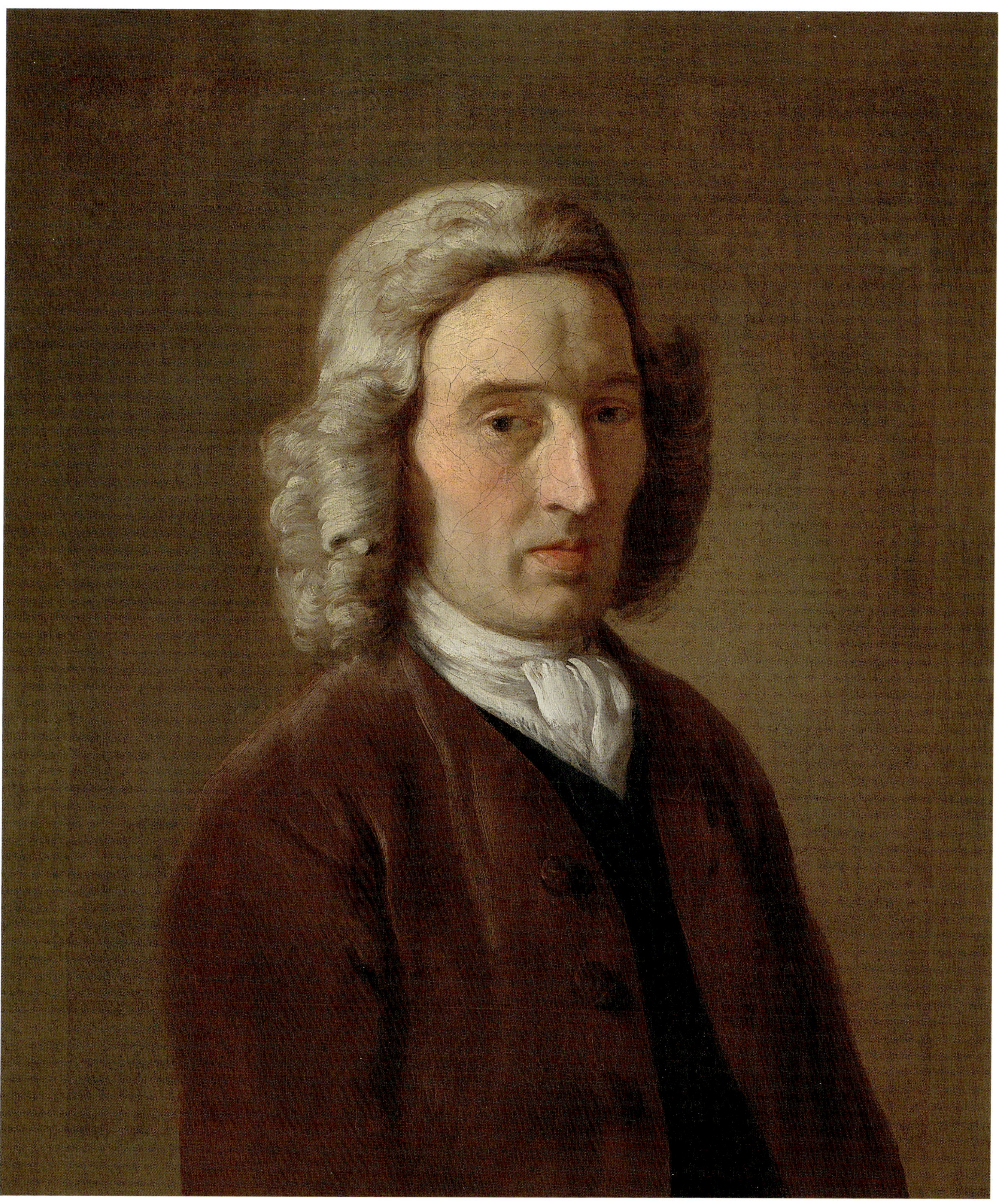

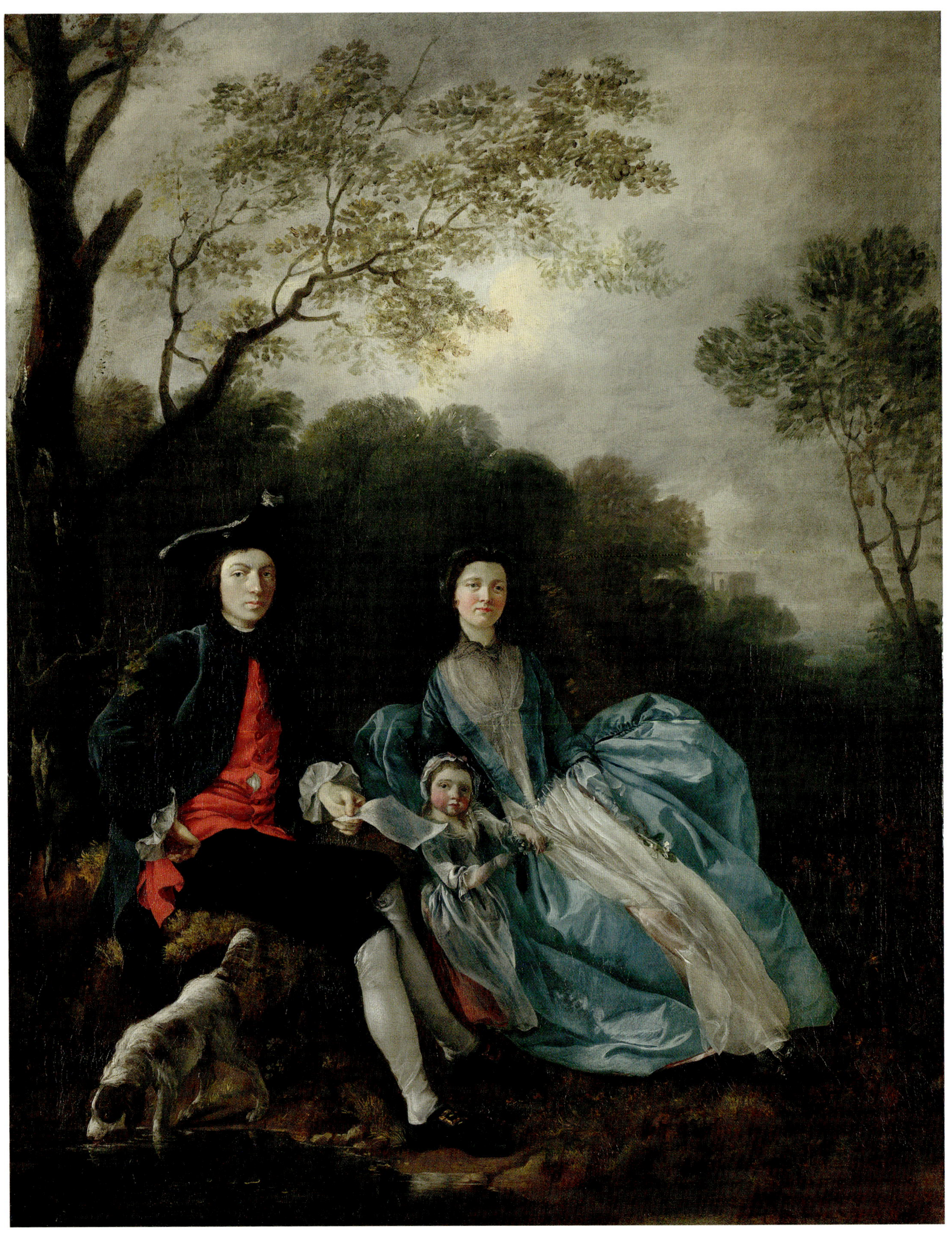

2

The Artist with his Wife
Margaret and Eldest
Daughter Mary

1748?
Oil on canvas, 921 x 705mm

Painted when he was no more than twenty years of age, this conversation piece shows Gainsborough and his young wife Margaret as fashionable gentlefolk taking their ease in the countryside. A slightly later addition to the scene was the figure of their eldest child Mary, who must have been born shortly after their wedding on 15 July 1746, but who died early in 1748. This picture supplies the earliest evidence of the family's determination to assert their claims to being the social equals of Gainsborough's affluent patrons – quite a bold assertion, given the relatively humble status of the youthful artist and his wife's problematic origins as the illegitimate daughter of a duke. In what may or may not be an indication of their subsequent marital difficulties, the couple would never again appear within the boundaries of a single canvas.

Although now worn away by abrasions suffered in the past, the sheet of paper that Gainsborough is shown holding in his left hand probably once bore the outlines of a landscape sketch. This, together with the prominence given the rural setting, indicates his personal and professional interest in landscape art, a genre for which his special talent had already been recognised by his London contemporaries. However, few outside his family circle are likely to have been shown this picture, given its unfinished state. The provocative glimpse of Margaret Gainsborough's right calf through her muslin apron further underlines the image's private character.

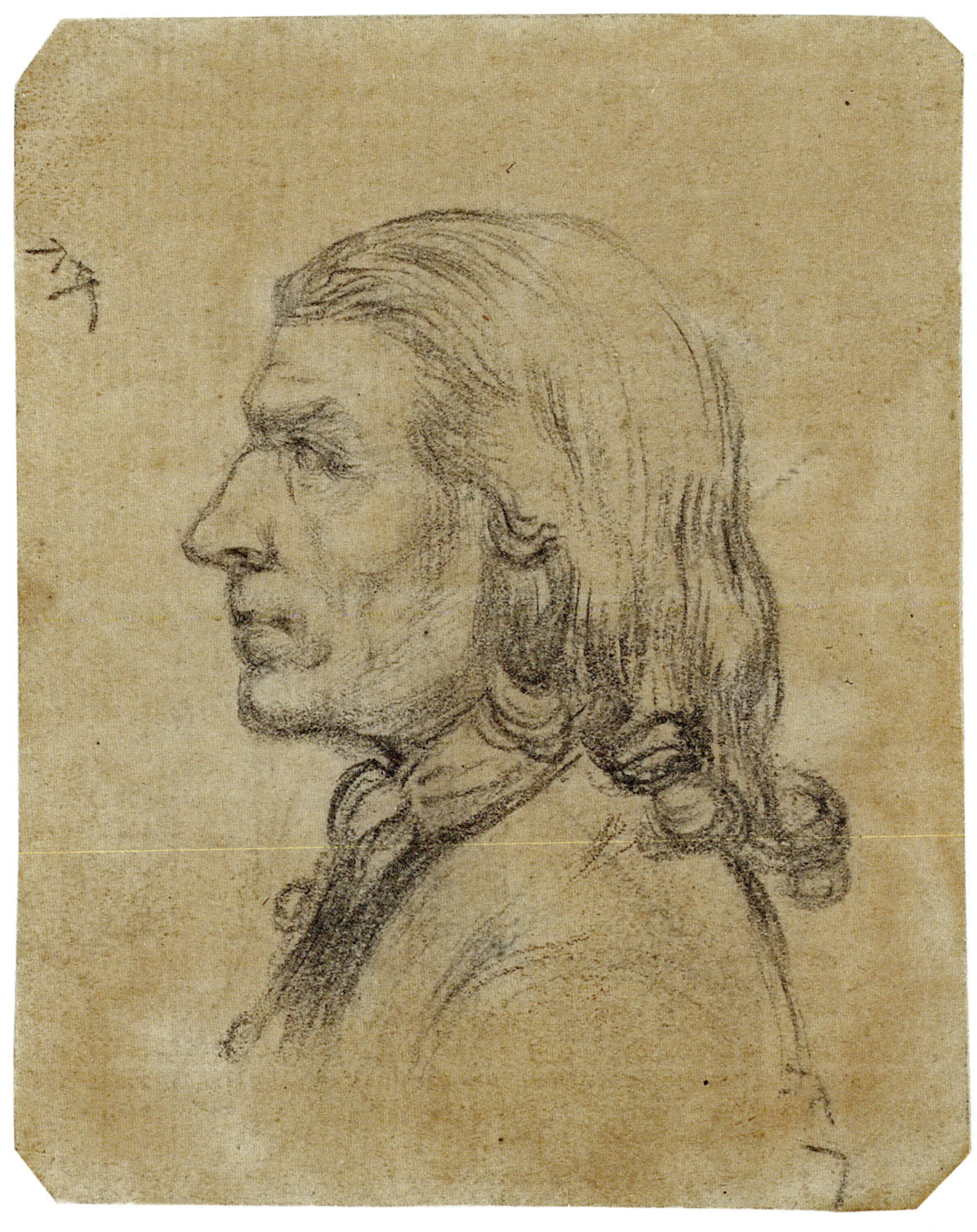

3

John Gainsborough, the Artist's Father

1751
Pencil, 94 x 74mm
Reproduced larger than actual size

Gainsborough's House, Sudbury, Suffolk

Fixed to the back of the frame of this little drawing is a label inscribed by the artist's wife Margaret with the following words: 'My Father Gainsborough's Picture, Drawn by my Husband three years after his Decease, and is extremely like him'. In mid-eighteenth-century Britain, the profile format was often used for commemorative portraits, of which this is an unusually intimate example. John Gainsborough is shown wearing his own hair (by contrast with his bewigged appearance in cat. 1) and on the small scale of a miniature. One of the remarkable features of Gainsborough's practice as a portraitist of his own relations is his strong preference for painting over drawing. The posthumous study of his father is one of the few exceptions that proves the rule, and the care with which it was preserved by his wife and successive generations of the artist's descendants (who retained ownership of the drawing until as recently as 1989) speaks for its value to the family.

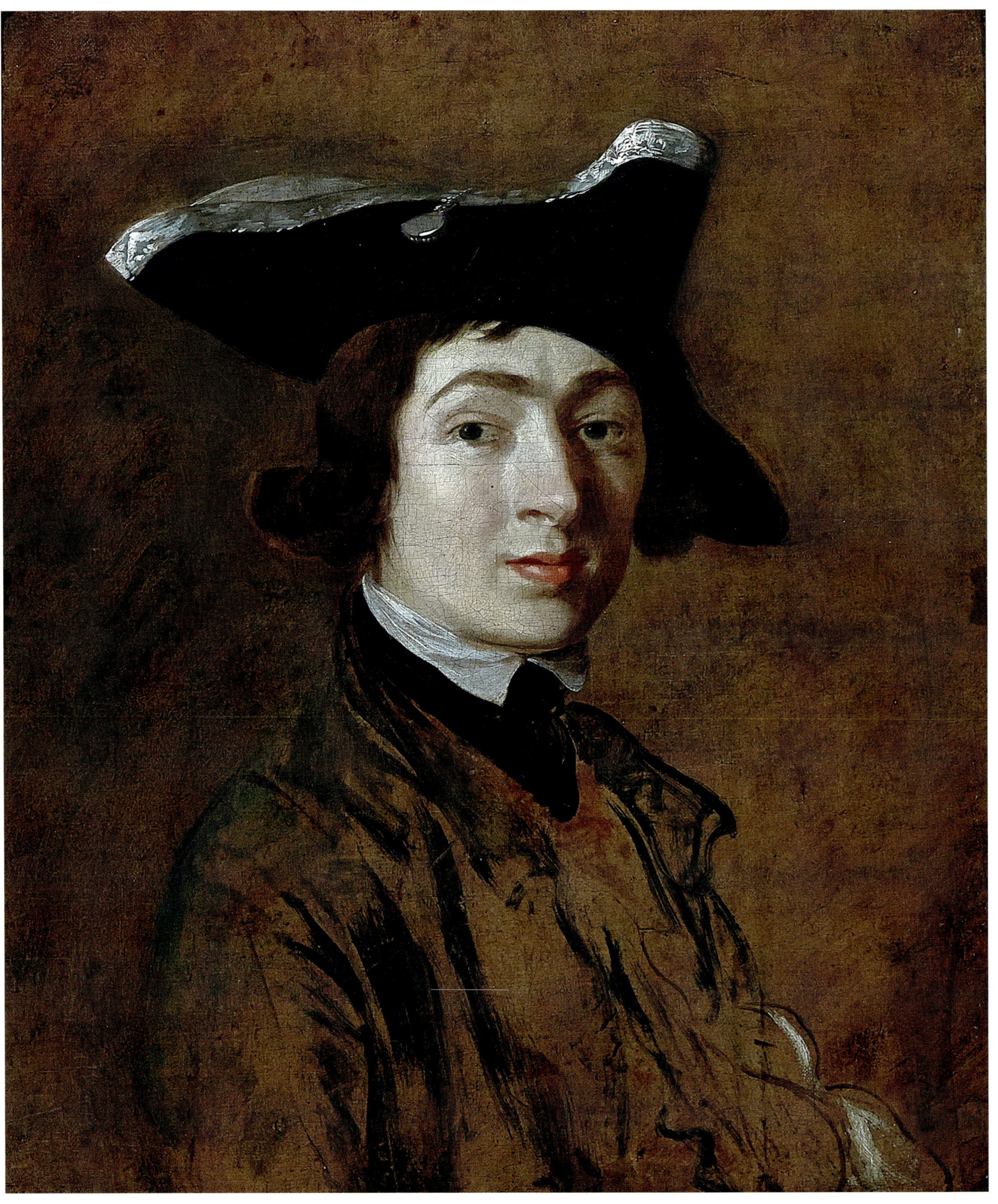

4

Self-portrait

*c.*1754
Oil on canvas, 584 x 483mm

Private Collection

A nineteenth-century inscription on the back of
this unfinished picture, which is a rare example of
an eighteenth-century canvas that has never been
relined, reads: 'Painted by Thomas Gainsborough at
Ipswich about the year 1754 (2nd sitting of himself)
aged 28'. The first sitting may have been related
to a drawing (cat. 5), the pencil self-portrait that
he then attached to a landscape background (cat.
6), or possibly an earlier painting that is otherwise
unrecorded. For an artist to depict himself without
any identifying signs of his trade was not unusual;
nor is it odd to find self-portraits from this period
that incorporate a pose that was understood to
signify the character of polite gentility – in this
instance, the 'hand-in-waistcoat' pattern, probably
the single most popular choice for male sitters
from the 1730s through the 1750s. The frock coat
he is wearing, so deftly sketched in, had only
recently come into fashion for country gentlemen;
as a member of a family of clothes merchants and
milliners, Gainsborough was always acutely aware
of sartorial signs and their implications. A case in
point is his decision to represent himself wearing

a three-cornered hat perched at a rakish angle – a
motif hardly ever encountered in contemporary
portraiture outside the outdoor or sporting
conversation-piece, where it contributed to an
air of casual rustic ease and elegance. Similarly
worn fashion accessories can be found in several
group portraits 'in little' by Francis Hayman, who
employed the young Gainsborough to work for him
in the early to mid 1740s; but there are also several
close precedents in Gainsborough's own work, such
as the *Muilman, Crokatt and Keable* conversation
piece of *c.*1750 (Gainsborough's House/Tate), and
the picture of himself with his wife and first-born
daughter (cat. 2). In this later autonomous self-
portrait, he surely must also have intended to
represent himself in a rural setting, possibly with a
tall tree just behind him and a more distant clump
of foliage on the right (judging by the faint traces
of rough brushwork on either side of his body).
But it was not until four or five years later that
Gainsborough seized the opportunity to take this
idea forward on a separate canvas (cat. 12), and
bring it to a completed form.

5

Self-portrait

1754?
Pencil on laid paper, 280 x 210mm

Andrew Clayton-Payne

This recently discovered sketch may have served as a template for the unfinished oil self-portrait (cat. 4), which follows it faithfully in all but one or two details. At a time when Gainsborough was still learning how to produce head-and-shoulders portraits on a scale approaching life-size, he may have found it easier to paint his own likeness by copying a pencil study, as opposed to working with brushes, palette and canvas directly from a mirror. Another possible explanation – albeit one that raises further questions – is that he executed the drawing to record the appearance of the oil in its incomplete state. If so, this suggests that he intended to finish the oil while retaining an aide-memoire of its process of production. It is also conceivable that Gainsborough had in mind to develop the pencil study itself into a more finished work, as he may well have done with the figure in another drawn self-portrait from his Ipswich period (cat. 6).

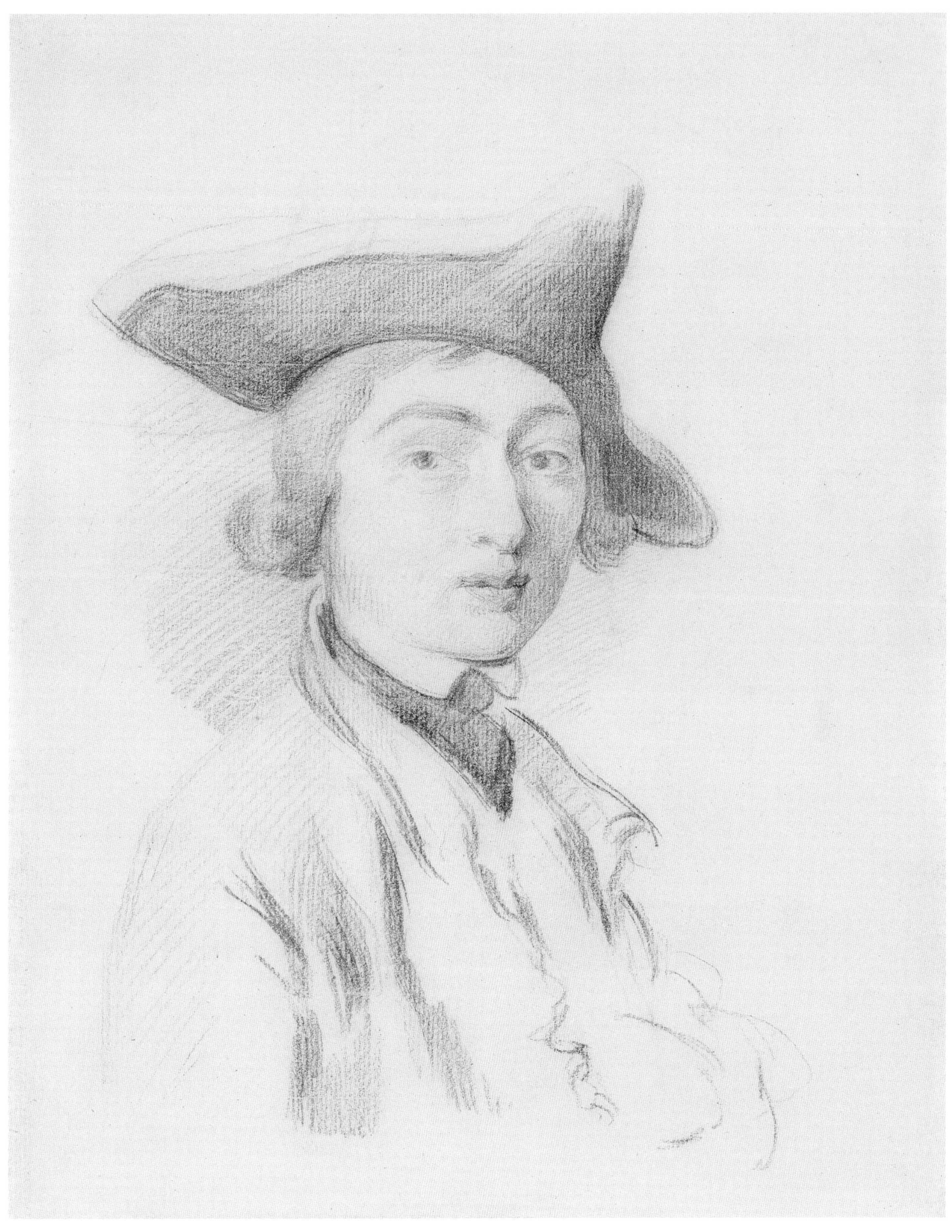

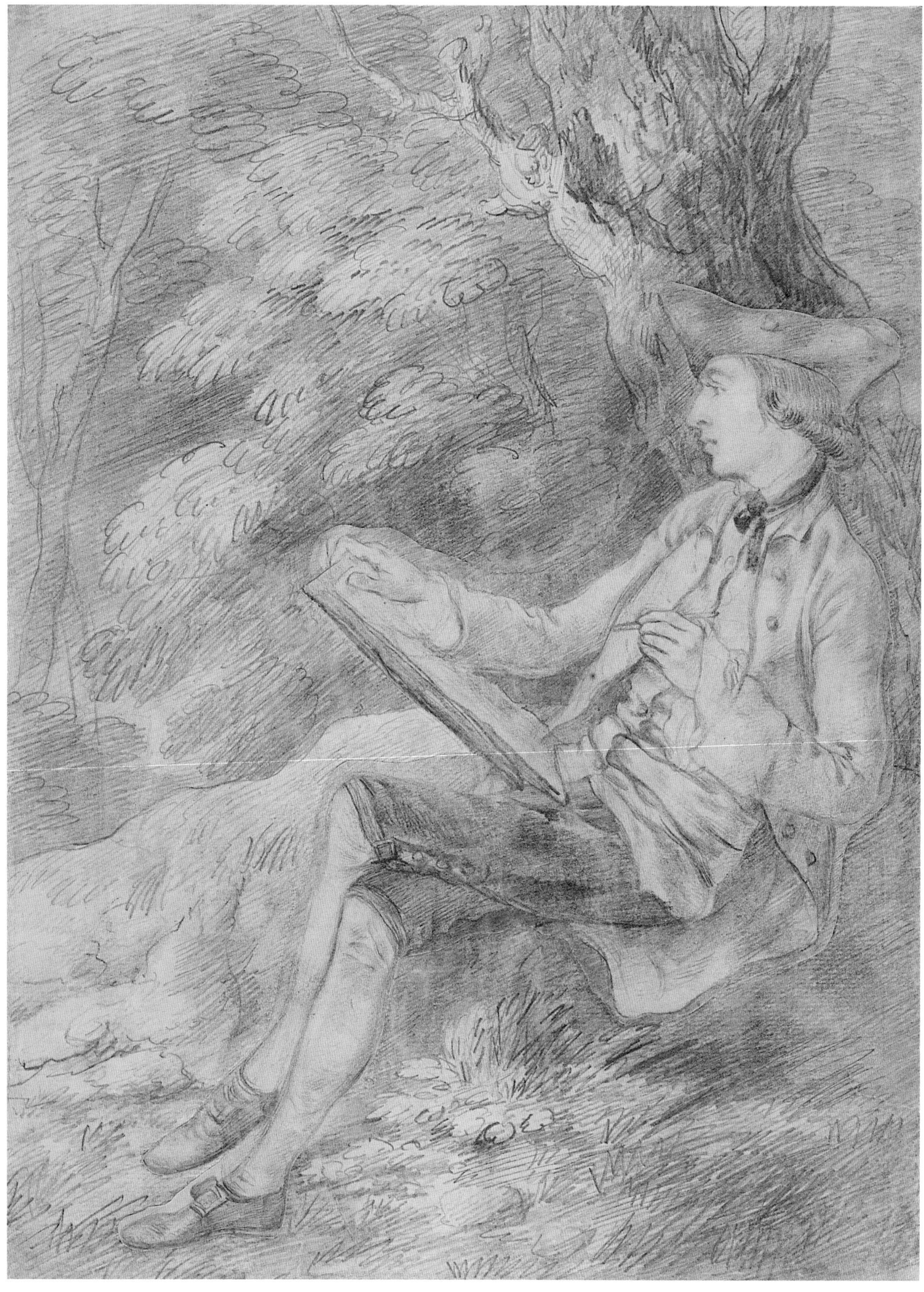

Self-portrait in a Wooded Landscape

*c.*1754–8
Pencil, 359 x 258mm

The British Museum, London
Exhibited in London only

Given the depth of Gainsborough's love for both landscape art and drawing, one imagines that he and his family must have regarded this self-portrait with particular fondness. The figure, which may have been executed a few years earlier than its setting, has been cut from another sheet of paper and carefully glued on to its current background. Although Gainsborough then used his pencil to try blending the two parts into a fully integrated whole, their independent origins are highlighted by the impossibility of determining what the artist is sitting on, if indeed anything at all. The resultant lack of unity unwittingly challenges the credibility of the fiction that the self-portrait seeks to project, of an artist fully absorbed in, and by, the natural world. Later in life, when writing to his friends, Gainsborough would invoke this fantasy as an ideal of free creativity, which the business of portraiture and the demands of his wife and daughters prevented him from achieving – sentiments that he may already have begun to feel by the mid 1750s.

Humphrey Gainsborough,
the Artist's Brother

c.1754–6
Oil on canvas, 580 x 480mm

National Gallery of Ireland, Dublin
Exhibited in London only

This is the first portrait that Gainsborough is known to have painted of any of his siblings, and the only example that survives from his time in Ipswich. By then, his brother Humphrey, a nonconformist minister with a talent for engineering, had long been absent from Suffolk. He had left Sudbury to train in London in 1736, and twelve years later had secured a pulpit in Henley-on-Thames, Oxfordshire, where he was to remain until the end of his life. His reputation as a man of learning probably helps to explain why he has been represented in profile – a format sometimes employed for commemorative purposes (see, for example, cat. 3), but that earlier eighteenth-century British portraitists had also used on more than one occasion to honour the achievements of scholars or men of letters. In its classical severity and colouristic sobriety, Humphrey's likeness may also have been designed to suggest a character of personal modesty and antipathy to showiness, consistent with the identity of a clergyman.

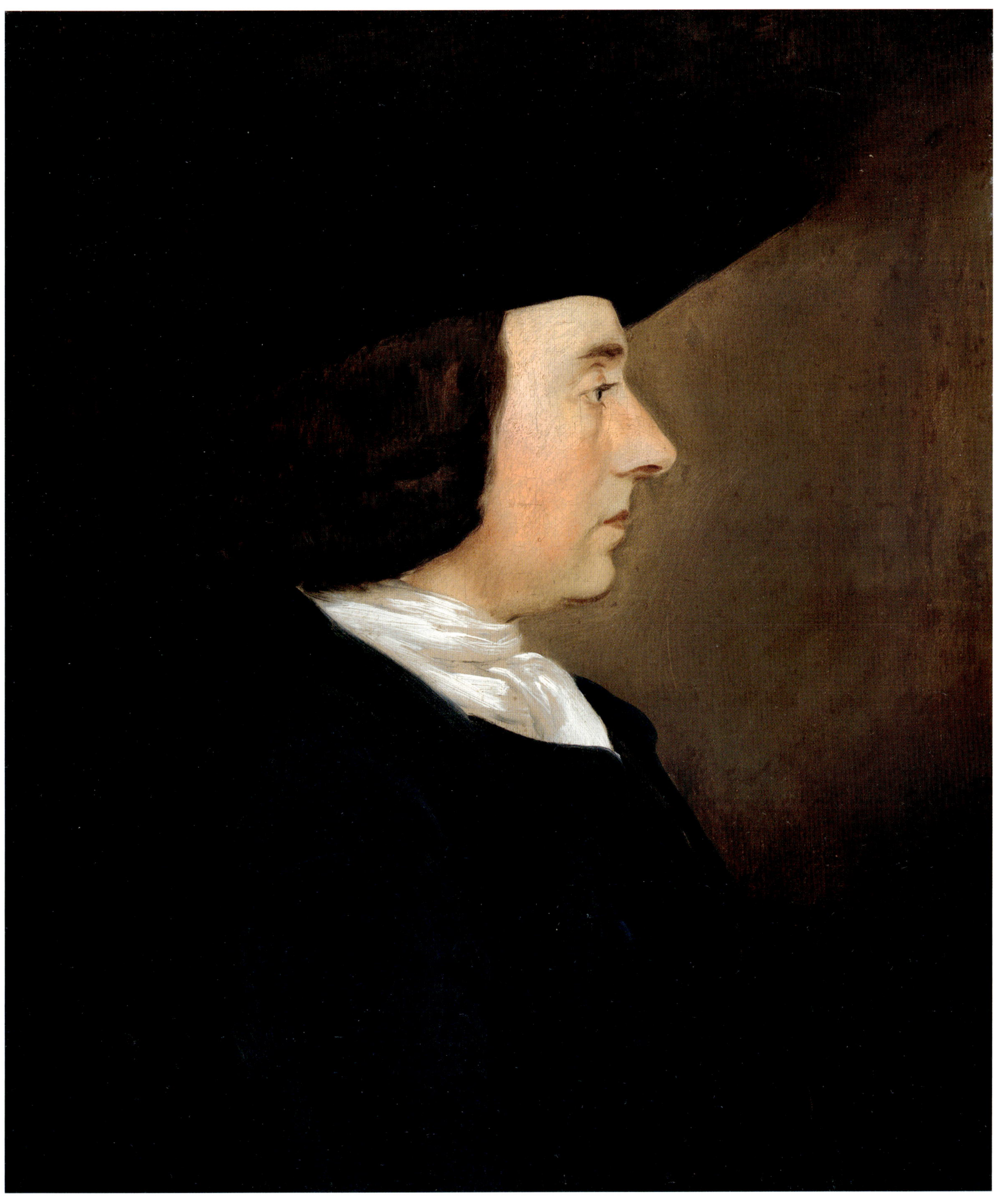

8

Henry Burrough,
the Artist's Cousin

*c.*1756
Oil on canvas, 760 x 640mm

Guildhall Art Gallery, City of London

Few head-and-shoulders portraits of eighteenth-century Anglican clergymen stray far from a simple standard pattern, and Gainsborough's image of Henry Burrough, his first cousin on his mother's side, and the Vicar of Wisbech in Cambridgeshire, is no exception to the rule. Both the artist and the sitter may have used this notably conservative image to advance their respective careers: Burrough, by presenting a copy (by another hand) to his Cambridge college and Gainsborough, by advertising his skills to potential patrons, clerical and otherwise, in the Reverend's circle.

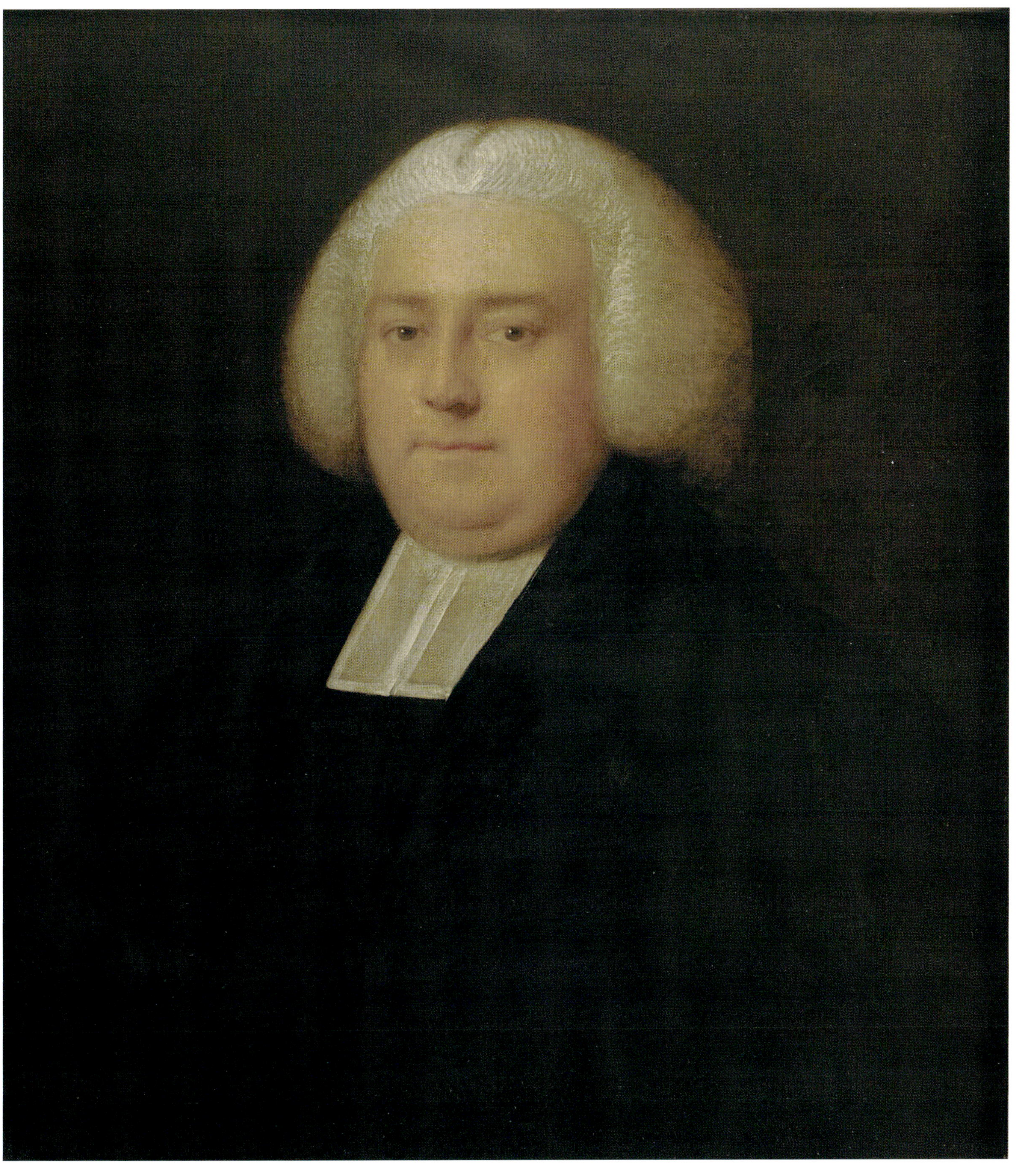

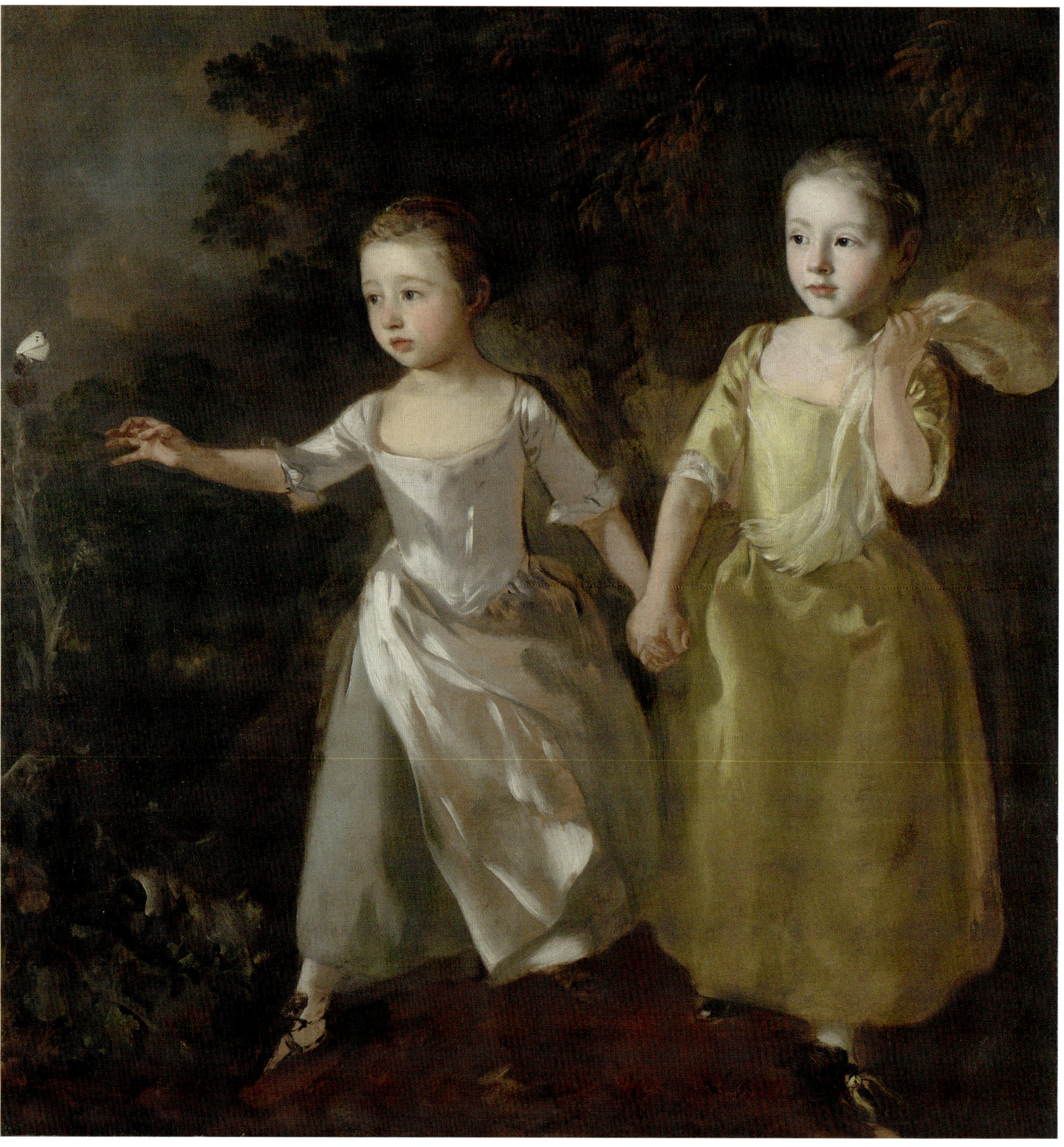

9

**Mary and Margaret Gainsborough,
the Artist's Daughters,
Chasing a Butterfly**

c.1756
Oil on canvas, 1135 x 1050mm

The National Gallery, London
Exhibited in London only

This is the earliest in the sequence of six double portraits in oils of the artist's daughters, who must have been around five and six years old at the time. Mary is shown restraining her younger sister as she reaches out towards a butterfly that has landed on a thistle, which threatens to prick her fingers with its sharp thorns. Originating in seventeenth-century emblem books, this motif symbolised the dangers inherent in a child's pursuit of its own thoughtless impulses, whilst also invoking the more general idea of the transience of human life and its pleasures. The introduction of this moral dimension, and the image's obvious tenderness, are just two of several features that make this picture stand apart from the body of portraits from Gainsborough's Ipswich period.

No less unusual in this context is the large scale of the figures, their representation in motion, and the breadth and freedom of the artist's brushwork – all of which indicate that the girls' father was taking full advantage of the opportunities to experiment that only a private, uncommissioned portrait could offer. But the pressure to attend to paying customers probably also helps to explain why Gainsborough left the painting in an incomplete state. Surprisingly, given the intimate depiction of his children, he did not take this picture with him when he moved with his family to Bath in 1759. Instead it stayed behind in Suffolk, in the possession of his friend the Reverend Robert Hingeston, the headmaster of Ipswich School.

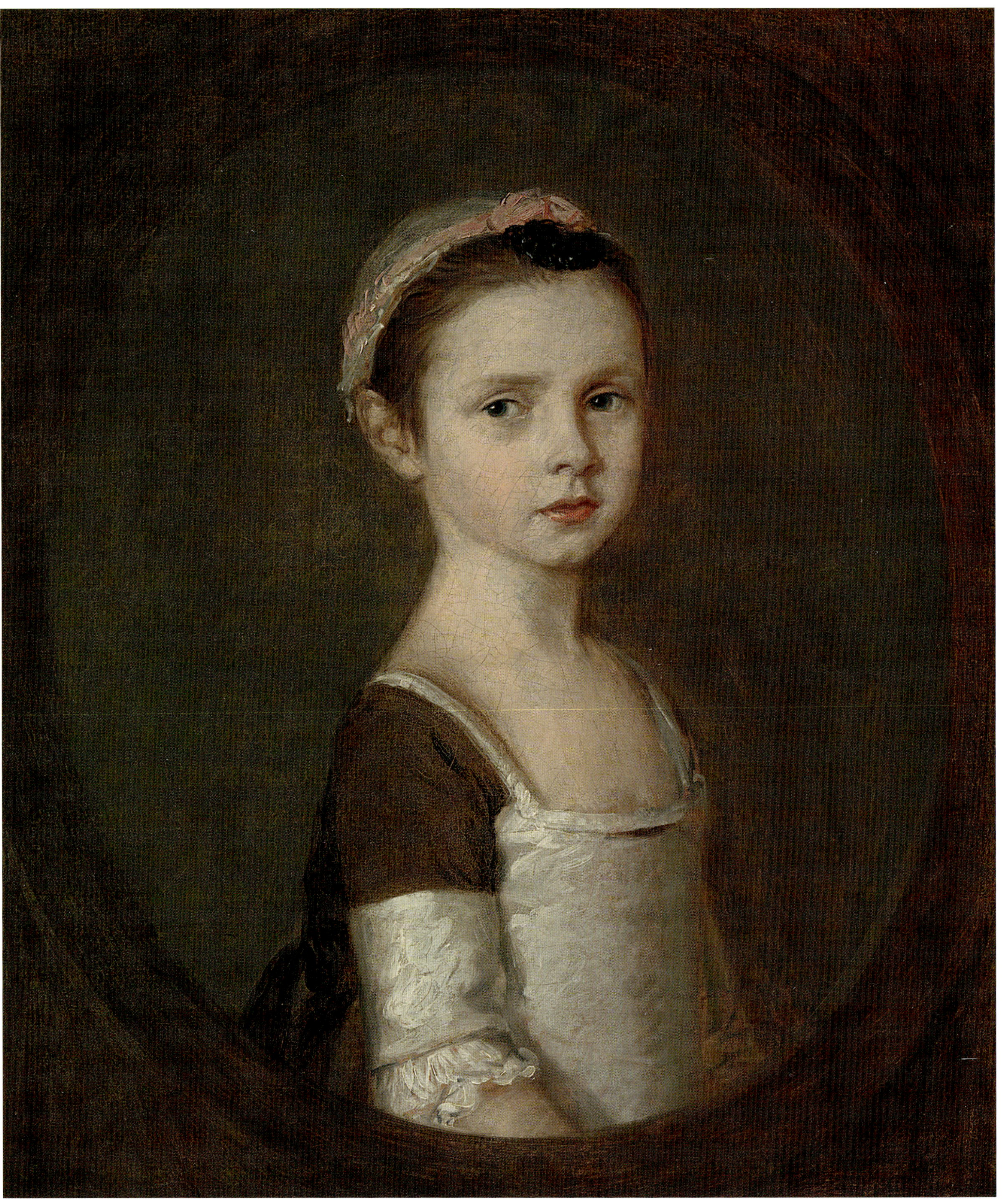

10

Susan Gardiner, the Artist's Niece

c.1758–9

Oil on canvas, 619 x 511mm

Yale Center for British Art, Paul Mellon Collection,
New Haven, CT

This is the first of many head-and-shoulders portraits by Gainsborough of his relations where the sitter is positioned within an oval surround that mimics the appearance of masonry. The device works simultaneously to create an enclosing sense of intimacy, and to place the subject and the viewer at a respectable distance from one another. Indeed, we know that Gainsborough wanted pictures like this to be seen from several feet away because, in 1758, when one of his patrons complained about the 'roughness' of his portrait's 'surface', the artist responded by insisting that this served to 'giv[e] force to the effect at a proper distance'.[1] In its degree of finish as well as its pastel-like handling, the *Susan Gardiner* compares closely with the commissioned portraits that Gainsborough had begun to paint by the end of his time in Ipswich. On this occasion, however, it is most unlikely that any money was involved. Susan's mother was the artist's sister Susanna Gardiner (cat. 42), who, together with her husband, Richard, ran a millinery business in Sudbury. The entirely plausible suggestion has been made that Gainsborough presented the Gardiners with this portrait of their eight- or nine-year-old daughter as a parting gift, just as he was on the verge of moving with his family to Bath. X-rays have recently revealed that the picture has been painted on a recycled piece of canvas, cut at both sides and at the top from a small landscape – an economy that the artist is unlikely to have taken when working for any of his paying clients.

11

Mary Gainsborough, the Artist's Daughter

c.1758–9
Oil on canvas, 360 x 310mm

Private Collection

Although traditionally identified as a likeness
of Margaret Gainsborough, the face in this little
unfinished head study (perhaps cut down from a
larger canvas?) bears a closer resemblance to that
of her older sister, Mary. Particularly striking are
the similarities to the left-hand figure in the double
portrait showing Mary playing with Margaret's
hair (cat. 15), although there she looks just slightly
older. In both pictures Mary's head is decorated
with an ornate brown rosette attached to a pink
hair ribbon, a fashionable combination that (with
the addition of a cap) can also be found in the
contemporaneous portrait of her cousin Susan
Gardiner (cat. 10).

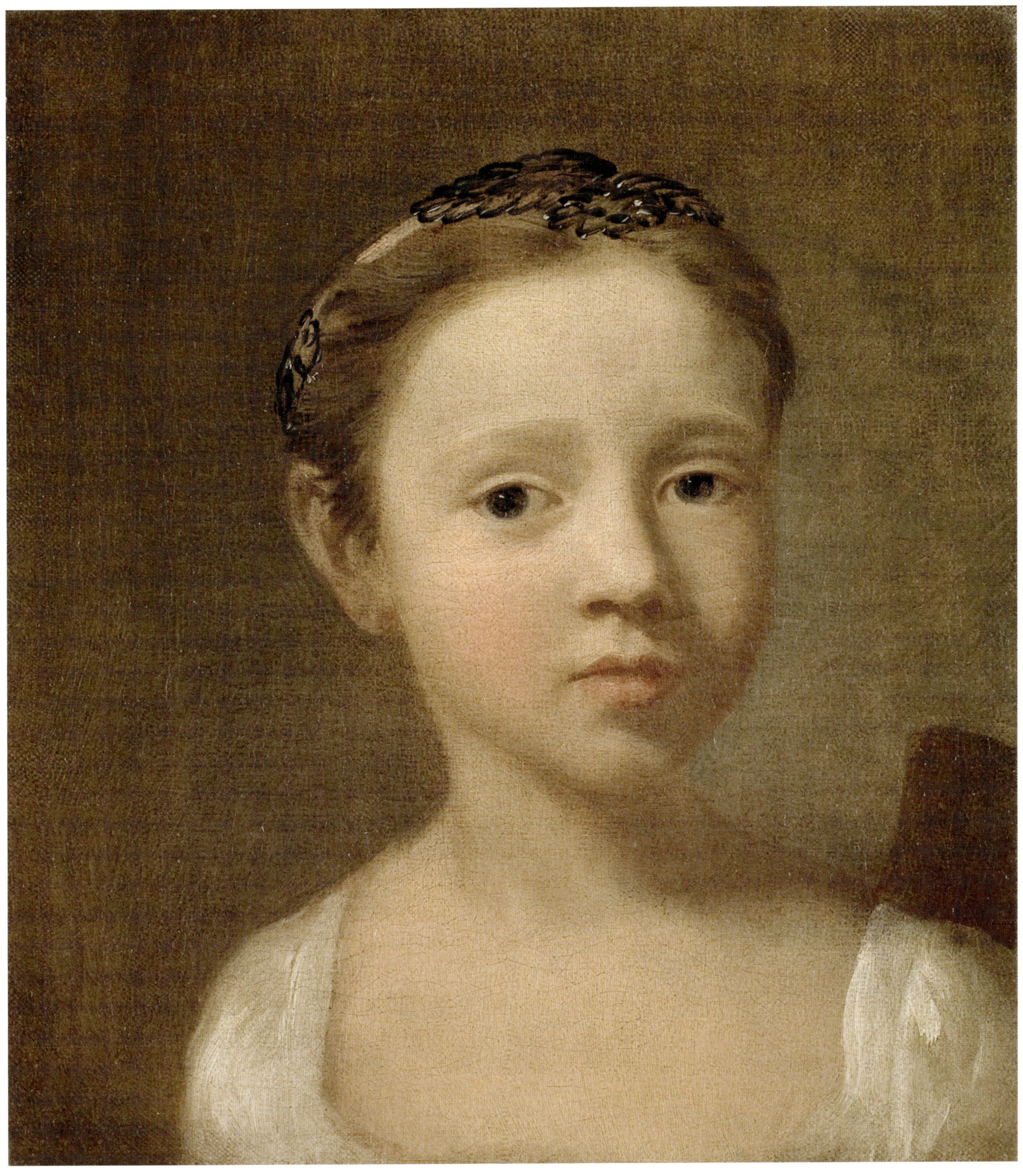

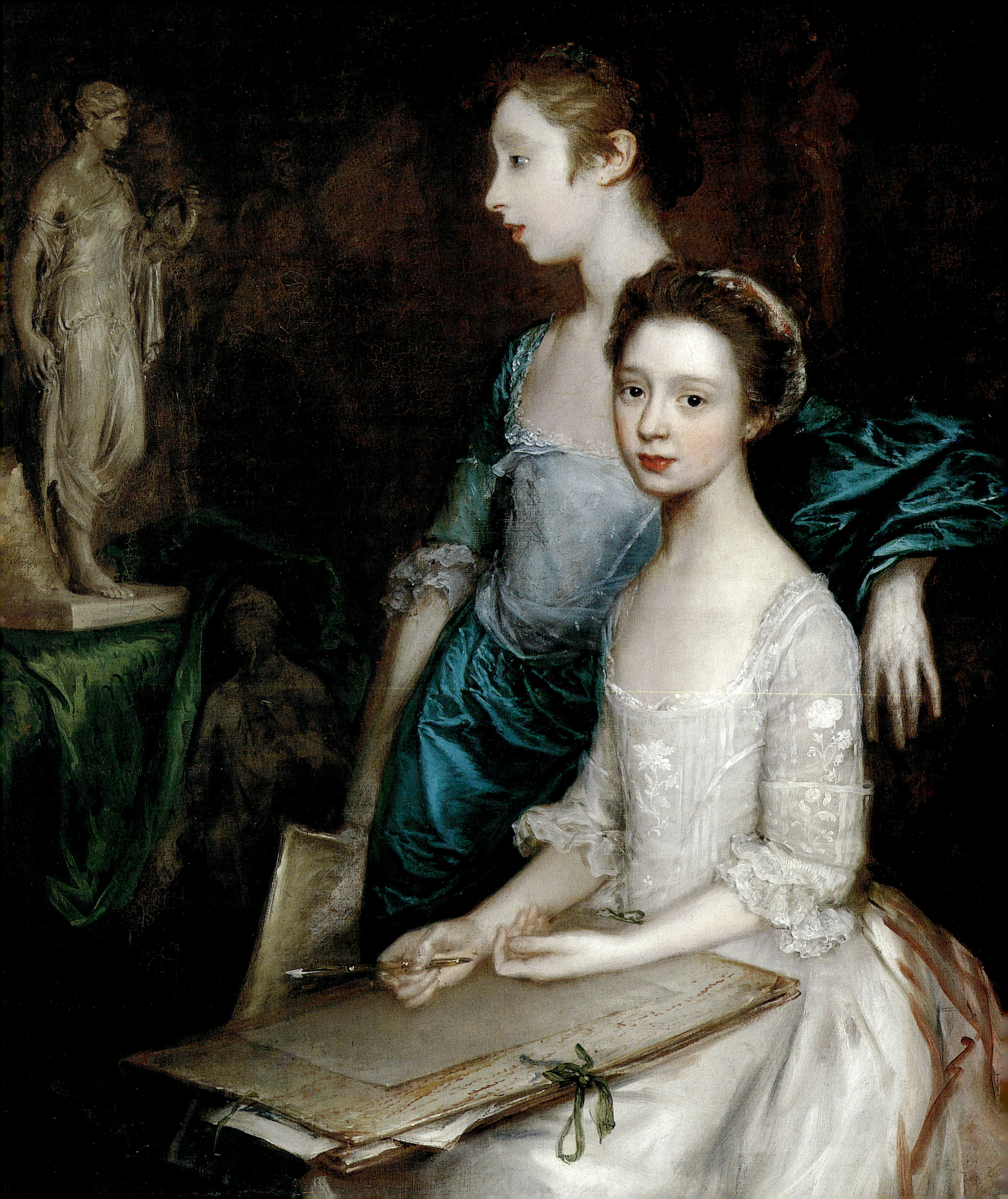

BATH

1759–1774

At Bath, Gainsborough's career went from strength to strength. In June 1760, less than a year after arriving with his family, the artist took on the lease of a mansion in Abbey Street, one of the most visited and expensive parts of town. In addition to the advantages offered by its prominent location, this grand house contained a studio space large enough to accommodate the production of full-length portraits. It also had a sizeable parlour, where potential clients were invited to admire a selection of Gainsborough's 'show pictures' – mainly eye-catching likenesses of Bath celebrities, among them, quite probably, the artist and his wife. Rooms not required for the portrait business or for the family's use were let out to visitors, thus providing an independent income stream.

In 1762 his widowed sister Mary Gibbon moved in, and set up her millinery shop in a corner of the building. Four years later, after she and her brother had moved to near-adjacent houses in the fashionable Circus, the entire Abbey Street property became a lodging-house, which she assumed full responsibility for running. Meanwhile, fuelled by the regular appearance of his paintings at London's annual art exhibitions, the demand for Gainsborough's services as a portraitist continued to grow – to the point where he began to complain that it left him with no time to pursue interests that mattered far more to him, both personally and artistically. These pressures help to explain his development of a quicker and sketchier portrait style, and why, in 1772, he took on his first and only apprentice – his nephew Gainsborough Dupont.

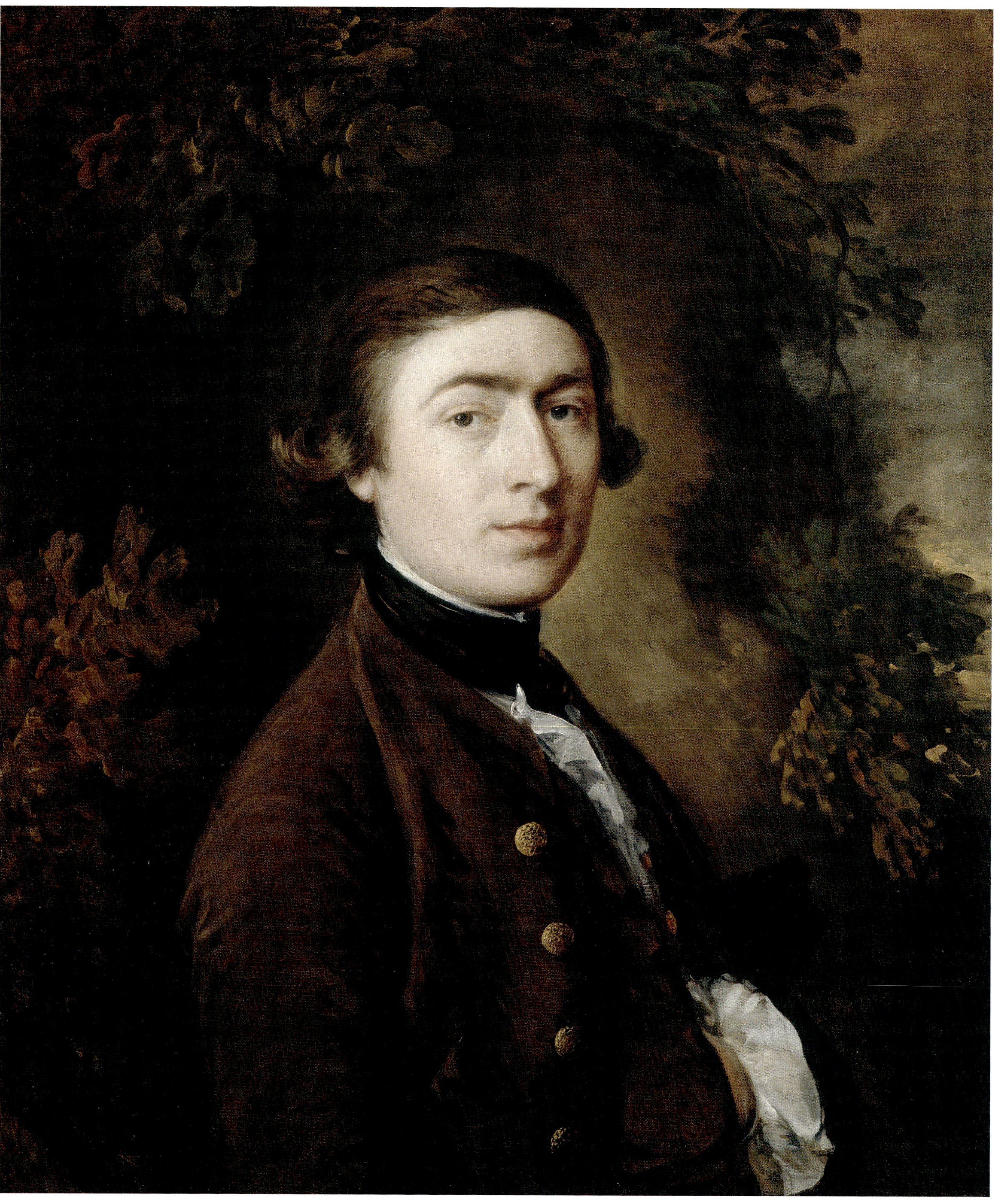

12

Self-portrait

*c.*1758–9

Oil on canvas, 762 x 635mm

National Portrait Gallery, London

This self-portrait and its pendant of the artist's wife look to have been painted just around the time when the family moved to Bath, where they would remain for fifteen years. Whereas Ipswich was a provincial town with limited opportunities for patronage, it was nonetheless a place where Gainsborough's numerous links with the local citizenry and gentry in the region of his birth enabled him to build the initial foundations of his career. Bath, however, presented him with great challenges. Although not entirely without connections in the city and its environs, as a virtually unknown portraitist he faced a daunting task in trying to attract the custom of Bath's affluent and cosmopolitan clientele, consisting mainly of tourists drawn by the health-giving waters and lively social life of what was then Britain's premier spa resort. In this context Gainsborough's earliest-known, finished self-portrait in oils was designed to function as a multi-layered advertisement – firstly, of the artist's gentlemanly status, secondly, of the type of product he could offer to potential male sitters, and last but not least, of his ability to produce an accurate likeness, which on this occasion invited comparison with the original. The artist shows himself wearing his own hair, styled to resemble a wig, and a brown coat enlivened with brass buttons and the elegant ruffles of a fine white linen shirt. Although the colour of his coat may have looked rather rustic to his viewers (at a time when red, blue, or green were regarded as much more fashionable), in all other respects Gainsborough cuts very much the figure of a confident member of the 1760s beau monde.

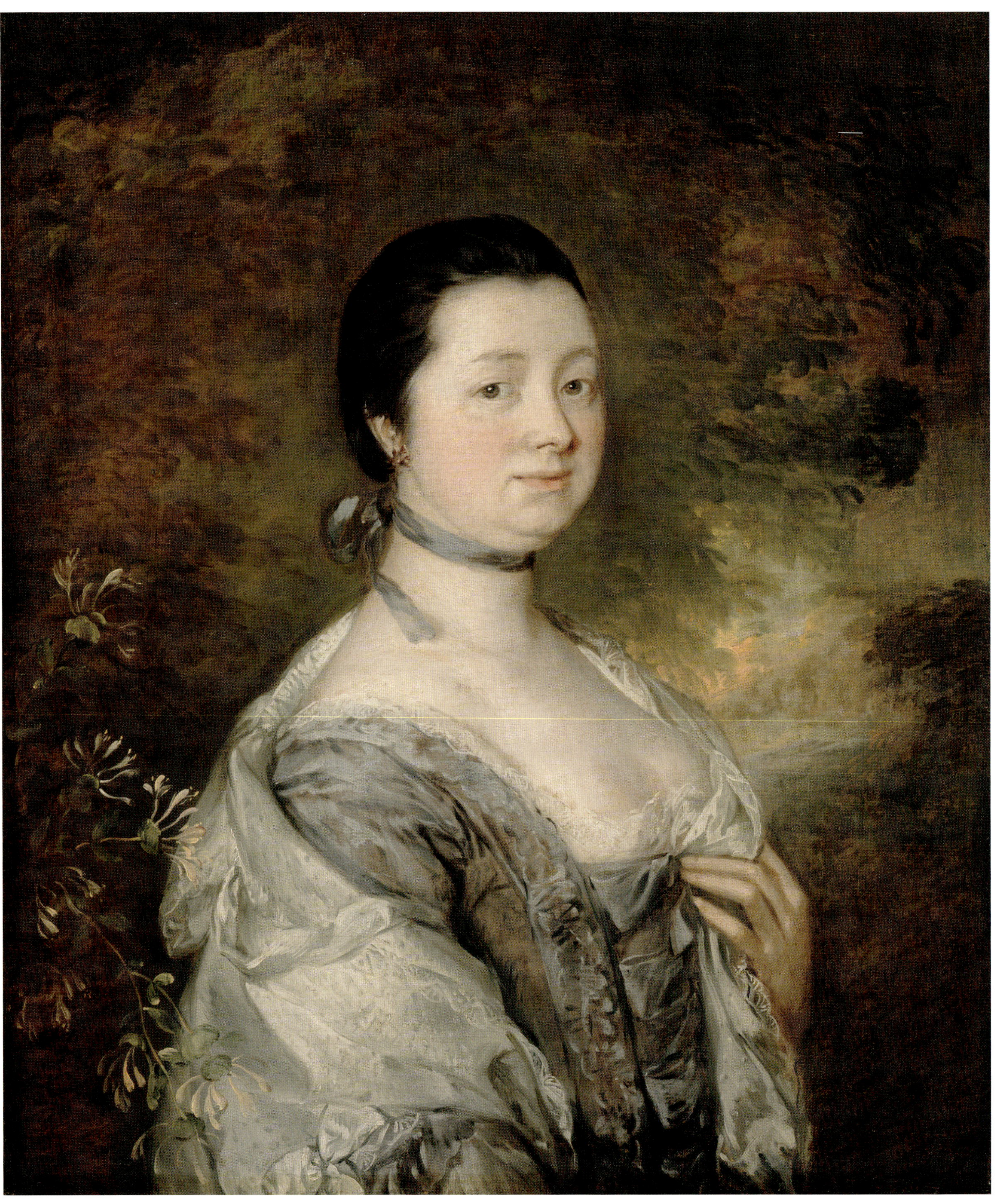

Margaret Gainsborough, the Artist's Wife

*c.*1758
Oil on canvas, 760 x 635mm

Gemäldegalerie, Staatliche Museen zu Berlin

Like its companion piece (cat. 12), this 'three-quarters' of Margaret Gainsborough is likely to have been produced shortly after the family's move to Bath, as a demonstration to a whole new set of potential clients of her husband's skill, in this case as a portraitist of fashionable women. Both works may well have been displayed in the artist's showroom, where visitors were invited to admire a variety of his works, including likenesses of local celebrities. In a composition that echoes the seventeenth-century courtly art of Sir Anthony van Dyck and Sir Peter Lely, Gainsborough has depicted his wife as an aristocratic 'Beauty', a status that she, as the illegitimate daughter of a duke, may well have felt was nothing less than she deserved. Her dress, with its ornate ribbons and silk trimmings, conforms to the French mode then popular with British women of the upper classes – though few of these, if any, would have dared to reveal quite so broad an expanse of décolletage to any man apart from their own husbands. It is unusual, though certainly not unheard of, for a pair of eighteenth-century British husband-and-wife portraits to show both sitters facing in the same direction. From this we can infer that the two paintings probably did not hang side by side, but opposite or above one another.

14

Study for a Portrait of the Artist's Wife and Daughters [?]

c.1759–62
Pencil, trimmed at all four corners, 379 x 244mm

Kupferstichkabinett, Staatliche Museen zu Berlin
Exhibited in London only

Although it cannot be stated with absolute certainty, the suggestion that the subjects of this drawing are Gainsborough's wife and daughters is highly plausible. The woman bears a marked resemblance to the Berlin portrait in oils of the artist's wife (cat. 13), while the two girls look to be the right ages: Margaret around nine or ten, and Mary about eighteen months younger. At a point in his career when Gainsborough had only just begun painting full-length portraits on the scale of life, he may well have thought of using his own family to experiment with the format. And although the composition – and the mother's pose in particular – owe much to the example of Van Dyck, Gainsborough may also have had in mind to emulate one of Sir Peter Paul Rubens's celebrated pictures of his own wife with one or more of her children. In any event, the idea seems never to have progressed beyond this single pencil sketch, which would go on to form part of the small group of drawings that were retained by the artist's family after his death. As far as we know, he never again represented his wife with any of their offspring, so this is where her maternal role in the story told by his 'family album' comes to an end.

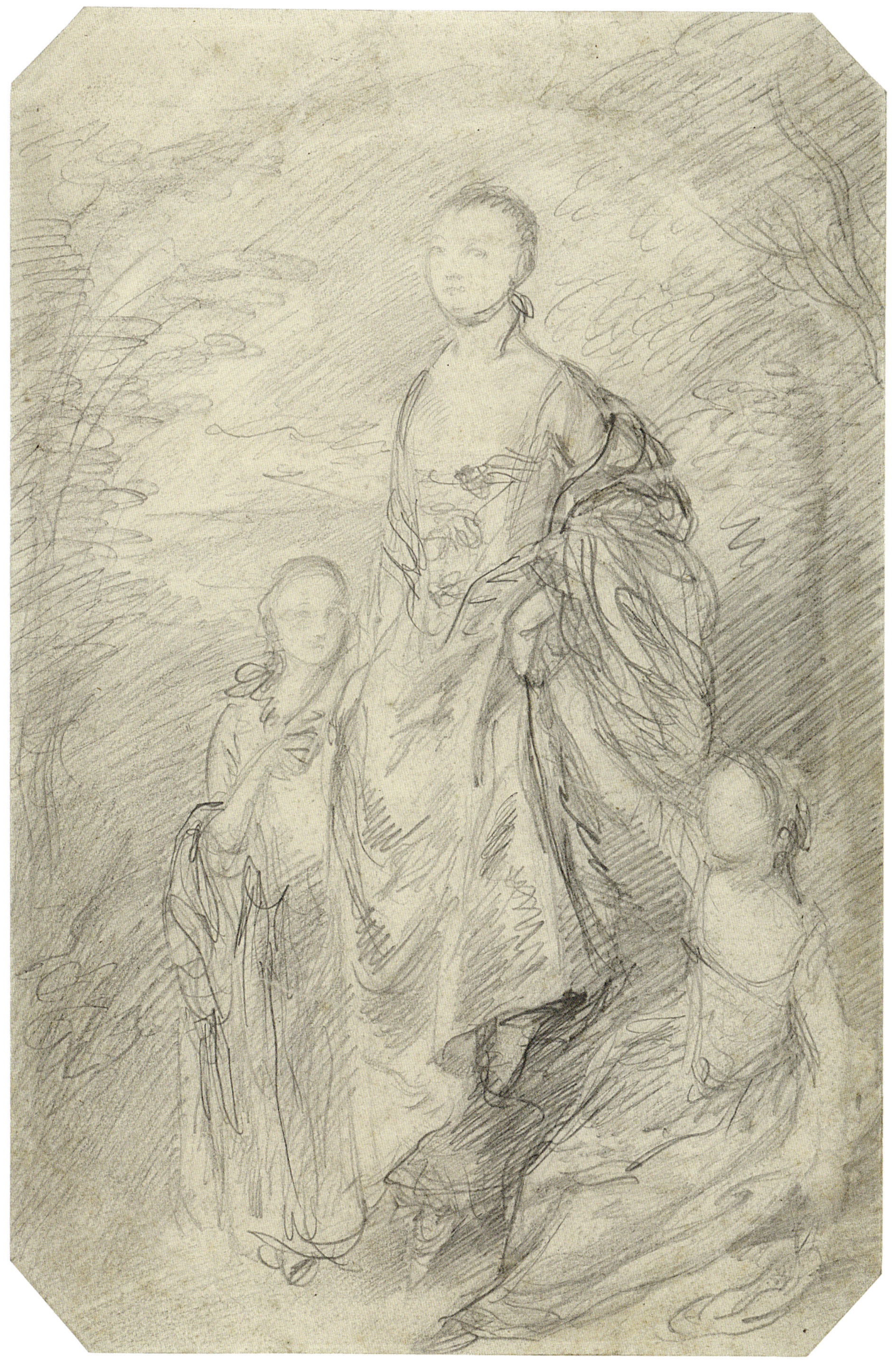

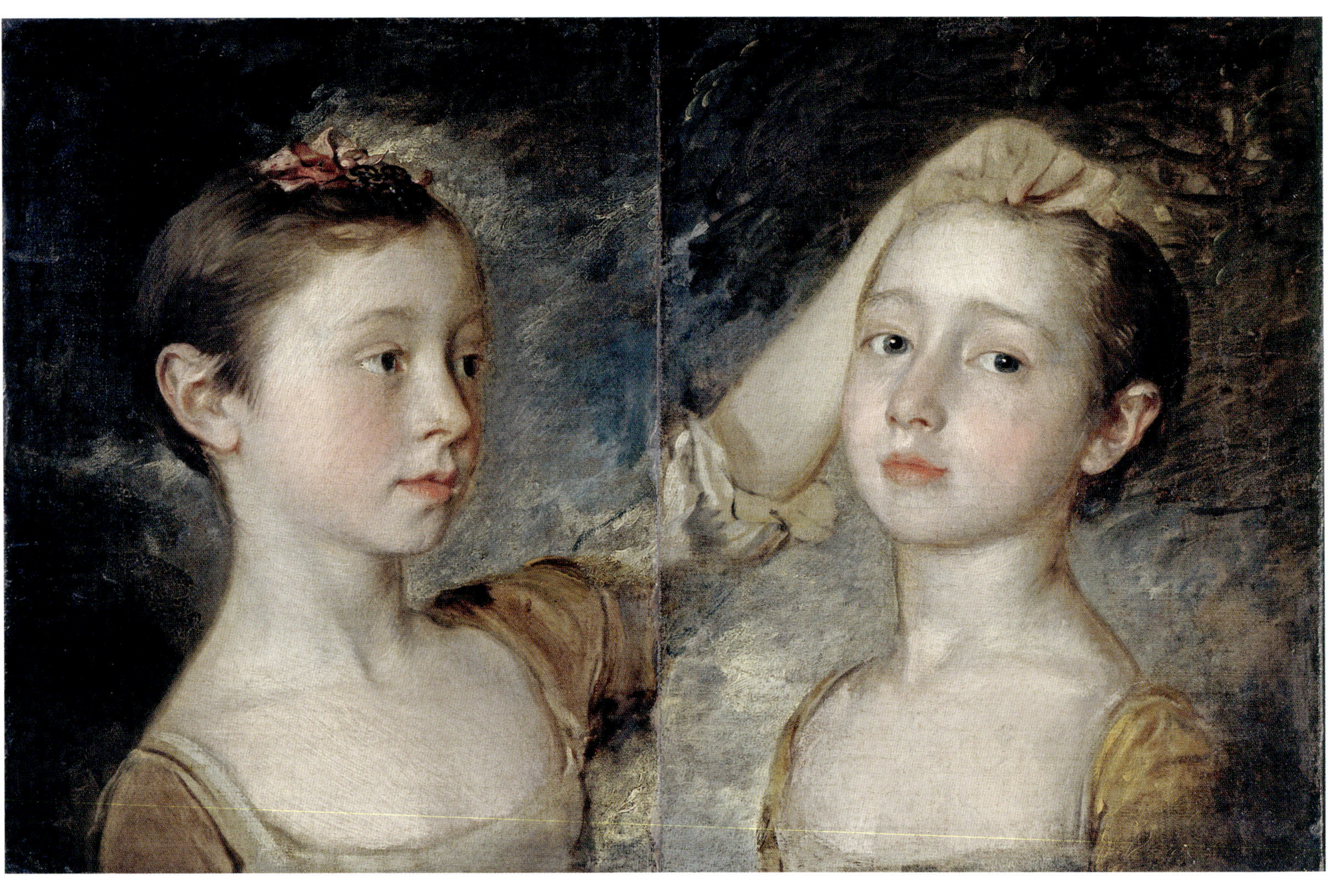

15

Mary and Margaret Gainsborough, the Artist's Daughters

*c.*1760–1
Oil on canvas, 406 x 584mm

Victoria and Albert Museum, London

One of a cluster of three double portraits of Mary and Margaret Gainsborough painted soon after the family had settled in Bath, this example bears the traces of its difficult nineteenth-century afterlife. Left in an unfinished state at the time of the painter's death, the canvas was cut in two a few decades later and divided between two different collectors. After one of these died in the 1870s, the fragment he had owned was purchased by the other, who then commissioned a restorer to reunite the two parts. At this point the understandable decision was made, for the sake of pictorial coherence, to place the girls' heads on the same level, and to add a few black outlines to join Mary's shoulder with the rest of her outstretched arm. Only now has it been recognised that originally Mary would have been shown looking down at her younger sister from a somewhat greater height, and from a slightly further distance than we see at present. For a proposed reconstruction of Gainsborough's intended configuration, see fig. 33. As in most of the double portraits of his daughters, 'Molly and the Captain' – as he fondly nicknamed Mary and Margaret respectively – appear joined to one another, in an attitude of emotional intimacy that cannot be found in any of the likenesses of their parents.

FIG. 33
Reconstruction of the original alignment of *Mary and Margaret Gainsborough, the Artist's Daughters* (cat. 15)

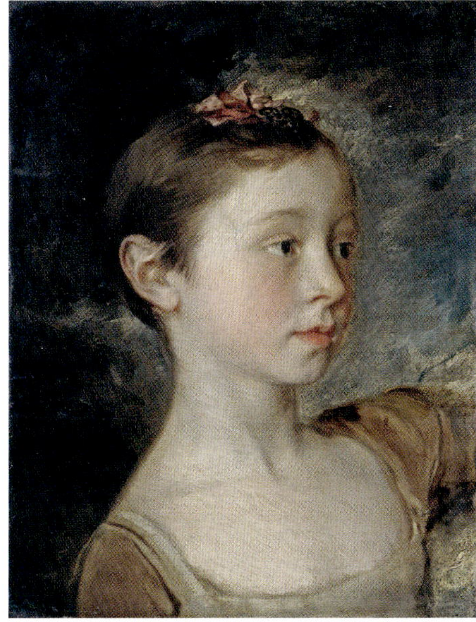
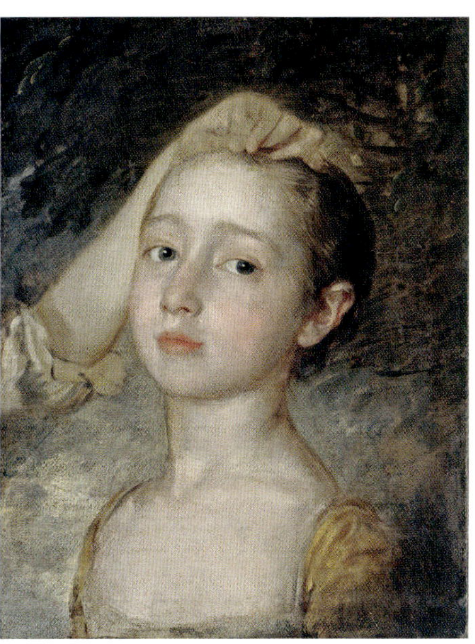

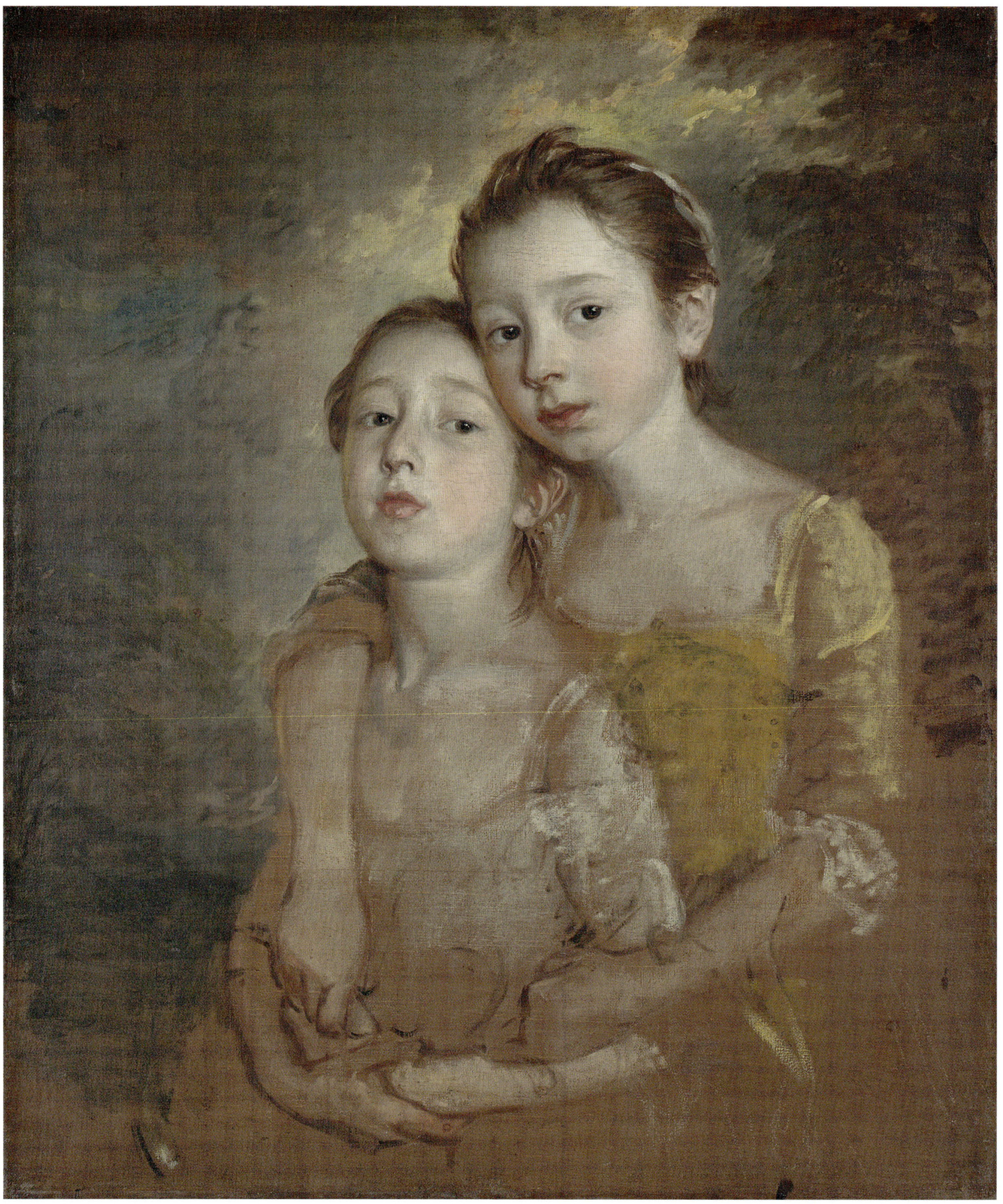

16

Mary and Margaret Gainsborough, the Artist's Daughters, Playing with a Cat

c.1760–1
Oil on canvas, 756 x 629mm

The National Gallery, London

During the years immediately following the family's move to Bath, Gainsborough's daughters posed for three double portraits, none of which was brought to completion. Although this may well have been the sketchiest of the trio, it is the only canvas that has survived in what can confidently be assumed to be its original proportions. Indeed, by 1923, when it was put up for sale by the artist's descendants, the painting had still to receive its first coat of varnish. The technical evidence indicates that after covering the surface with two layers of priming – first a pinkish-brown, then a darker brown – Gainsborough quickly drew the principal outlines in white chalk or pastel before applying oils to work up the girl's faces and chests – but nothing else – to a relatively high degree of finish. Their expressions seem inexplicably calm, given that Mary has grasped the tail of the cat, shown snarling as it struggles to free itself from the sisters' arms. The fleeting nature of this action combines with the seemingly spontaneous character of the brushwork to create the highly compelling impression of a momentary encounter quickly observed, and just as swiftly recorded. Even in its unfinished state – and partially because it remained in that state – *The Artist's Daughters with a Cat* may well have impressed 1760s cognoscenti as a bravura demonstration of its author's virtuosity; but for the painter himself and the members of his family, the picture's value must have resided first and foremost in its character as a highly personal memento of his daughters and their close relationship to one another.

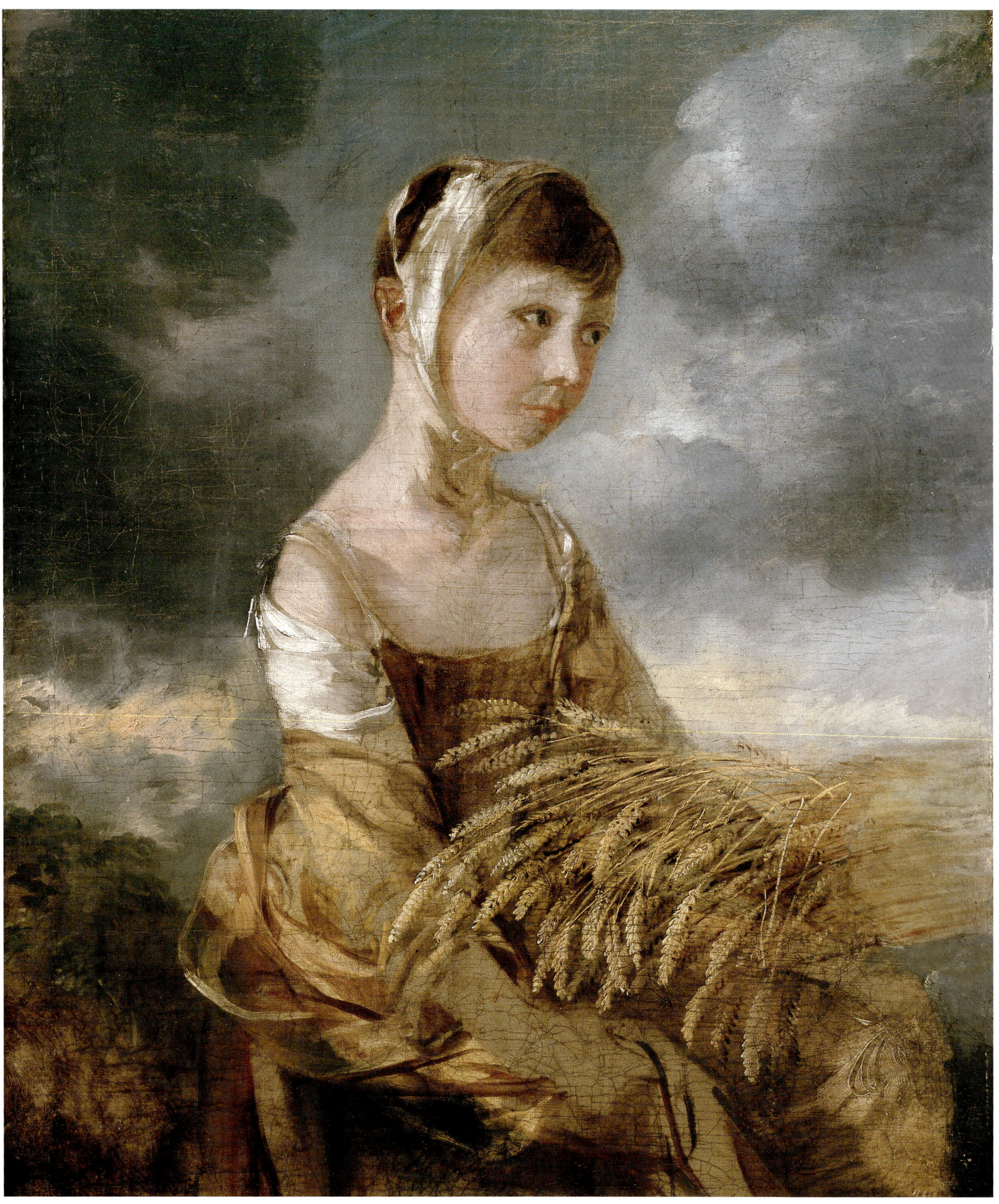

17

Margaret Gainsborough,
the Artist's Daughter, as a Gleaner

*c.*1760–1
Oil on canvas, 730 x 630mm

Ashmolean Museum of Art and Archaeology, University of Oxford

This is the only fragment now known to survive of an unfinished picture which in 1824 was described as representing 'portraits of [Gainsborough's] two daughters, in the garb of peasant girls, on the confines of a corn-field, dividing their gleanings' (see page 48, n. 29). From Margaret's posture and the direction of her glance we can presume that she is looking up towards her older sister Mary, who is passing her some stalks of wheat (surely not corn), and whose figure would have occupied the lost right-hand side of the composition. The element of portraiture is arguably of less importance here than in any of Gainsborough's other depictions of his daughters. On this occasion his prime concern was to try his hand at the relatively new genre of 'fancy painting', using Mary and Margaret as his models. Eighteenth-century 'fancies' typically featured anonymous figures from everyday life, such as children or rustic types, engaged in characteristic activities, and depicted on or near the scale of life. By the 1780s, the genre would become one of Gainsborough's major preoccupations, but on this much earlier occasion, his interests were focused on experimenting with a curious *mélange* of portraiture and subject-painting, and on imagining his daughters in a role that could hardly have been more foreign to the realities of the family's increasingly affluent circumstances in Bath. Apart from her rather stylish bronze-coloured silk mantle, which has slipped down from her right shoulder, Margaret's dress closely corresponds to the actual garb worn by peasant girls of the period, Clearly, Gainsborough's extensive knowledge of clothing encompassed the poor as well as the rich.

18

Study for Mary and Margaret Gainsborough, the Artist's Daughters, at their Drawing

c.1763–4
Black chalk heightened with white on blue-grey paper
377 x 262mm

Gainsborough's House, Sudbury, Suffolk

Still relatively new to the task of painting portrait groups on a large scale, Gainsborough struggled with the design for *The Artist's Daughters at their Drawing* (cat. 19), the most formal likeness he had yet attempted of his girls Mary and Margaret. X-rays of the Worcester canvas (fig. 34), not to mention the ghost-like pentimento in its upper left quadrant of a young girl's profile, show that Gainsborough originally intended to position Margaret so that she faced her seated older sister instead of standing behind her. Having rejected this idea once the work was well advanced, the painter used this study to test out an alternative design that went on to serve as the basis for the final composition. Both the painting and the drawing remained in the family's possession after Gainsborough's death.

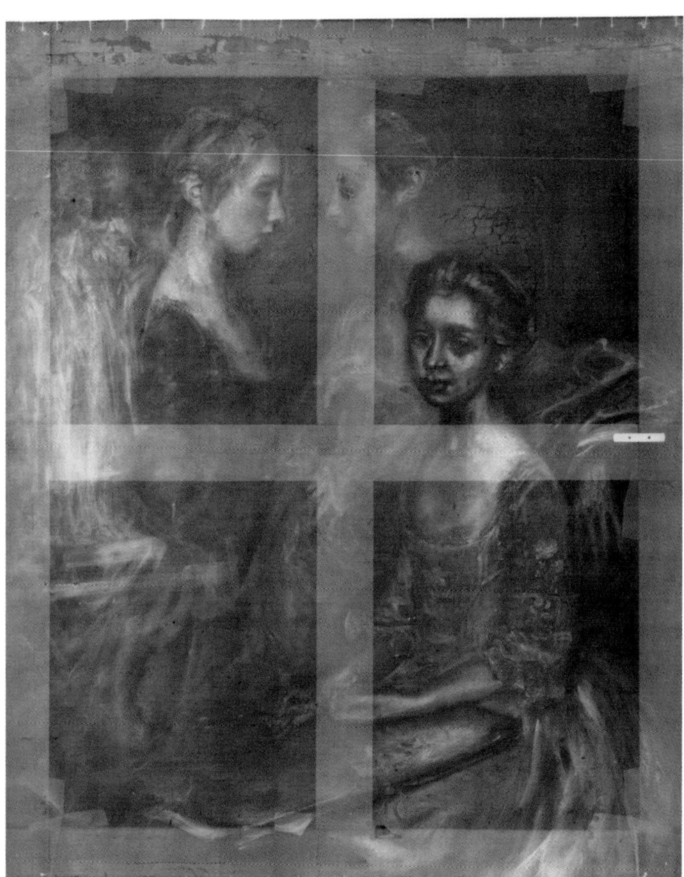

FIG. 34
X-ray of *Mary and Margaret Gainsborough, the Artist's Daughters, at their Drawing* (cat. 19)
Worcester Art Museum, Worcester, MA

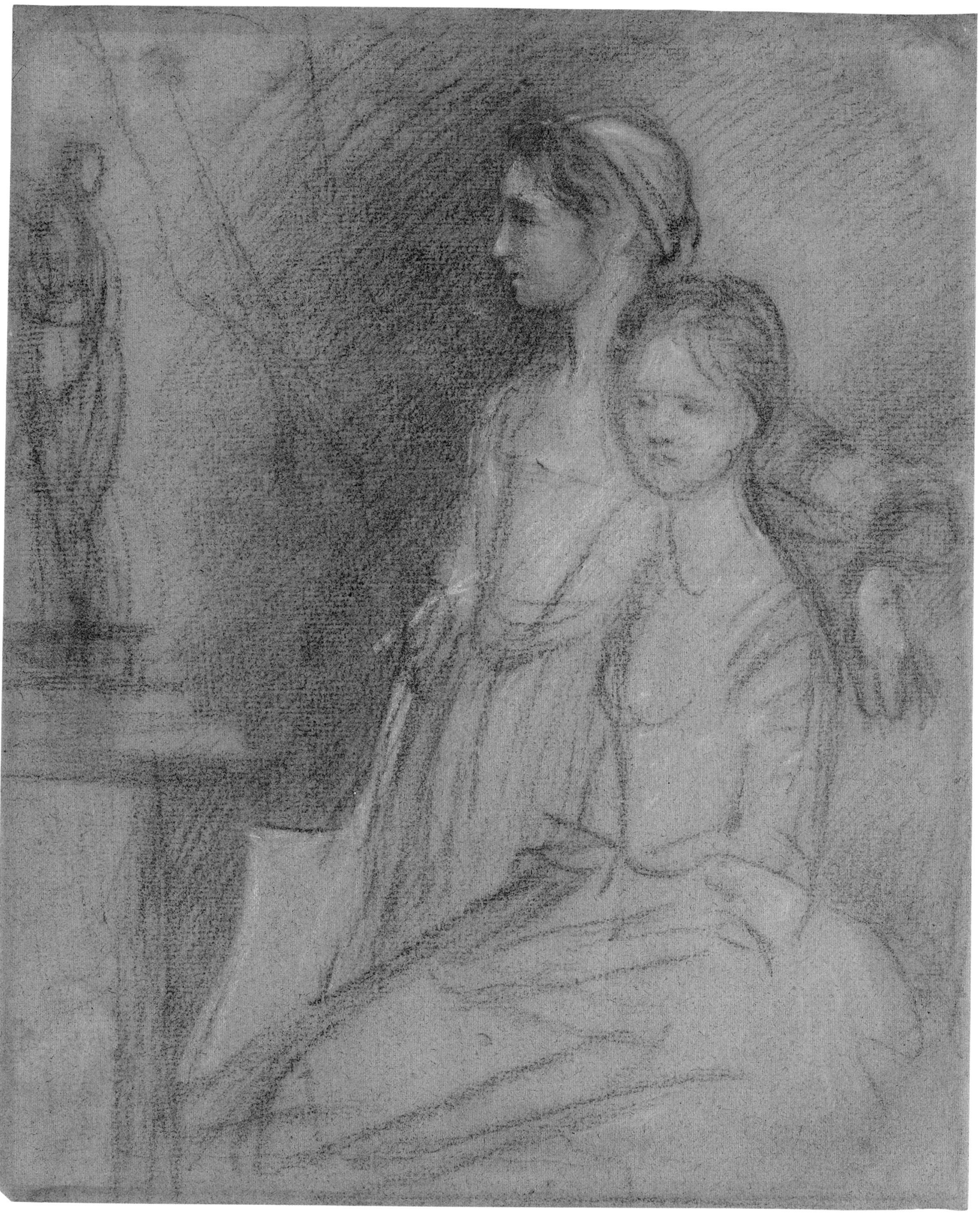

19

Mary and Margaret Gainsborough,
the Artist's Daughters, at their Drawing

c.1763–4
Oil on canvas, 1273 x 1017mm

Worcester Art Museum, Worcester, MA

After his recovery from a life-threatening illness in 1763, Gainsborough's thoughts turned to the future of his daughters. Uncertain of his own longevity, and anxious that neither daughter should find herself with no option but dependence on a husband, he set in motion plans to have them educated as artists. His hope was that the girls would be able to support themselves by producing and selling landscapes, as he himself, paradoxically, had signally failed to do. We know of these ambitions from Gainsborough's correspondence, and from this image of his daughters as young art students: Mary is shown seated holding a porte-crayon and a portfolio of drawings, while Margaret stands behind her gazing at a reduced plaster cast of the Farnese Flora, a celebrated classical sculpture representing the goddess of spring (the other female statue below is too sketchily rendered to be identifiable, but looks to represent a more mature draped female figure, possibly Juno or Ceres). In this context, the Flora operates on at least three different levels of meaning: as an embodiment of the art that the girls have been set to study; as a signifier of nature, and thus implicitly of landscape; and finally, as the harbinger of a future full of promise – a message echoed by the embroidered flowers on Mary's whitework bodice. Margaret's clothing owes more to Van Dyck than to current fashions: the great swathe of rich blue satin that seems to encompass both her dress and the fabric spilling over her left arm looks more like an artfully arranged piece of studio drapery than a garment that could actually have been worn. Likewise her posture – especially the placement of her left arm and hand – comes straight out of the Flemish master's repertoire.

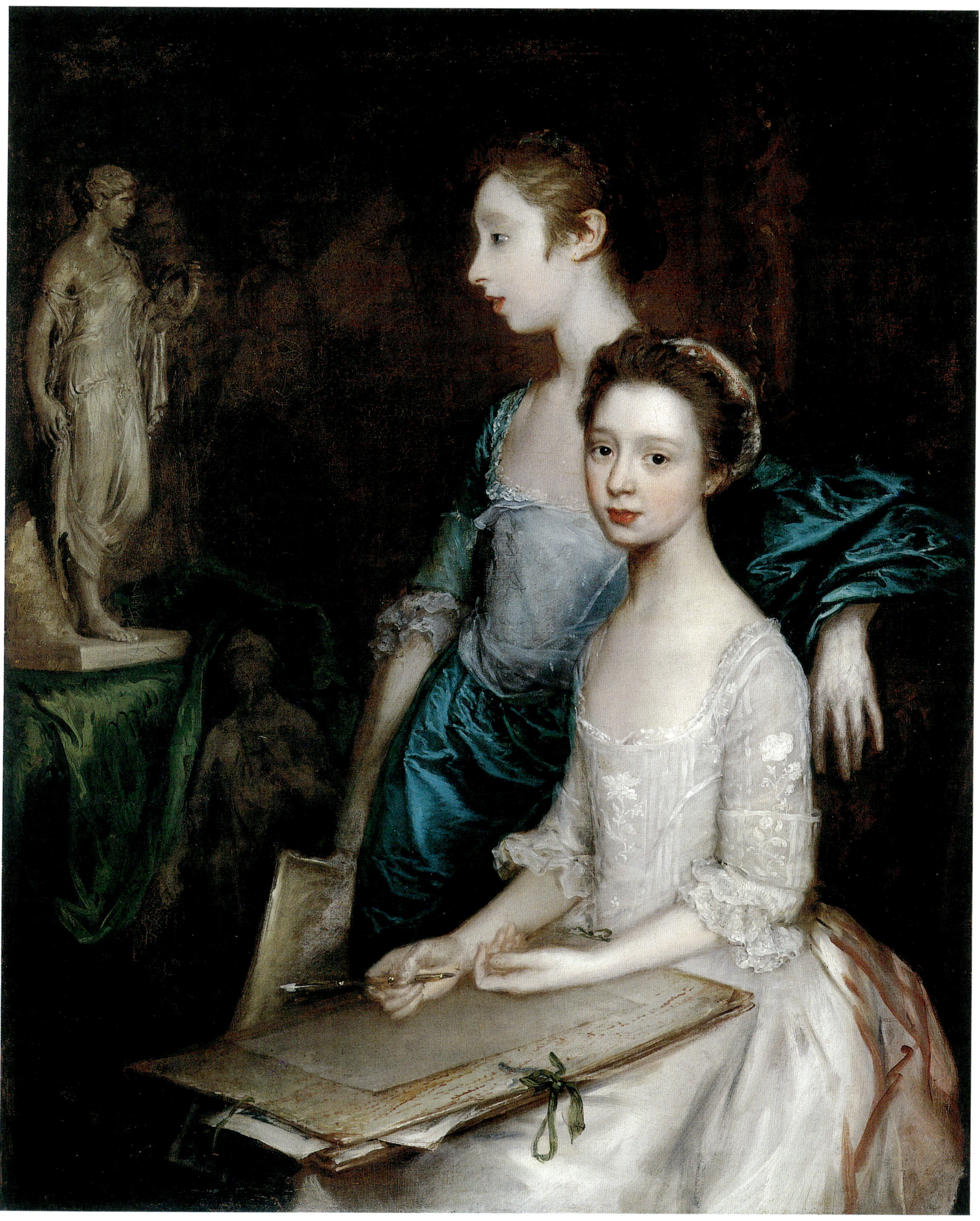

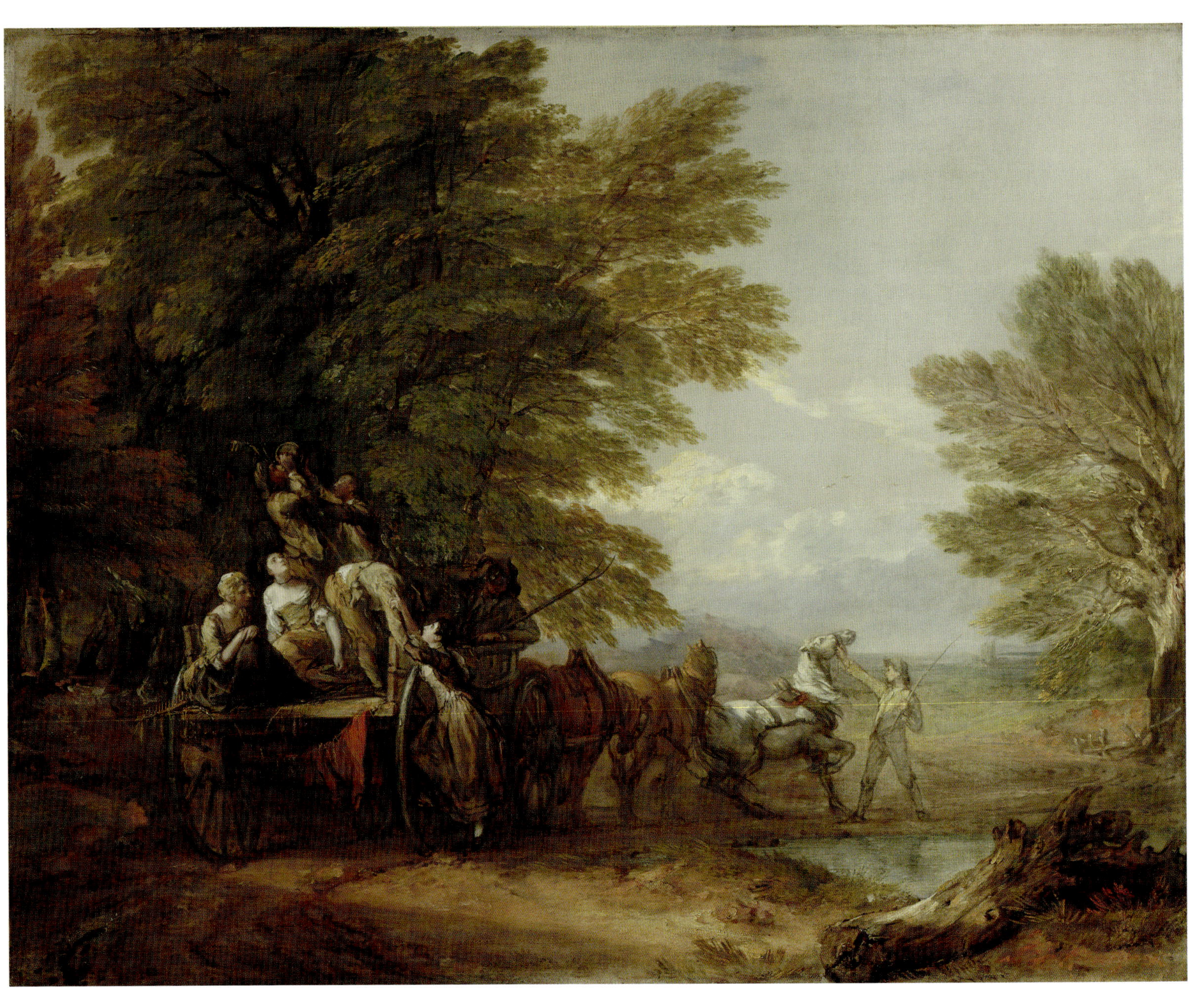

The Harvest Wagon

exhibited 1767
Oil on canvas, 1225 x 1475mm

The Henry Barber Trust, The Barber Institute
of Fine Arts, University of Birmingham
Exhibited in London only

One of Gainsborough's major exhibition landscapes of the 1760s, *The Harvest Wagon* owes its inclusion in his 'family album' to the plausible traditional belief that the painter depicted his daughters as two of the farm-girls in the scene. The earliest published source for this claim appears to be *The Royal Gallery of British Art* (*c*.1850), an illustrated volume compiled by the engraver Edward Finden, whose information came directly from the elderly son of Walter Wiltshire, a close friend of the artist and the picture's original owner. Modern scholars have generally agreed that comparisons with other portraits of the sisters support the identification of Margaret as the model for the figure being helped on to the cart, and of Mary as the seated young woman looking up at the rustics fighting over a barrel of beer. Given the artifice of their inclusion, it is perhaps not entirely surprising that neither fits seamlessly into the design. Of the eight human faces on view, only those of the Gainsborough girls are fully highlighted and described with portrait-like specificity. Their fashionable hairstyles and

the gold buckles on Margaret's shoes further set the pair apart from their rather more 'common' companions, and from the three loutish men especially. Some six or seven years previously, Gainsborough had depicted his daughters as gleaners attired in the humble garb worn by the lowest ranks of the rural poor (cat. 17); but now, as they were approaching marriageable age, he assigned them roles of somewhat greater dignity, in a landscape that celebrated the mythic delights of the age-old harvest ritual. As Ann Bermingham has observed (see page 59), the dream of finding refuge in the simple life of the countryside was Gainsborough's fantasy, not that of his daughters. In *The Harvest Wagon* he projected Mary and Margaret into an Arcadian realm that he himself longed to inhabit, an imagined place where his children (and he) would be protected from the evils of 'Tea drinkings, Dancings, Husband huntings &c'. But as we are invited to infer from their hairstyles and those buckles, Mary and Margaret had grander social aspirations, as their father must have been all too aware.

'The Pitminster Boy'

late 1760s
Oil on canvas, 608 x 504mm

Private Collection, on loan to
Gainsborough's House, Sudbury, Suffolk

The term 'family' in eighteenth-century Britain was understood to include not just relations by blood or marriage, but servants and other members of the household. This image is of one of Gainsborough's studio assistants. Although his name has not been recorded, this depiction of him is traditionally known as *'The Pitminster Boy'*, after his home village in Somerset. According to the artist's earliest biographer, this youth 'used to carry Gainsborough's materials when he went into the country to sketch' while visiting friends at Barton Grange, near Taunton in Somerset.[2] Apparently, it was here that the likeness was executed. In its relatively small size, sketchy finish and the use of a feigned oval, *'The Pitminster Boy'* is very much of a piece with Gainsborough's contemporaneous paintings of his relations (see *Edward Richard Gardiner*, cat. 27), and was obviously painted at speed. On this occasion, however, we are less likely to be dealing with a portrait per se, but instead with a study of expression in the tradition of a Dutch *tronie* (face), a category of imagery associated with Rembrandt and other seventeenth-century Netherlandish masters (fig. 35). In 1769, at the inaugural exhibition of the Royal Academy (of which he was a founding member), one of Gainsborough's submissions was *A boy's head*, which could well have been this canvas. He would certainly have been aware that expressive heads had long played an important part in the teaching offered by art academies; but whereas such studies had traditionally served as a stepping stone to the epic sublimities of history painting, Gainsborough characteristically confined himself to a subject no more dramatic than a studio assistant's tentative glance as he offers up a brush to his master.

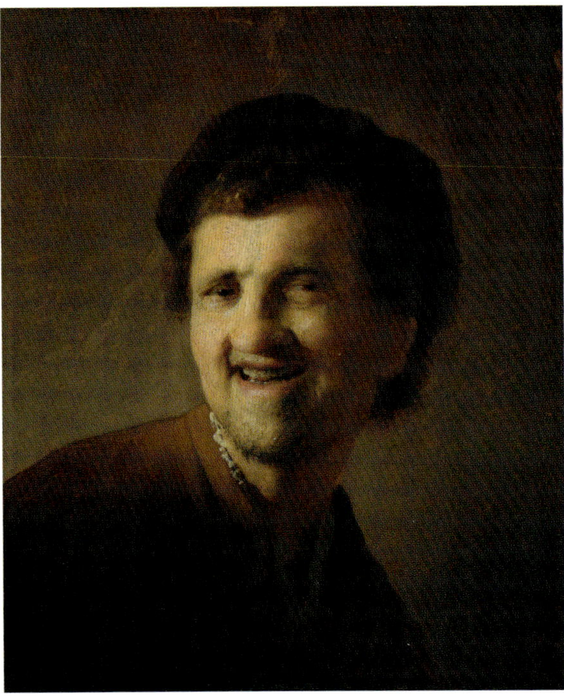

FIG. 35
Circle of Rembrandt van Rijn
Tronie of a *Laughing Young Man*
c.1629–30
Oil on panel
412 x 338mm
Rijksmuseum, Amsterdam

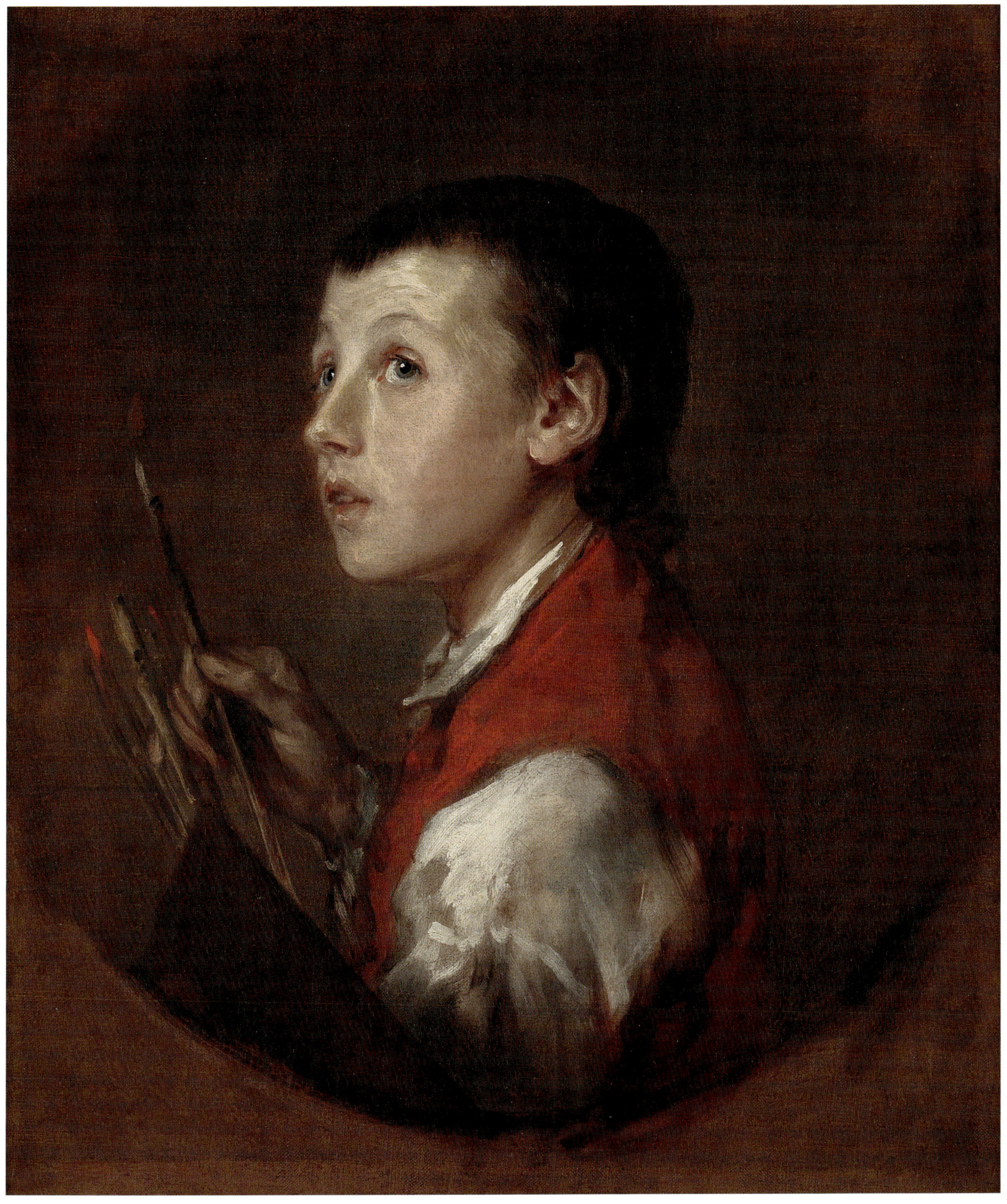

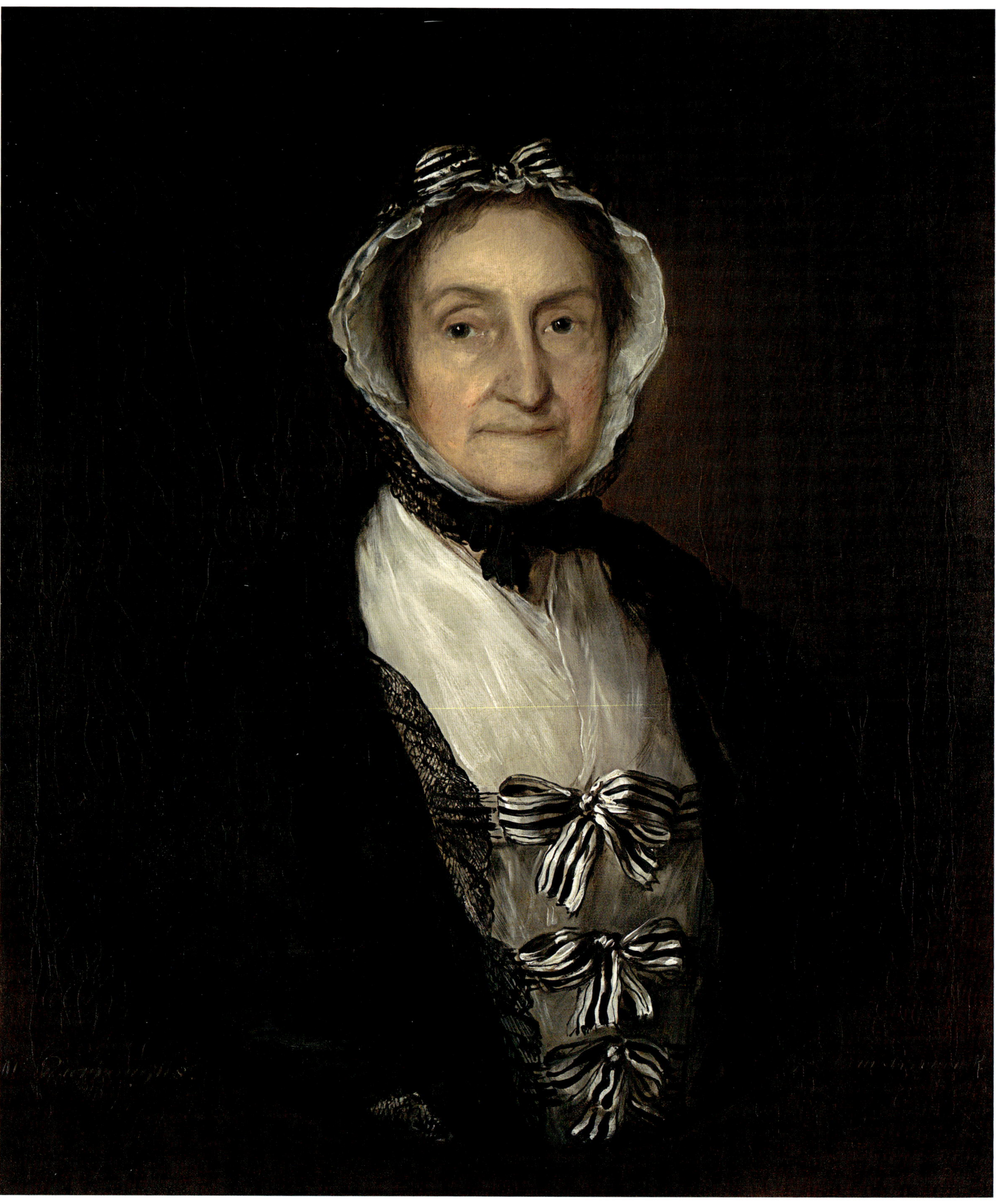

22

Lucy Audley, the Artist's Cousin's Mother-in-Law

Late 1760s
Oil on canvas, 730 x 606mm
Inscribed in a later hand lower left, *Mrs Burroughs*;
lower right, *Gainsborough / 176...*

USC Fisher Museum of Art, Los Angeles,
Elizabeth Holmes Fisher Collection

Long believed to represent Philippa Burrough, the mother of the artist's cousin the Reverend Henry Burrough (cat. 8), the subject of this portrait has been reidentified by Gainsborough scholar Hugh Belsey as Lucy Audley, the mother of Henry's second wife, Jane. This, then, would make her the most distant relation whom Gainsborough is known to have painted. The picture's exceptionally high degree of finish raises the possibility that we are dealing with a rare instance when a family portrait was executed on commission – a possibility strengthened by the existence of a second version, recently acquired by Gainsborough's House, which looks to be an early copy by another hand. Although the inscriptions in the lower corners are much later additions, and given that the subject's name is evidently wrong, the manner in which the long-widowed Mrs Audley is dressed (her husband died in 1733) would be entirely consistent with a date in the late 1760s. The close attention that the artist has paid to the details of satin, ribbons and lace reminds us that he came from a family of milliners; but the characterful face of his 64-year-old sitter also helps to explain why Gainsborough was so greatly admired for the consummate sensitivity of his likenesses.

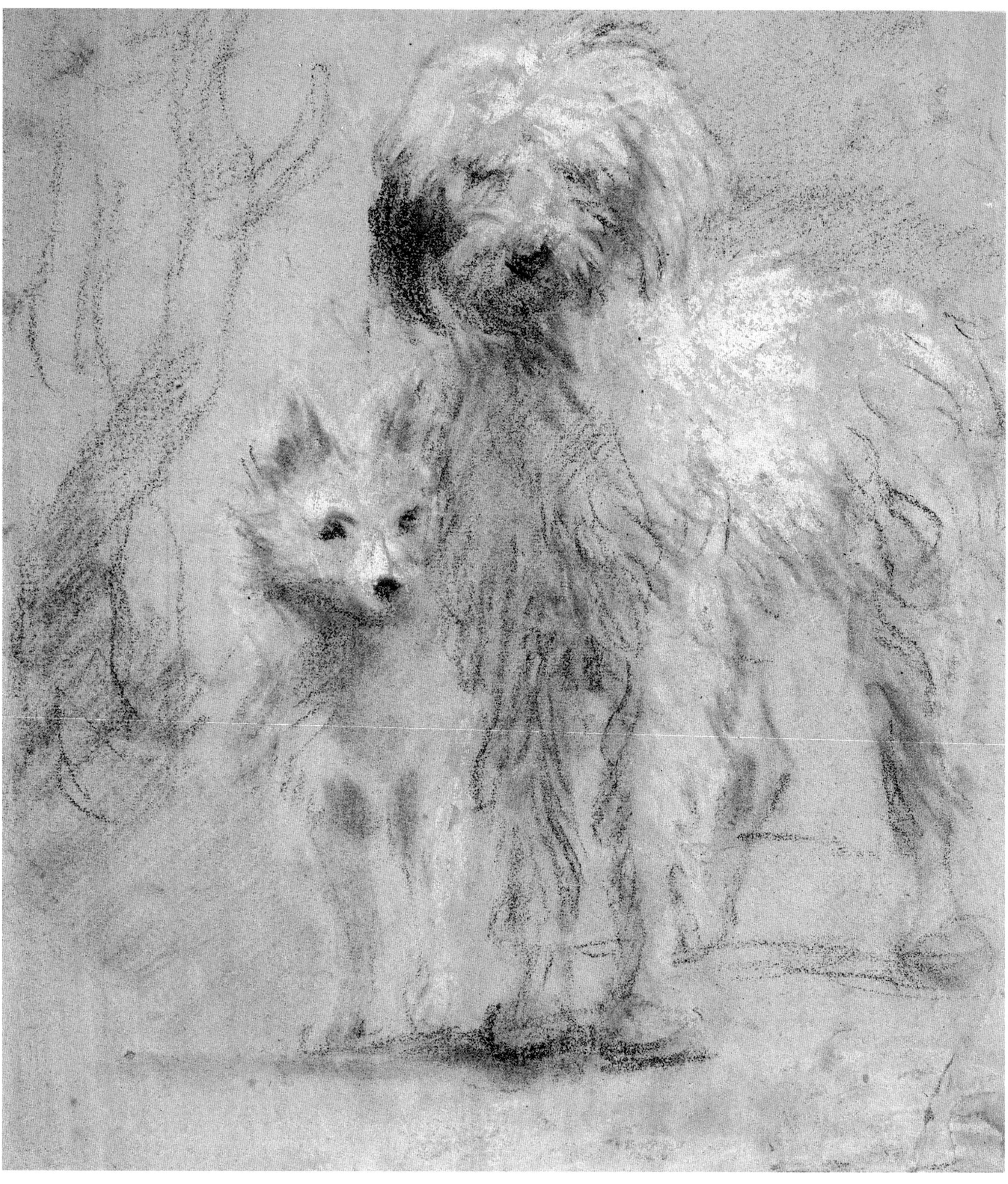

124   BATH

23

Tristram and Fox

1760s
Black chalk and stump, heightened with
white, on prepared paper, 212 x 180mm
Reproduced larger than actual size

Private Collection

In the lithographic reproduction of this drawing issued in 1827 by the artist's great-nephew Richard Lane, these dogs are identified as *Tristram and Fox (Favorites* [sic] *of Gainsborough)*. Since the print shows the original composition in reverse, in the chalk sketch it is Fox (a fox-like Spitz or Pomeranian) who appears on the left, with the larger Tristram (an old English sheepdog-type?) by his side. It must have been Lane or one of his relations who told the artist's first biographer, George Williams Fulcher, that Tristram (named after Laurence Sterne's anti-hero *Tristram Shandy*) had been Margaret Gainsborough's pet, while Fox had answered to her husband.[3] If, here, we take the dogs to be acting as surrogates for their respective owners, then Tristram would seem to be very much in charge. That the composition has strong echoes of a full-length double portrait strengthens the tantalising possibility that Gainsborough intended this drawing as a wry commentary on the dynamics of his marriage. The later portrait in oils of another pair of their pet canines (cat. 41) would appear to characterise the human couple's relationship in radically different terms.

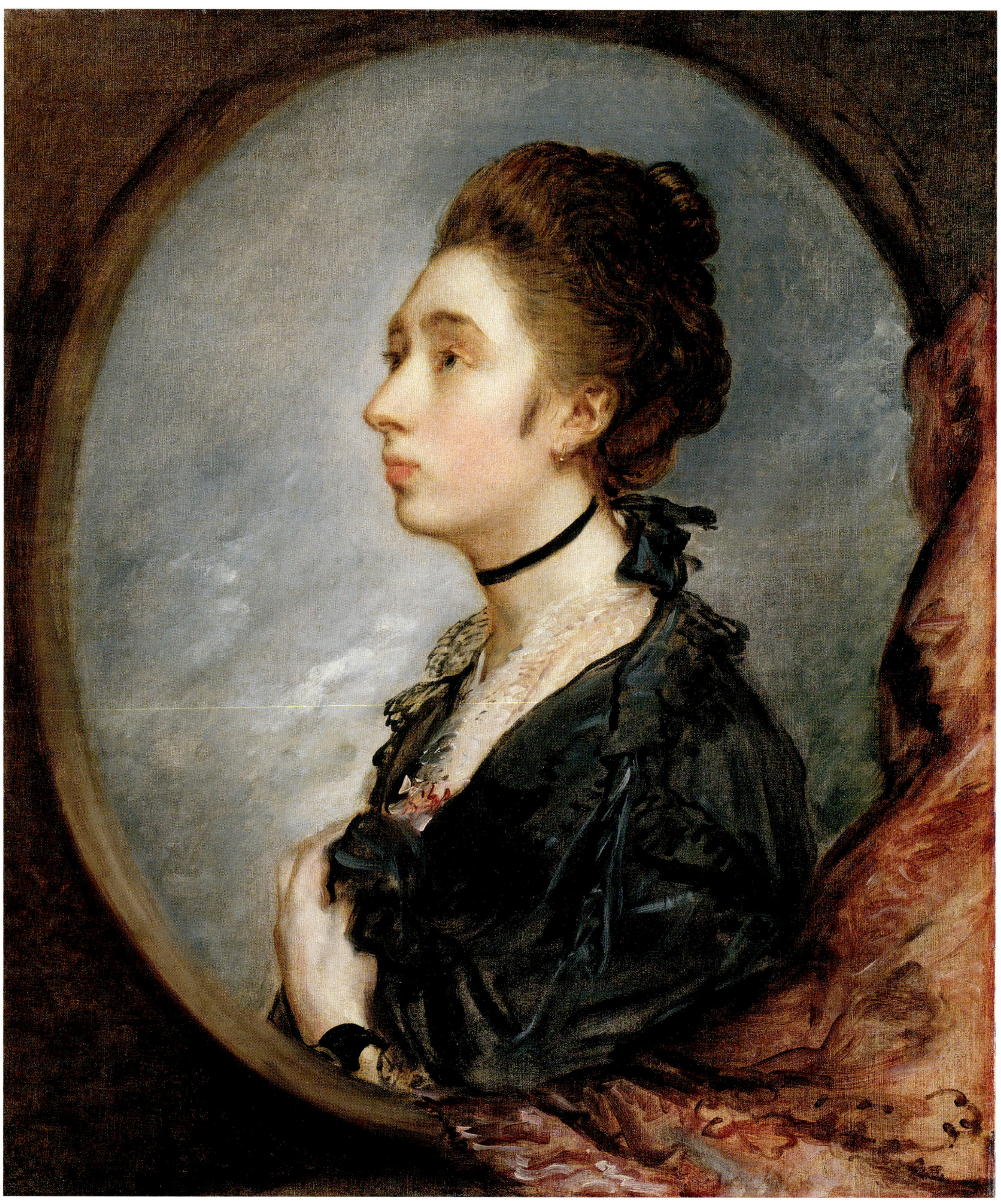

24

Margaret Gainsborough,
The Artist's Daughter

c.1772
Oil on canvas, 756 x 629mm

Tate

Like *'The Pitminster Boy'* of a few years earlier (cat. 21), this likeness of Gainsborough's younger daughter is as much a study of facial expression as it is a portrait per se. Silhouetted in profile against a dramatic sky, Margaret looks upwards in a pose reminiscent of a saint shown with hand on heart gazing up at the heavens, as depicted by Rubens, Murillo, or any number of other seventeenth-century European Old Masters. Here, however, rather than signifying religious devotion, the dramatic attitude would probably have been read as invoking sensibility – a quality as fashionable in the 1770s as Margaret's hairstyle and black mantle, which serve to highlight the delicate pallor of her skin. The great swathe of pink drapery that overlaps the *trompe l'oeil* oval 'frame within a frame' draws on the illusionistic conventions of earlier engraved frontispieces.[4] This conceit, together with the forms of the short cape known as a 'pelerine', gave Gainsborough the opportunity to demonstrate his painterly virtuosity. Although Margaret's head has been fully modelled in layers of semi-transparent glazes that create extraordinarily subtle transitions from whites to pinks to reds, the remainder of the composition looks to have been sketched at remarkable speed.

Gainsborough Dupont,
the Artist's Nephew

*c.*1773
Black chalk and stump, coloured chalks and
watercolour, varnished, 171 x 143mm
Inscribed bottom in a later hand: *T Gainsbg^h* and
Gainsborough Dupont, Painter; verso, in Gainsborough
Dupont's hand: *Portrait of/Gainsborough Dupont/drawn
in chalks by Gainsborough/Bath about the/Year 1775*

Victoria and Albert Museum, London

This rapidly executed study of a boyish
Gainsborough Dupont, the son of the artist's sister
Sarah, shows him from almost the same angle as
the oval now at Waddesdon Manor (cat. 26), and
against a background similarly divided into shaded
and brighter areas. The fact that all four corners
of the small sheet of paper have been left empty
suggests that here, too, Gainsborough had an oval
format in mind, thus raising the possibility that this
drawing served a preparatory function in relation
to the oil. If this was indeed the case, it prompts
two observations: firstly, that when Gainsborough
set about transforming his teenaged apprentice
into a Van Dyckian aristocrat, he took considerable
liberties with the likeness; and secondly, that he
may have wished to give himself a head start
before attempting a demonstration of his ability to
complete a portrait at a single sitting.

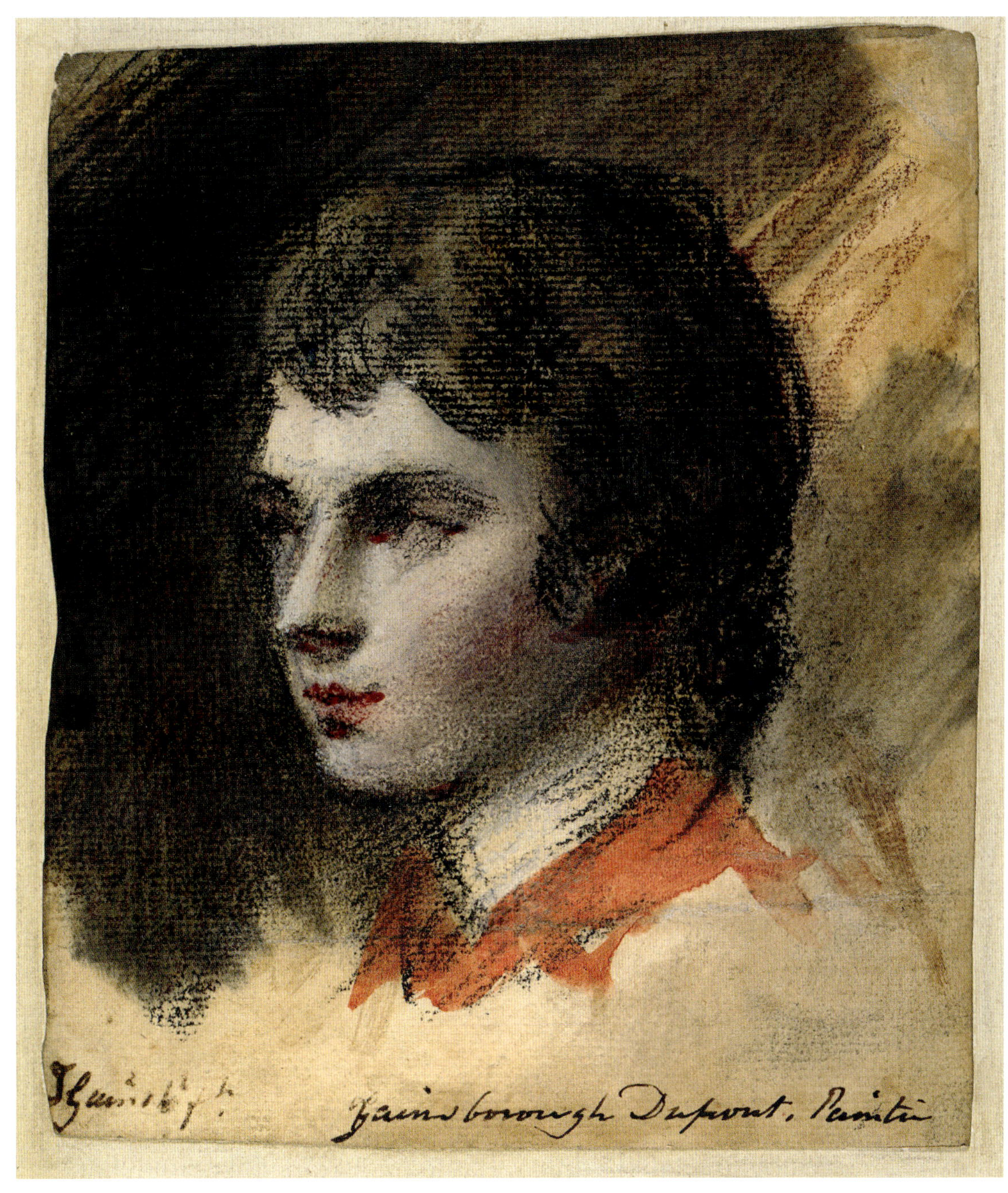

26

Gainsborough Dupont,
the Artist's Nephew

1773
Oil on canvas, 516 x 388mm
Signed in initials lower left: *TG*

In 1773 Gainsborough offered a bravura display of his powers as a portraitist by taking less than an hour to create this oval of his nephew and apprentice Gainsborough Dupont. Although the picture was praised by the artist's friend Philip Thicknesse as 'more like the work of God than man' (see page 32), Gainsborough's choice of Van Dyck dress suggests that it was the seventeenth-century master, not the Divinity, whom he had in mind to emulate. By presenting the teenaged offspring of a humble Suffolk carpenter (cat. 39) as a Van Dyckian gilded youth, Gainsborough demonstrated not only the transformative power of his genius, but also his ability to elevate portraiture to the level of great art. These ambitious claims appear to have met with immediate acceptance, for he gave away the painting once it had been completed, and soon afterwards it entered the collection of an aristocratic connoisseur.

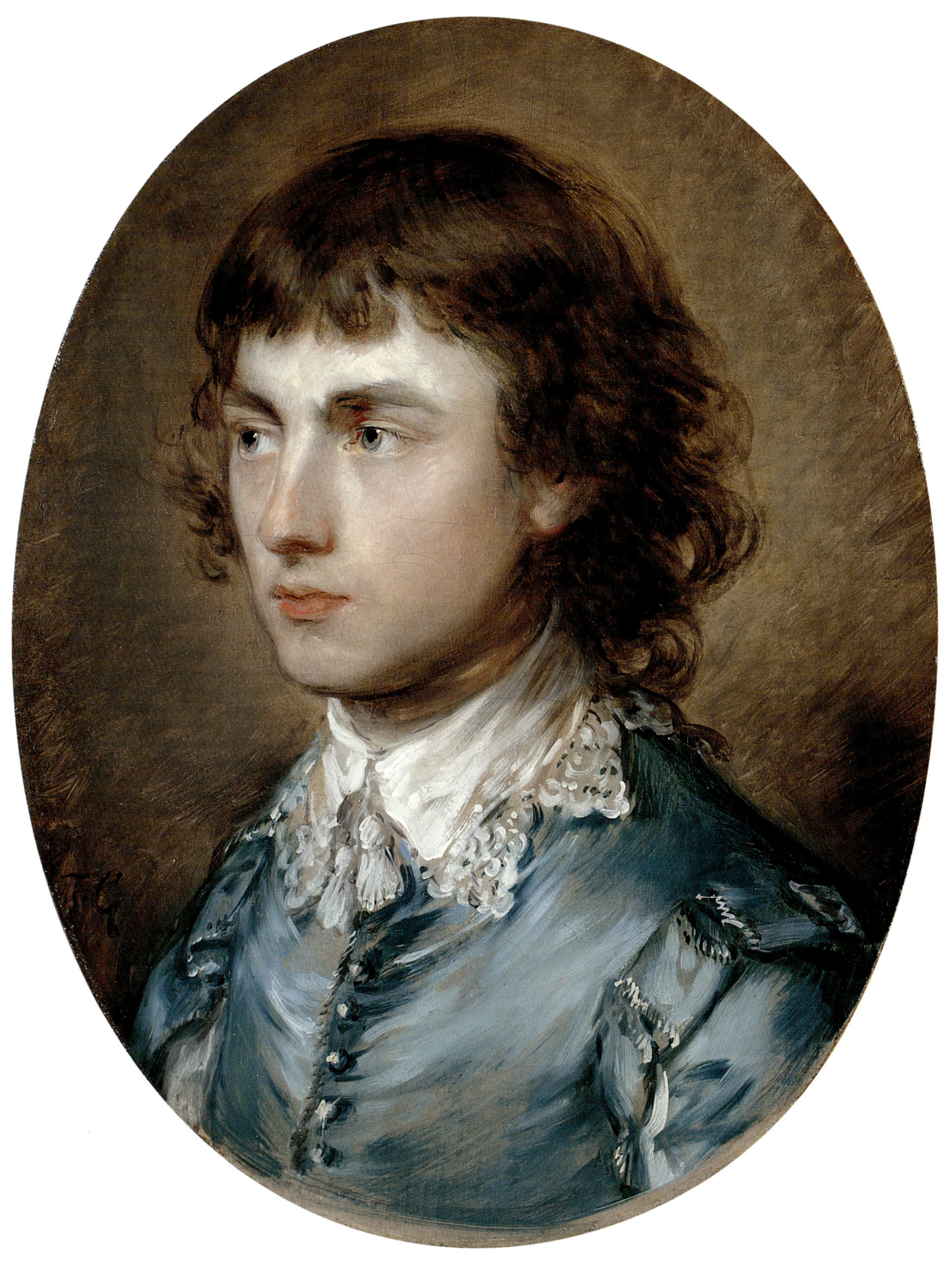

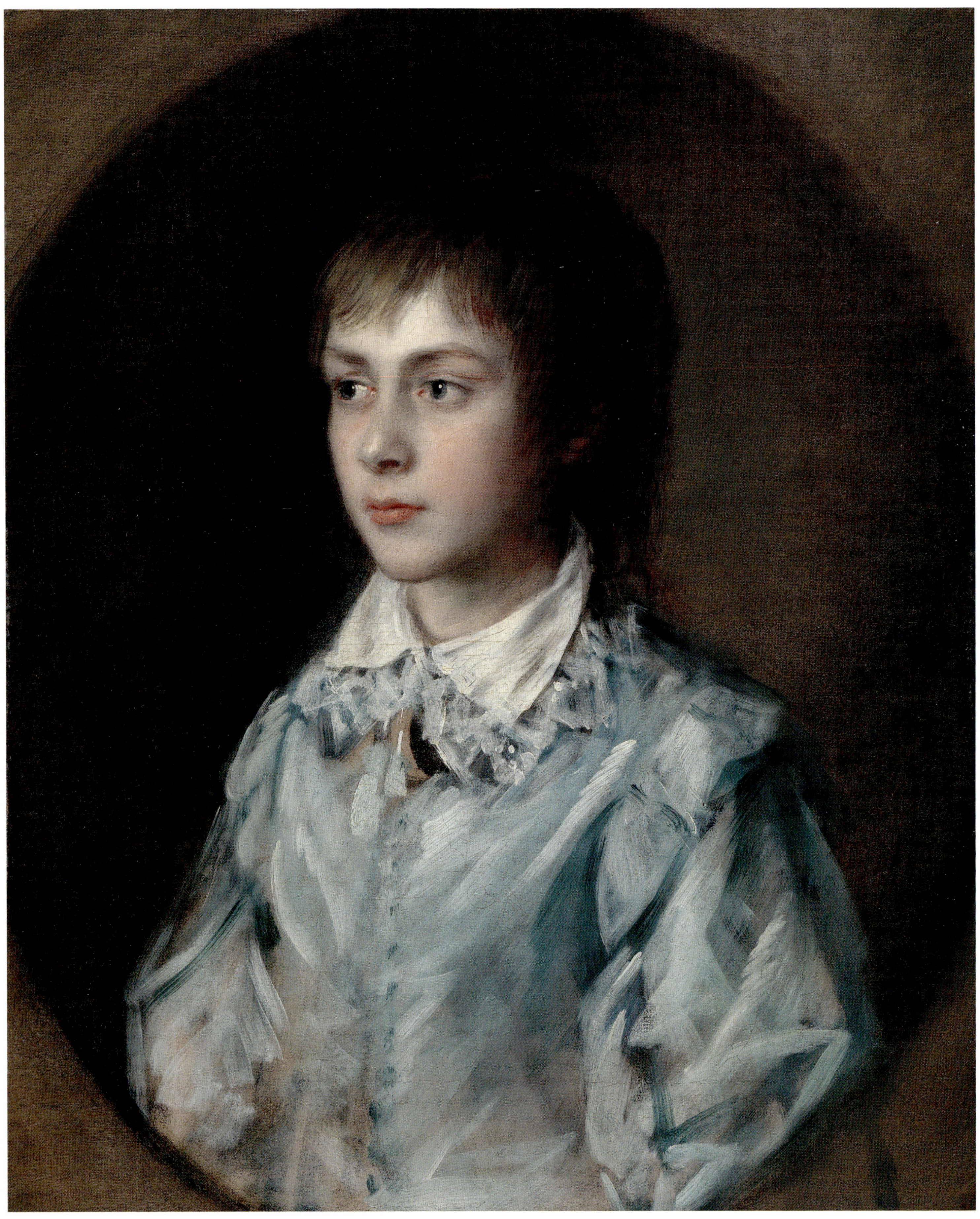

27

Edward Richard Gardiner, the Artist's Nephew

*c.*1772–4
Oil on canvas, 622 x 502mm

Tate

Gainsborough probably painted this likeness of Edward Richard Gardiner (b.1764), his nephew, as a pendant to the earlier portrait of the boy's sister Susan (cat. 10). Since the same period of time had elapsed between the births of the two siblings, the paired images would have shown each child at the same age, around eight or nine, a coincidence that is unlikely to have escaped either Gainsborough or the children's mother (cat. 42). The same juxtaposition would also have highlighted just how dramatically Gainsborough's art had changed since he had moved from Ipswich to Bath. Whereas the late 1750s had seen him rather timidly developing his own version of contemporary French and British trends, by the early 1770s he had become one of the nation's leading artists, a painter utterly confident in his virtuoso skills and more than willing to pit himself against any rival, past or present. On this occasion, as in the two roughly contemporaneous depictions of another nephew, Gainsborough Dupont (cats 26, 48), the object of his emulation was Sir Anthony van Dyck. The Van Dyck dress worn by the young Gardiner may have been a studio prop, since the same garment features in the Waddesdon oval of Dupont (cat. 26), and probably also in *'The Blue Boy'* (fig. 12). The Gardiner is the least finished of these three compositions: apart from the white collar, the boy's costume remains little more than a sketchy array of sweeping angular brushstrokes, which barely cover the salmon-coloured ground. When it came to painting the head, it was the child's likeness that mattered, but the draperies are all about Gainsborough and Van Dyck.

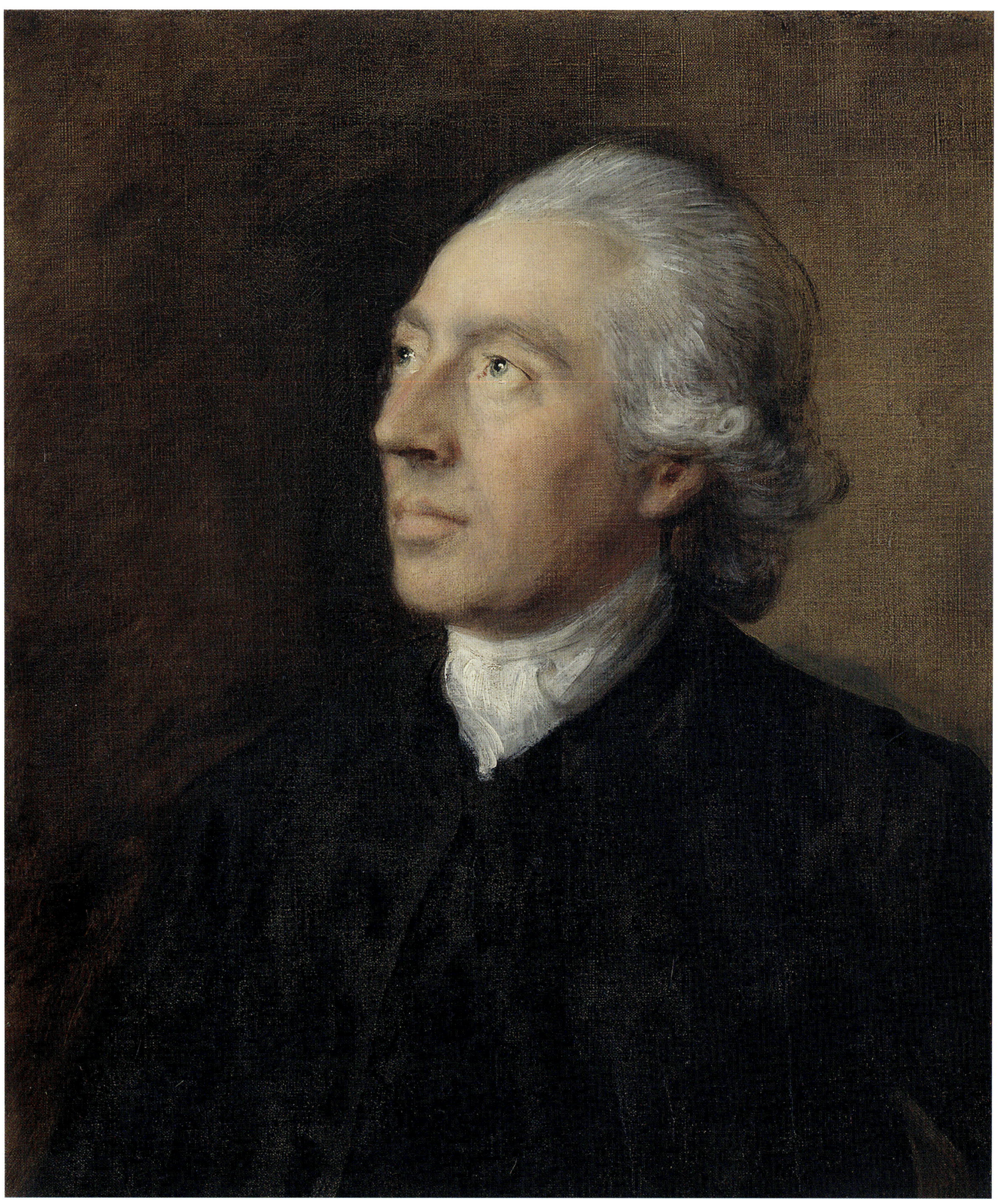

28

Humphrey Gainsborough,
the Artist's Brother

early 1770s

Oil on canvas, 597 x 495mm

Yale Center for British Art, Paul Mellon Collection,
New Haven, CT

Gainsborough's older brother Humphrey, a Congregational minister at Henley-on-Thames from 1748 until his death in 1776, was the only one of his siblings whom he painted twice – first in Ipswich (cat. 7) and then towards the end of his time in Bath. Although something similar can be found in the contemporaneous head-and-shoulders of his daughter Margaret (cat. 24), this is a rare instance in Gainsborough's portrait oeuvre of a sitter being shown gazing up and to one side. The attitude carries echoes of Old Master images of saints in ecstasy, and presumably on this occasion was meant to honour Humphrey as a deeply religious man. That compliment probably helps to explain why one of his Henley parishioners commissioned Gainsborough to paint a second version (now in a private collection) – the only time he was ever paid to replicate one of the portraits of his relations.

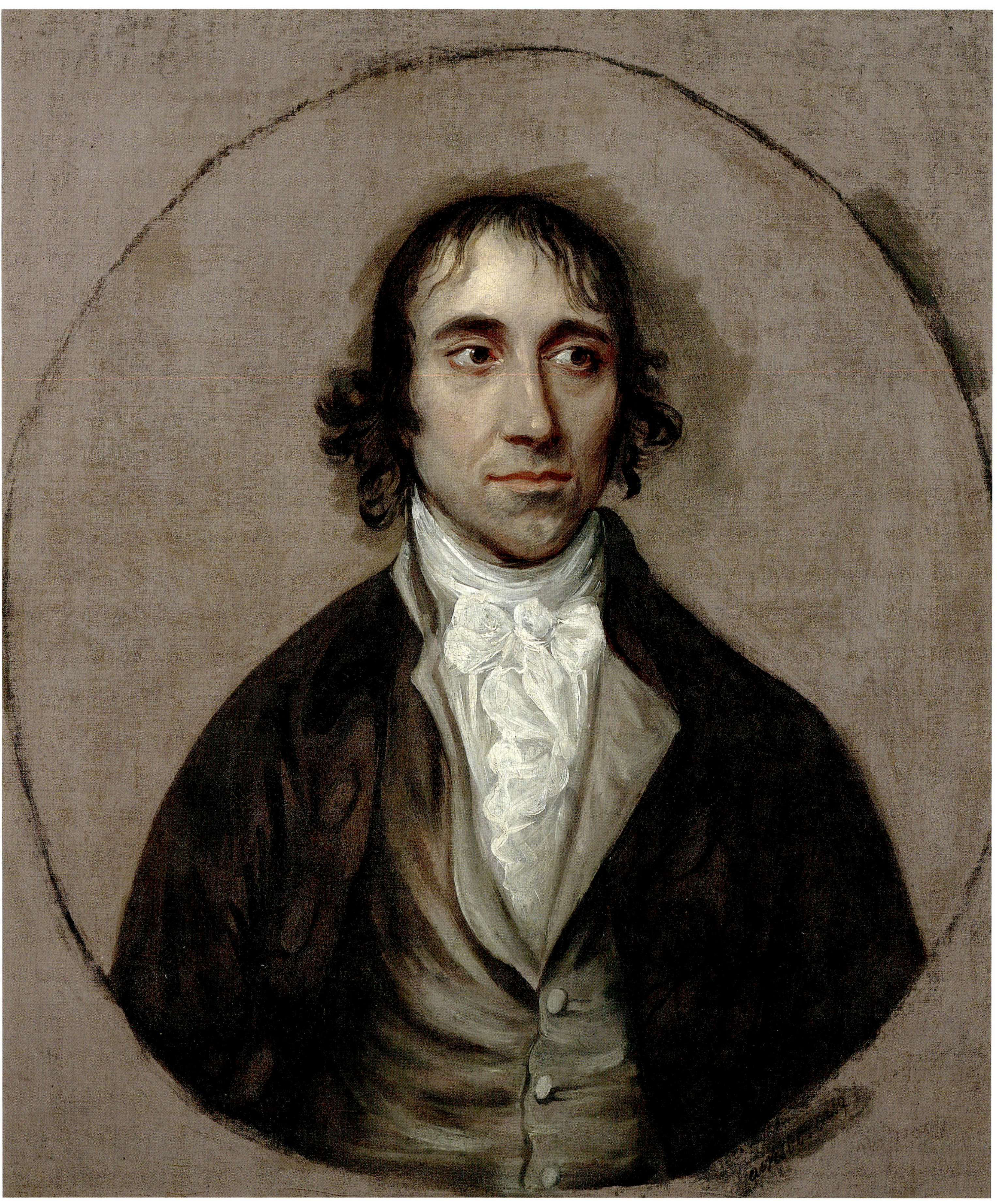

29

John Gainsborough ('Scheming Jack'), the Artist's Brother

early 1770s
Oil on canvas, 724 x 597mm
Signed (?) lower right: *Gainsborow*

Private Collection

Recent cleaning of this picture has shown that it is unfinished in a way that differs from what we find in other Gainsborough portraits of his relations. Here the figure looks virtually complete, but the setting, apart from one roughly painted line that demarcates the beginnings of an oval surround, consists of nothing more than an expanse of primed canvas, with hardly any indication of shading except immediately around the head. It is possible that Gainsborough painted his brother's features, and that, at a later date, the body was filled in by Dupont, whose handling lacks the lightness and fluidity characteristic of his uncle. In any event, it is hard to resist the temptation of reading into this likeness what we know of John Gainsborough's history, as a failed inventor who came to depend financially on his much younger (and far more successful) brother Thomas. But even if it would be wrong to characterise this as the image of a ne'er-do-well, 'Scheming Jack's' dishevelled locks suggest his almost complete lack of concern for the niceties of appearance, and place him in a social rank beneath that of a 'fine gentleman'. He would, in fact, have been on much the same level with his brother-in-law, Philip Dupont, whom Gainsborough also depicted wigless and even more plainly dressed (cat. 39). If the 'Gainsborow' inscription is original and not a later addition, the curious spelling may have been the artist's way of punningly referring to his brother's chronic pleas for financial support.

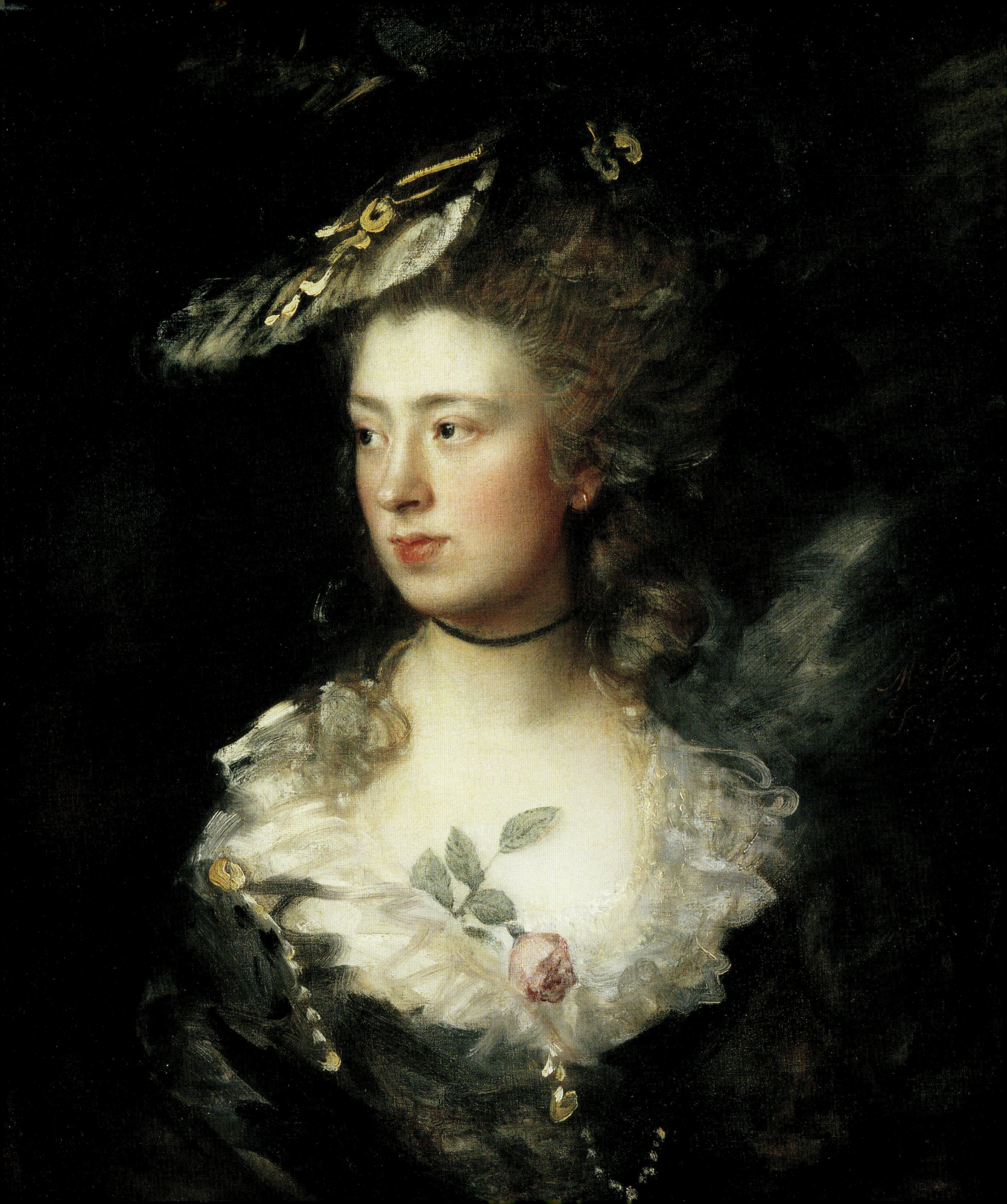

LONDON

1774–1788

Gainsborough's move to London in 1774 inaugurated the final, triumphant phase of his career – and by taking up residence in Schomberg House, Pall Mall, he placed himself and his family at the very heart of West End high society. Judging from the evidence provided by their portraits, not only the artist but also his relations were eager to claim a share of the elevated social status that had come with his hard-won rise to fame. Gainsborough's desire to promote his own and their ambitions is nowhere better shown than in the remarkably formal full-length portrait of his daughters, which may well have been designed to adorn the family's prestigious new surroundings. On this canvas, for the first time, Mary and Margaret have been made to look indistinguishable from the fine ladies who populate so many of their father's commissioned works. Arguably, they deserved nothing less as the grandchildren of a duke (on their mother's side), and as the offspring of one of Britain's most popular – and wealthiest – artists, who could boast the additional cachet of being a founding member of the Royal Academy.

By the end of the 1770s, Gainsborough had achieved the highest goal of any eighteenth-century portraitist, when he secured the patronage of the royal family, who would continue to employ him throughout the remainder of his life. Over the same period he painted no fewer than five likenesses of his wife Margaret, who, according to a family story of somewhat dubious reliability, he depicted every year on their wedding anniversary. All the pictures in this late series strike a note of personal tenderness, but the two diminutive oil sketches from the mid to late 1780s – perhaps the most unambiguously private of all Gainsborough's portraits – must surely have been meant for his and Margaret's eyes alone.

Mary and Margaret Gainsborough, the Artist's Daughters

c.1774
Oil on canvas, 2487 x 1500mm

Private Collection

Of all the six (actually five and a half) double portraits of Gainsborough's daughters, this is the only one that can be described as entirely finished. It is also the largest, the most formal and the least personal of the series – that is to say, the only one that could easily be taken for a work commissioned by one of the artist's paying customers. As Ann Bermingham has observed (see page 55), Mary and Margaret are shown here as they might themselves have wished to be seen – namely, as the fashionable subjects of a conventionally beautiful Gainsborough portrait – and not, as had hitherto been the case, as vehicles for, or projections of, their father's ambitions and desires. The only unexpected feature of the picture may be the accompanying dog, an age-old symbol of fidelity more usually encountered in double full-lengths of married couples. Its inclusion may have been the painter's way of signalling the emotional closeness of the sisters' relationship.

The occasion for the production of this grand image may well have been the family's move in 1774 from Bath to London, where they took up residence at Schomberg House in Pall Mall. Here, one imagines that Gainsborough's sumptuous double full-length of his daughters would have looked entirely at home, in a setting where their depiction as fine ladies would have served to buttress the entire family's claims to gentility. Yet, for reasons that remain unexplained, this painting did not long remain with the Gainsboroughs. If it had not left their possession by the time of the artist's death in 1788, it certainly did so shortly thereafter.

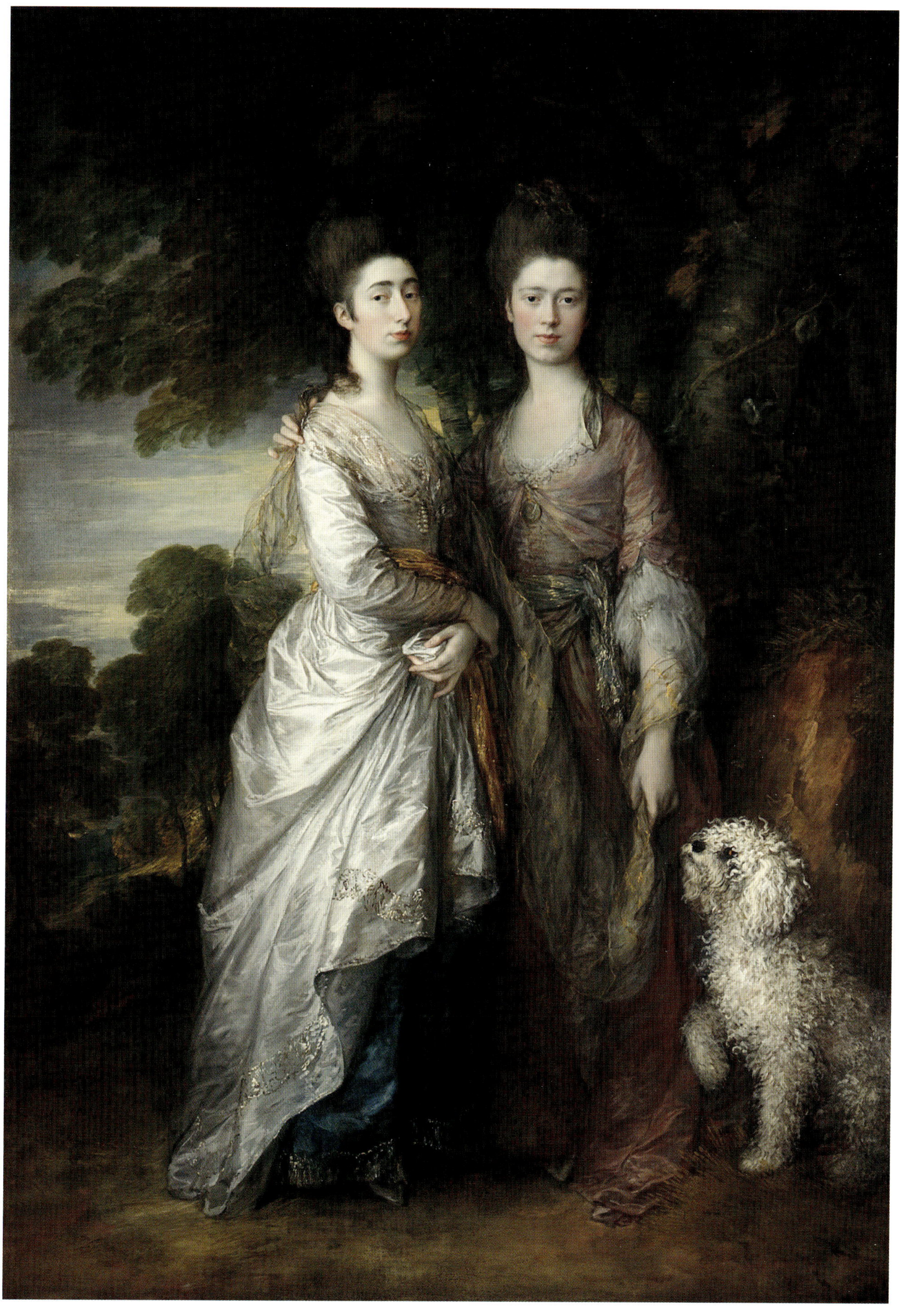

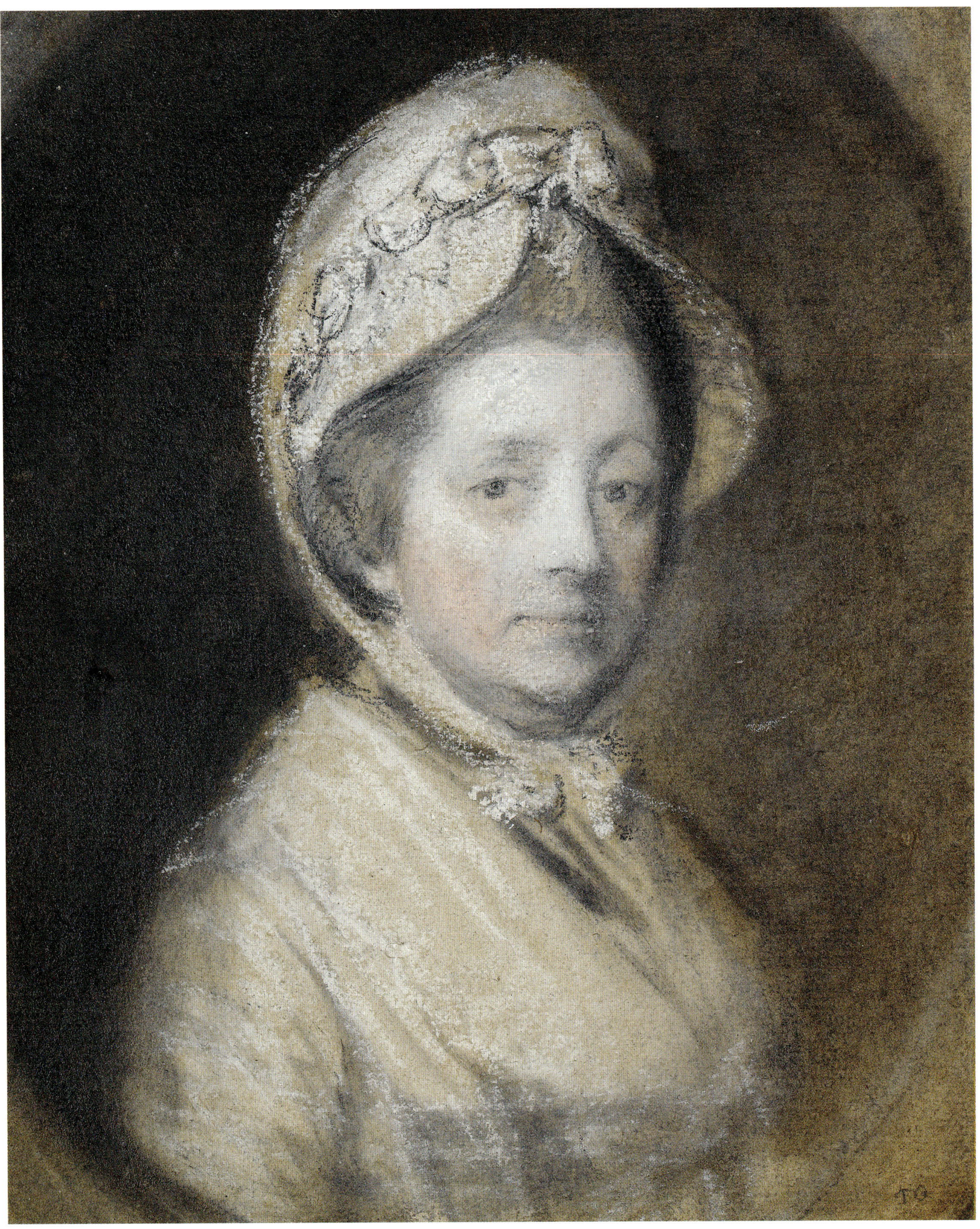

Margaret Gainsborough, the Artist's Wife

*c.*mid-1770s
Pastel over pencil, heightened
with gouache, 235 x 190mm
Signed (?) in initials lower right: *TG*

Private Collection
Exhibited in London only

Gainsborough is known to have produced only around half a dozen portraits in pastel, most dating from the years on either side of 1770. With these works he entered into direct competition with his older contemporary William Hoare, who, by then, had long been established as Bath's leading portraitist 'in crayons'. While the portability of the pastels and speed of execution made this technique particularly well-suited for the spa's transient clientele, the medium had the disadvantage of being easily susceptible to damage caused by rubbing, as this example clearly demonstrates. In a letter of 1771 to the Hon. Edward Stratford, a disappointed client, Gainsborough acknowledged the problem: 'I'm sorry your Chalk Drawings got Rubbed as they were muzzy [i.e. indistinct] enough at first, as indeed all Chalk Drawings of Portraits must be so Small and the Chalk so soft.'[5] On the other hand, both the scale and the 'muzziness' of the handling could be exploited to create an effect of remarkable intimacy, such as Gainsborough has achieved here. The type of high cap that Margaret is shown wearing came into fashion in the mid 1770s, so the pastel, rather than dating from the Gainsboroughs' time in Bath, as has hitherto been assumed, may well be the first in the series of six portraits of his wife that are known from the family's time in London.

Gainsborough Dupont, the Artist's Nephew

*c.*1775–6
Oil on canvas, 762 x 632mm

Memphis Brooks Museum of Art, Memphis, TN

This is one of two portraits of Dupont that Gainsborough painted in the years soon after the family's move to London; the other portrait (fig. 36) has not been seen since the 1950s. Whereas previously he had used his nephew as the subject for virtuoso performances in the manner of Van Dyck (cats 26, 48), in the capital he depicted him as a fashionably dressed and bewigged beau, in a properly finished work that bears comparison with any of Gainsborough's commissioned likenesses of young gentlemen from the mid to later 1770s. This change in approach registered Dupont's elevation in status – from his uncle's apprentice to his paid assistant, student at the Royal Academy, and heir apparent to his practice. In his stylish new guise too, Dupont could take his place alongside his cousins (cat. 30) as a member of the affluent metropolitan elite, and as no less worthy an occupant of the family's opulent London quarters in Schomberg House, Pall Mall.

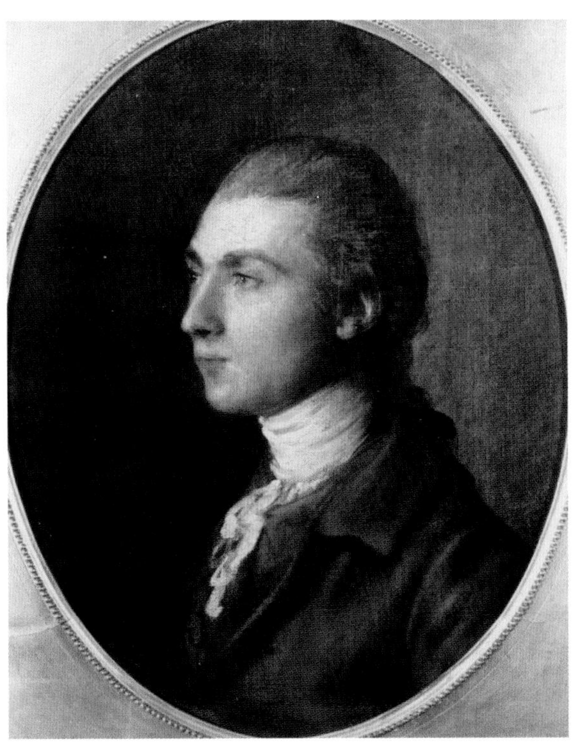

FIG. 36
Thomas Gainsborough
Gainsborough Dupont
c.1775–6
Oil on canvas
635 x 508mm
Present location unknown

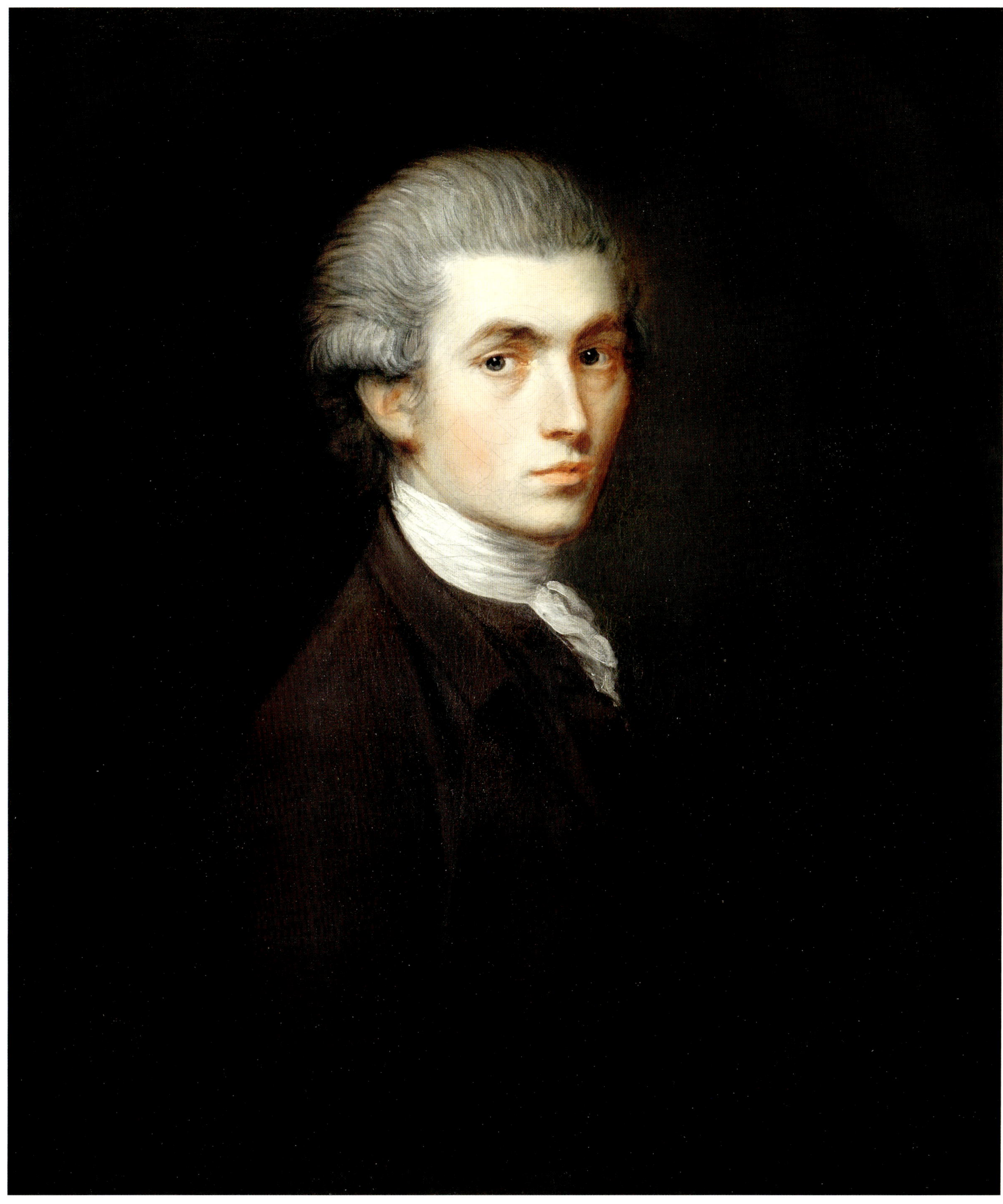

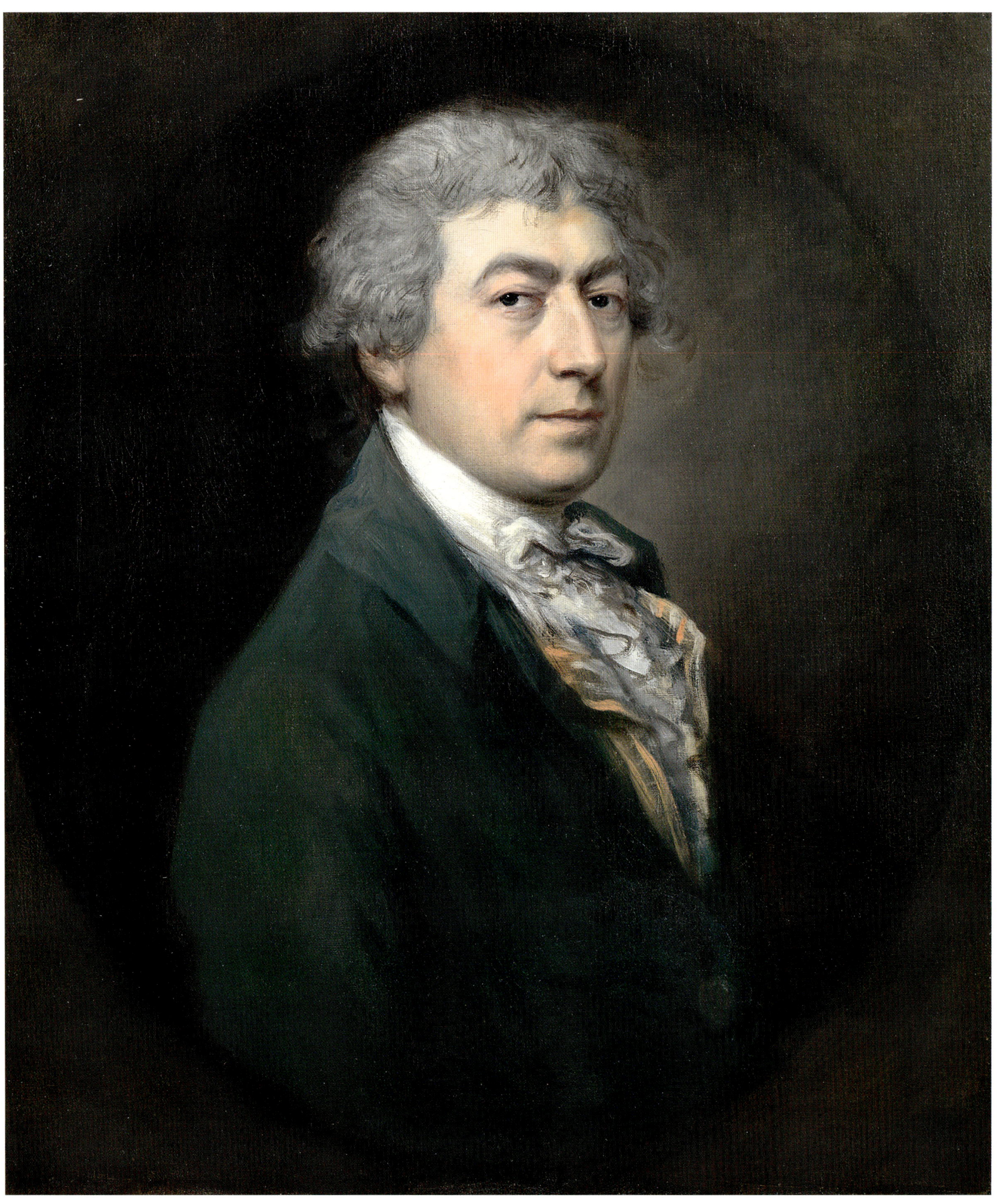

Self-portrait
(completed by Gainsborough Dupont)

mid-1770s and 1790

Oil on canvas, 766 x 635mm

The Samuel Courtauld Trust. The Courtauld Gallery, London

When this self-portrait was sold by Gainsborough's great-nephew Richard Lane in 1838,[6] it was noted in the catalogue that the picture had 'been worked upon by Gainsborough Dupont'. The extent and nature of his and his uncle's involvement remained unclear, however, until 2011, when extensive technical examination undertaken by Alysia Sawicka and Stefanie Lenk at the Courtauld Institute of Art uncovered evidence for an unusually complicated history.[7] Their findings indicate that the image began its life as a self-portrait in the years just after Gainsborough's move to London. At this point he worked the head up to a high degree of finish, and sketched in the outlines of the upper body. Initially, the artist's intention seems to have been to include his left arm, in much the same hand-in-waistcoat pose found in his two earlier self-portraits (cats 4, 12). Soon afterwards, however, he changed his mind. X-rays reveal that he raised the canvas to incorporate an unprimed area that gave him more space at the bottom, and this allowed him to introduce the oval surround. At a later date he sketched in the cuff of his right sleeve, and presumably painted out his left arm. It was in this unresolved state that the picture remained until Gainsborough's death, at which time Dupont undertook to transform it into a finished object. To do so, he repainted the body almost entirely, by copying the draperies and the hair from the late self-portrait that the artist's daughter Margaret subsequently presented to the Royal Academy (cat. 47). We can confidently assume that Dupont's aim was to fashion the unfinished likeness of his late uncle into a suitable pendant for the portrait of his aunt (cat. 34) – quite possibly at her behest. The two pictures were offered as successive lots at the Lane sale, and have remained together ever since.

Margaret Gainsborough, the Artist's Wife

*c.*1777
Oil on canvas, 766 x 638mm

This portrait of Margaret Gainsborough, possibly painted for her fiftieth birthday, is striking both for its compelling sense of emotional intimacy and a degree of intellectual ambition that is only very rarely found in Gainsborough's portrait oeuvre. As she holds back her black mantilla and fixes her gaze directly on her husband, Margaret strikes a pose based on a classical statue identified in the eighteenth century both as *pudicitia* (modesty) and the goddess Juno, the famously irascible spouse of the ever-philandering Jupiter. If Gainsborough was humorously (and learnedly) implying that his wife's temperament left something to be desired, the joke was at his own expense as well.

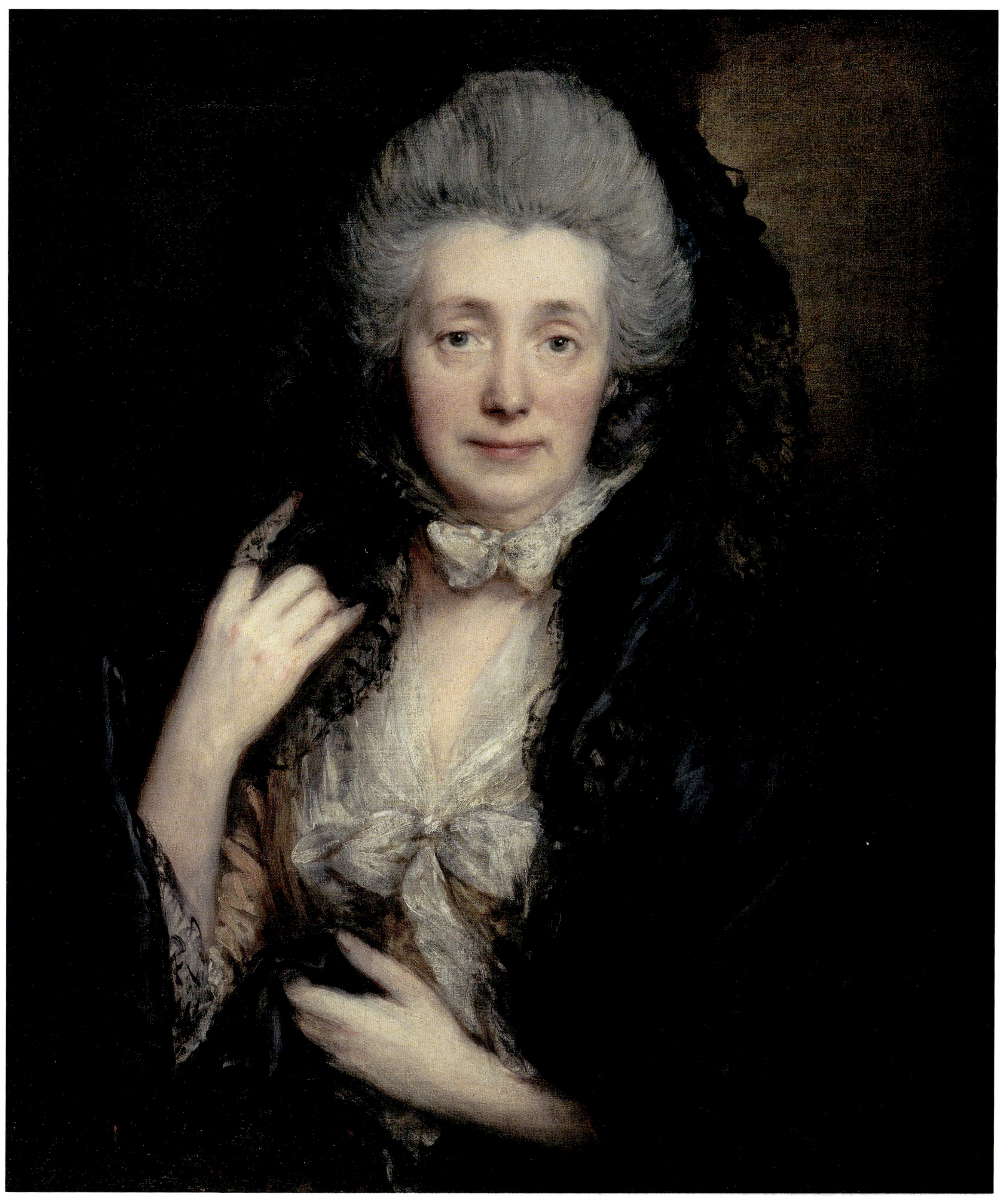

35

Mary Gainsborough, the Artist's Daughter

1777
Oil on canvas, 775 x 648mm
Inscribed at right: *M[y] G / T G fecit / 1777*

Tate

Gainsborough hardly ever signed and dated any of his painted portraits, never mind inscribe them with the name of his sitter; why he did so on this occasion we can only guess. What makes the signature all the more remarkable is that so much of the image, apart from the face, remains palpably unfinished, at least by normal eighteenth-century standards. Mary's ruff has been only roughly sketched in zigzag strokes of thick impasto, while the rest of her dress and her arms are given only the most rudimentary indication. Elsewhere, some of the freest passages of brushwork can be found on the highlighted brim of her feathered and ribboned hat, where the quick blobs and dashes of impasto call out for appreciation in their own right, independently of their descriptive function. Nonetheless, the signature tells us that the artist's work is done, indeed that such painterly exuberance is precisely what makes this a 'Gainsborough'. At an earlier point in his career, only portraits of a private character would have left his easel in so unresolved a state. By the late 1770s, however, even his exhibited likenesses were provoking complaints from critics that he was only bothering to finish his faces, and neglecting all the subordinate parts, the dress most obviously. In this instance, Mary's fanciful apparel owes less to contemporary fashions than it does to past art, and in particular to Rubens's famous portrait of his wife Helena Fourment (then believed to be one of Van Dyck's greatest masterpieces) now in the Gulbenkian Museum in Lisbon. Gainsborough strove to emulate the same Old Masters on a far grander scale in his spectacular full-length of *The Hon. Mrs Thomas Graham* (fig. 29), which he exhibited at the Royal Academy in 1777.

Throughout the nineteenth century, this portrait of Mary was kept by Gainsborough's descendants, together with a markedly less finished companion piece (now unlocated) of her younger sister Margaret, shown playing a theorbo (fig. 37).

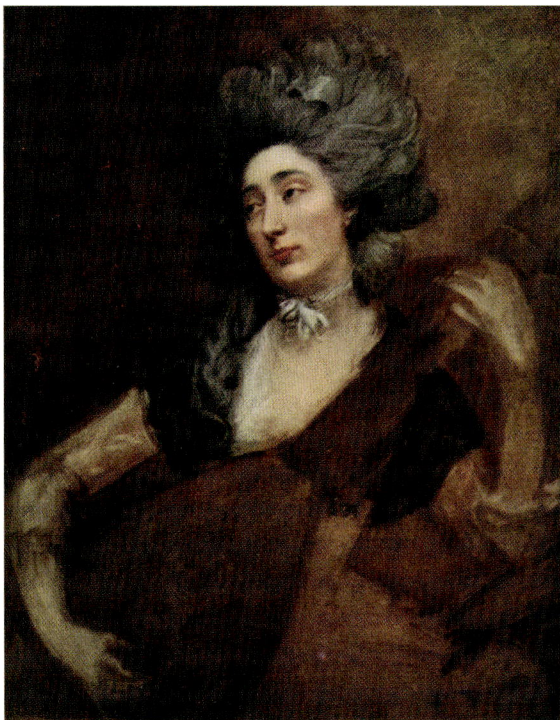

FIG. 37
Thomas Gainsborough
Margaret Gainsborough, the Artist's Daughter
c.1777
Oil on canvas
762 x 673mm
Present location unknown

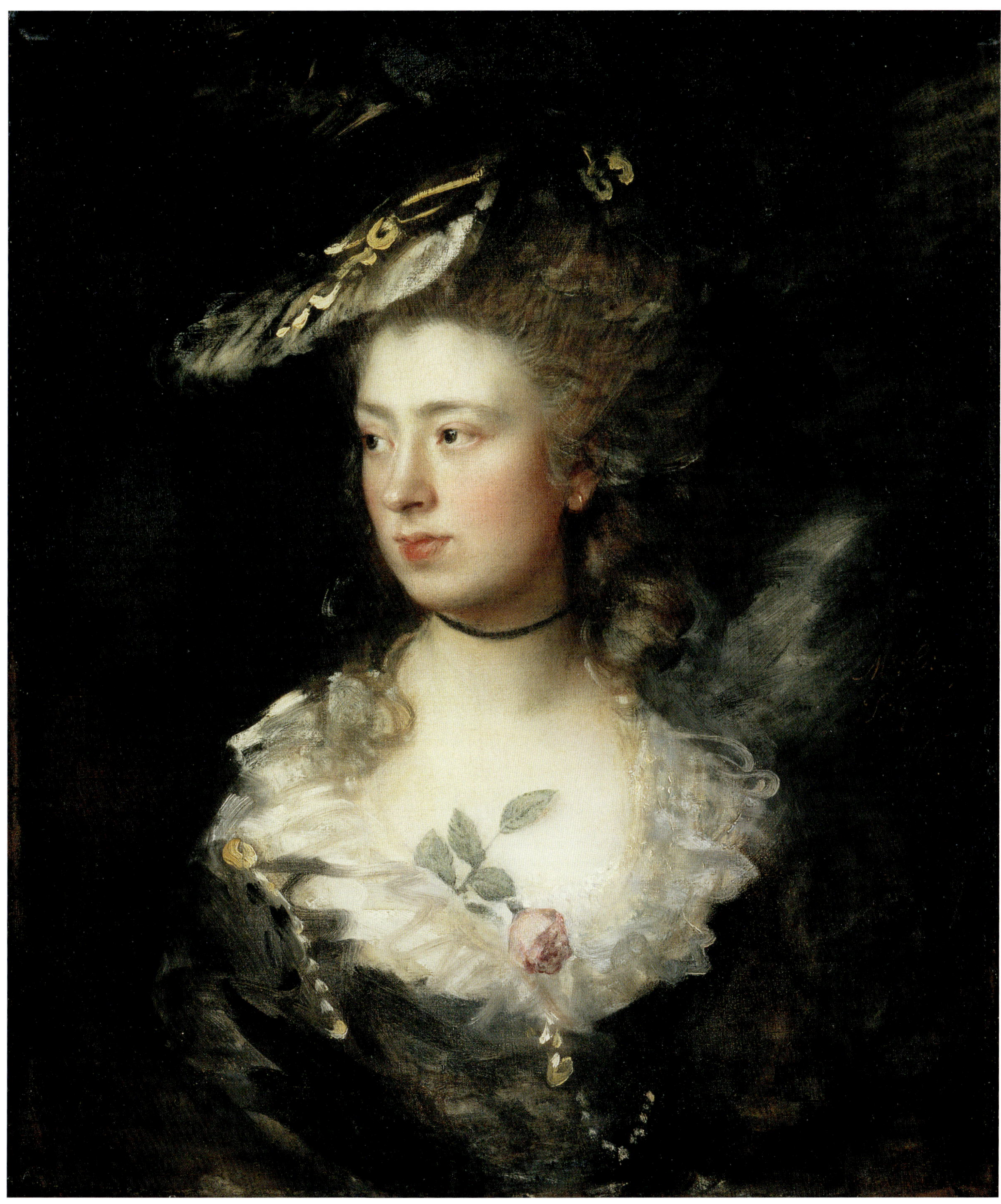

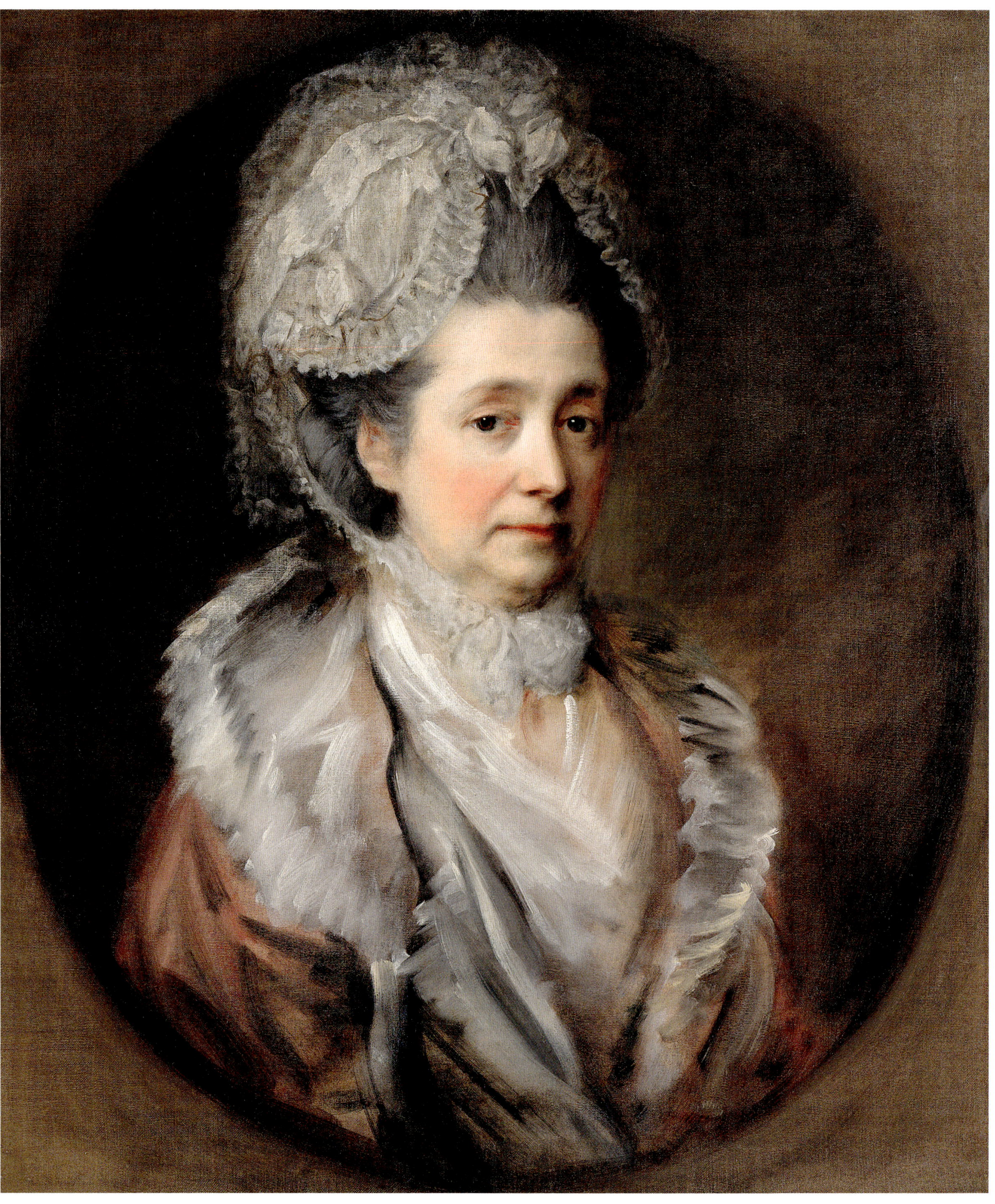

Margaret Gainsborough, the Artist's Wife

*c.*1777–8
Oil on canvas, 750 x 620mm

Arp Museum Bahnhof Rolandseck / Collection Rau for UNICEF

According to a story recounted by a late nineteenth-century member of the Burr family (presumably the child or grandchild of a nephew of Margaret Gainsborough, née Burr), Thomas Gainsborough painted his wife's portrait annually over a period of many years, as a way of marking the anniversary of their wedding in 1746. If this family tradition is true, the surviving evidence suggests that this might have become the artist's practice only during the last decade or so of his life, from which five likenesses in oil and possibly one drawing (cat. 43) of Margaret Gainsborough survive. Of these, the example in the Rau Collection is one of the earliest, the large lace cap adorned with ribbons that tie around the neck being very much *à la mode* in the later 1770s. Almost exactly the same hairstyle and headdress appear in a mezzotint of Mrs Catherine Frederick, published in 1777 by John Raphael Smith (fig. 38). This print is one of a series of six generally believed to depict a group of London's most exclusive prostitutes. The striking similarities between *Mrs Frederick* and *Margaret Gainsborough* should not lead us to suspect that Mr Gainsborough wished to cast aspersions on his wife's virtue – only that he wished to represent her as a beautiful and attractive woman with unerring taste for the latest in fashionable attire. Other evidence suggests that this is precisely how Margaret wished to see herself.

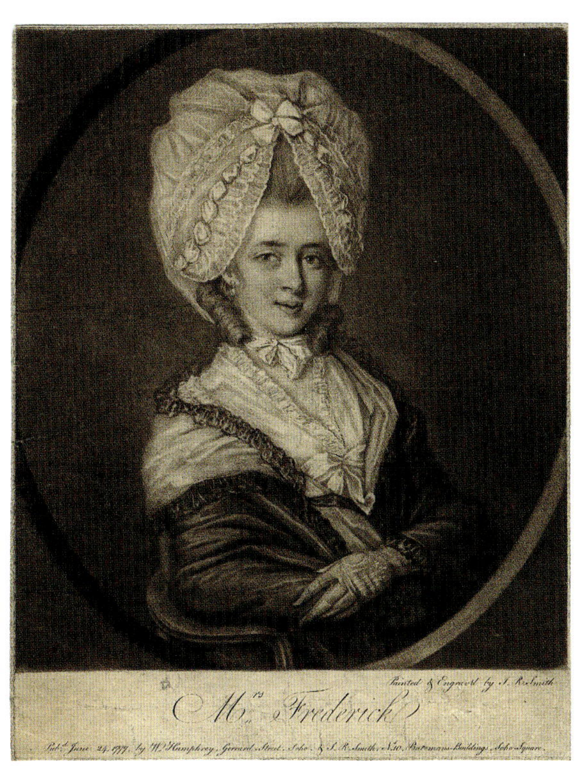

FIG. 38
John Raphael Smith
Mrs Catherine Frederick
1777
Mezzotint
267 x 203mm
National Portrait Gallery, London

Margaret Gainsborough, the Artist's Wife

c.1777–8
Oil on millboard, 240 x 222mm

Anthony Mould

The differences between Margaret Gainsborough's appearance in this and the Rau Collection portrait are small but significant enough to suggest that one was not copied from the other. The high quality of the little oil on millboard also argues in favour of its being an autograph work. Although Margaret's face looks somewhat fuller here, and perhaps just that little bit older, it is not inconceivable that both pictures were done at the same sitting. Another possibility is that they were painted in successive years, in line with the family story about annual anniversary gifts. It is not difficult to imagine pictures on the scale of this and the two later oils of Margaret (cats 44, 45) being presented as highly personal tokens of affection from an artist-husband to his wife.

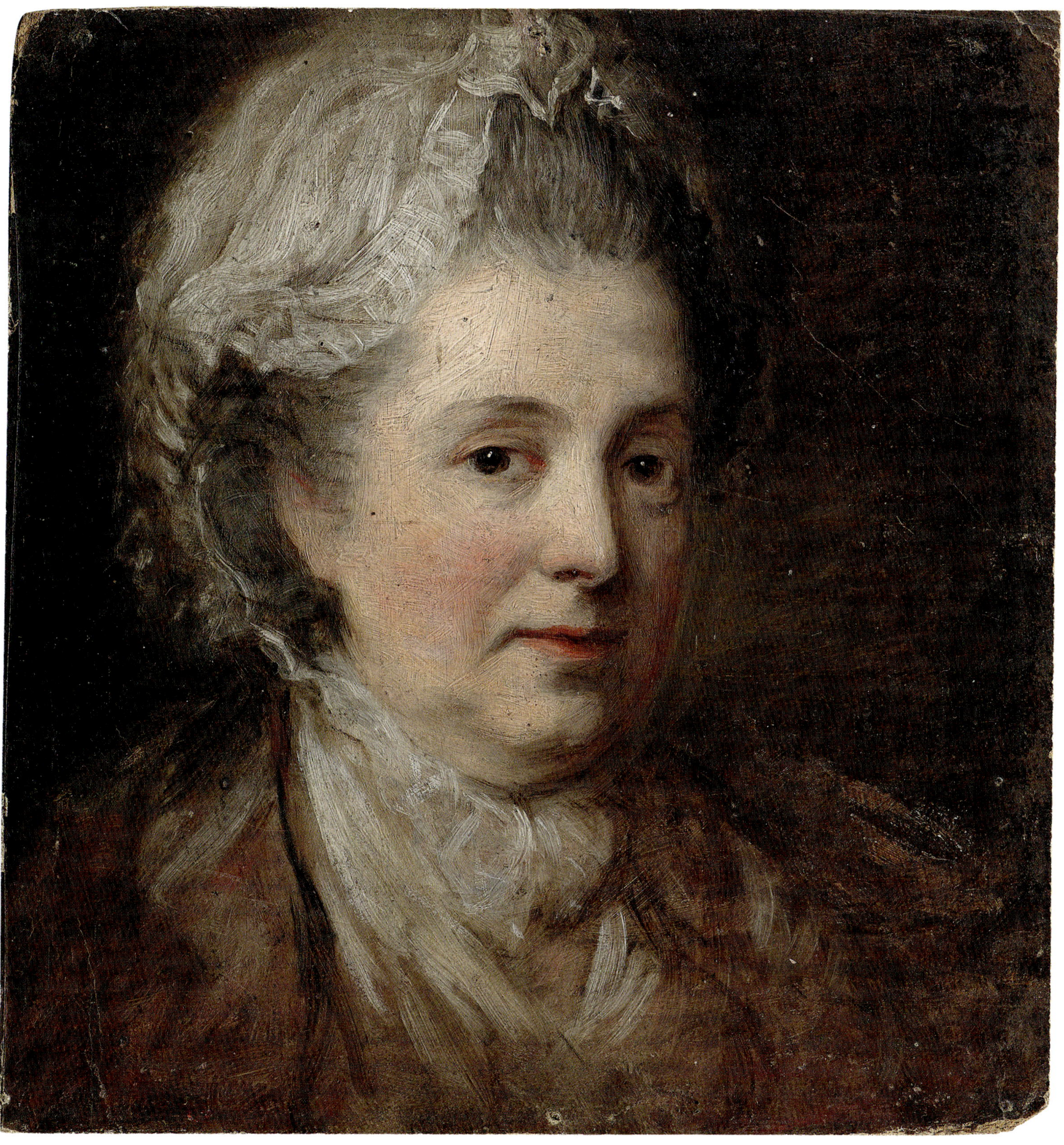

38

Sarah Dupont, the Artist's Sister

c.1777–9

Oil on canvas, 772 x 645mm

The Art Institute of Chicago, Charles H.
and Mary F.S. Worcester Collection

If Gainsborough gave his brother-in-law Philip Dupont an air of down-to-earth plainness bordering on bumpkin rusticity (cat. 39), he went to the opposite extreme when it came to painting Philip's wife Sarah, the artist's older sister by some twelve years, whom he fondly referred to as Sally. In what may or may not have been intended as a pointed riposte to the companion piece of her somewhat younger husband, she appears ornately coiffed and dressed, wearing an elaborate lace bonnet or *dormeuse* atop her raised grey hair, and a somewhat old-fashioned white kerchief tied with a large satin ribbon around her neck. The overall effect makes the similarly coiffed Margaret Gainsborough (cat. 36) look almost plain by comparison. Elderly women appear only infrequently in eighteenth-century English portraiture, and when they do, they tend to be endowed with a stronger sense of individual character than was considered suitable for their more youthful counterparts. The *Sarah Dupont* is no exception. But even if Gainsborough did not shy away from describing the wrinkles and lines on his sister's face, or of registering just how closely her features resembled his own, he also took great care that his treatment of her hair and clothing flattered the social pretensions of a carpenter's wife, and to play these off against the decidedly unpretentious character he assigned to her husband. In few eighteenth-century pendant portraits of a married couple do the spouses look as mismatched as they do here. Gainsborough, one suspects, must have been amused by the incongruity, though we can only guess whether his feelings were shared by the Duponts themselves.

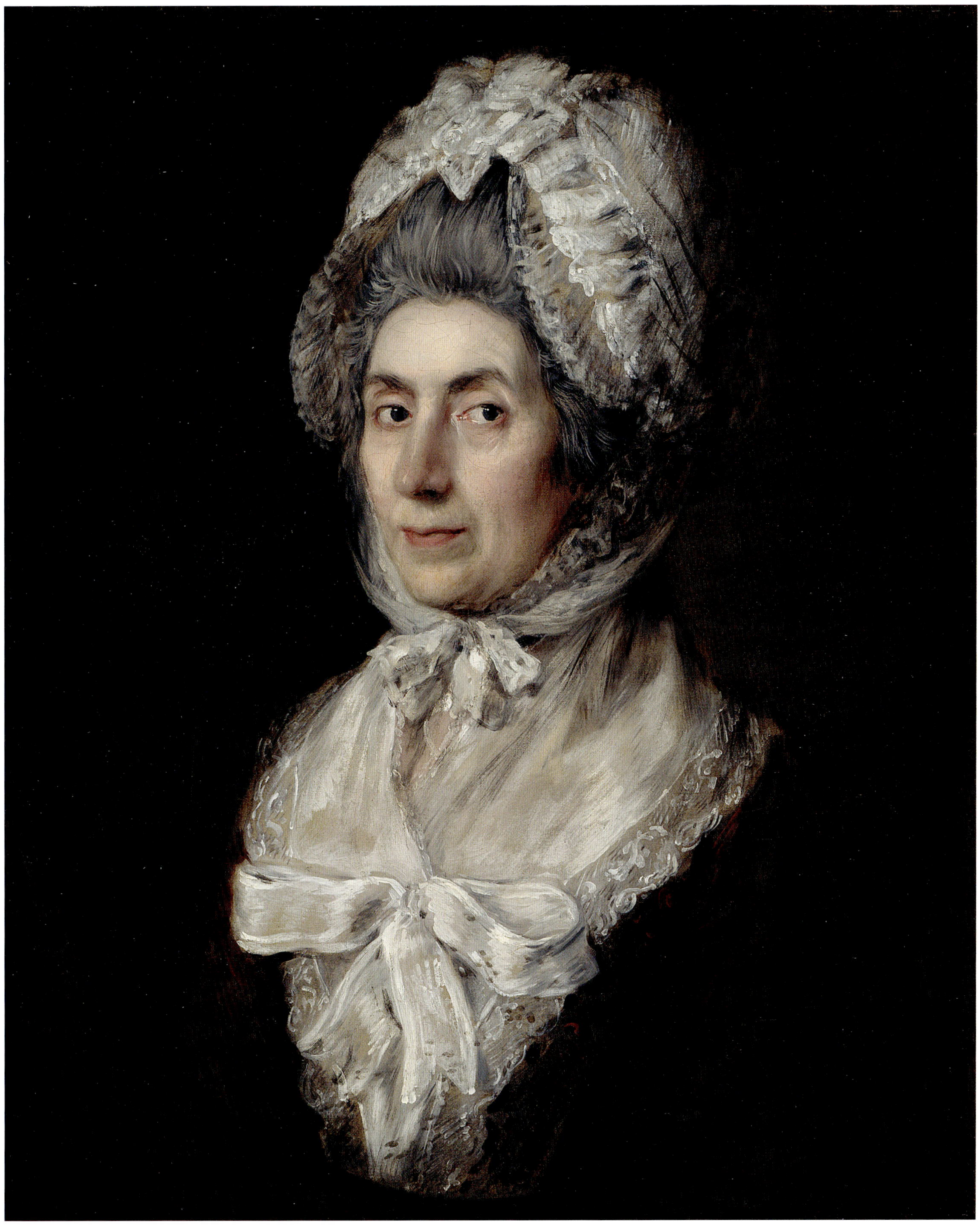

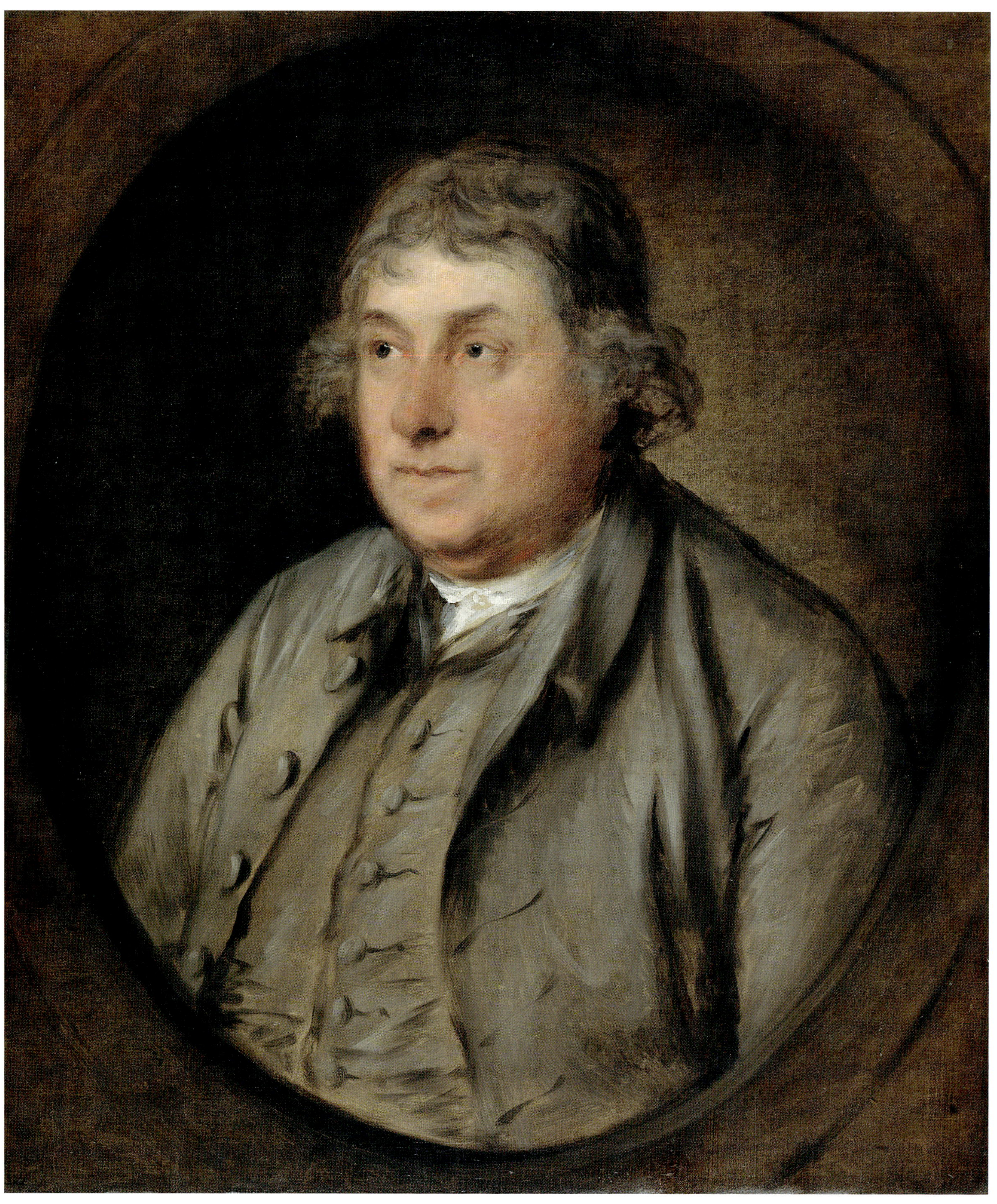

39

***Philip Dupont,
the Artist's Brother-in-law***

c.1777–9
Oil on canvas, 762 x 625mm

Fitzwilliam Museum, Cambridge

During the years following his move to London, Gainsborough seems to have settled on the head-and-shoulders in a feigned oval surround on a three-quarter canvas as his standard format for portraits of all his relations apart from his wife. The simplicity of the presentation meant that these works could be done quickly – quite possibly at a single sitting – especially given the facility of touch that the artist had acquired, and his use of semi-transparent, liquid pigments that required only the thinnest of coverage to achieve the effect required. On this occasion, the lively fluency of Gainsborough's brushwork offers a mute contrast to the plain, almost rough-and-ready character that he has given to the carpenter Philip Dupont, his sister Sarah's husband and the father of Gainsborough Dupont. Here, Philip is shown as a man strikingly unconcerned with matters of appearance. Having forsaken a wig in favour of showing his own unkempt hair, and dressed in the type of suit with a high-buttoned waistcoat that was totally out of fashion by then, he has more the look of a respectable working man than a member of the provincial middle class. A study in muted earth tones, this portrait looks even more modest when juxtaposed with its far brighter and more richly textured companion piece. In a reversal of the usual convention governing paired images of husbands and wives, Philip is shown looking to his right – and presumably towards his rather redoubtable spouse – while she ignores him in favour of gazing out at the viewer, reinforcing the impression that Sarah was the dominant partner in their relationship.

40

Unidentified Gentleman,
traditionally called Philip Dupont

c.1780–2
Oil on canvas, 762 x 635mm

Restoration House Collection, Rochester, Kent

Long supposed to represent Philip Dupont, this
portrait clearly shows a different sitter from the
individual in the Fitzwilliam painting (cat. 39).
Indeed, judging by his dress (especially the large
brass buttons and the bright yellow waistcoat),
he was a more fashionable man with at least
pretensions to gentility. The picture's provenance
suggests that its subject is likely to have been a
member of the Dupont family and Hugh Belsey has
suggested that it might be Philip's younger brother
Robert, about whom very little is known.

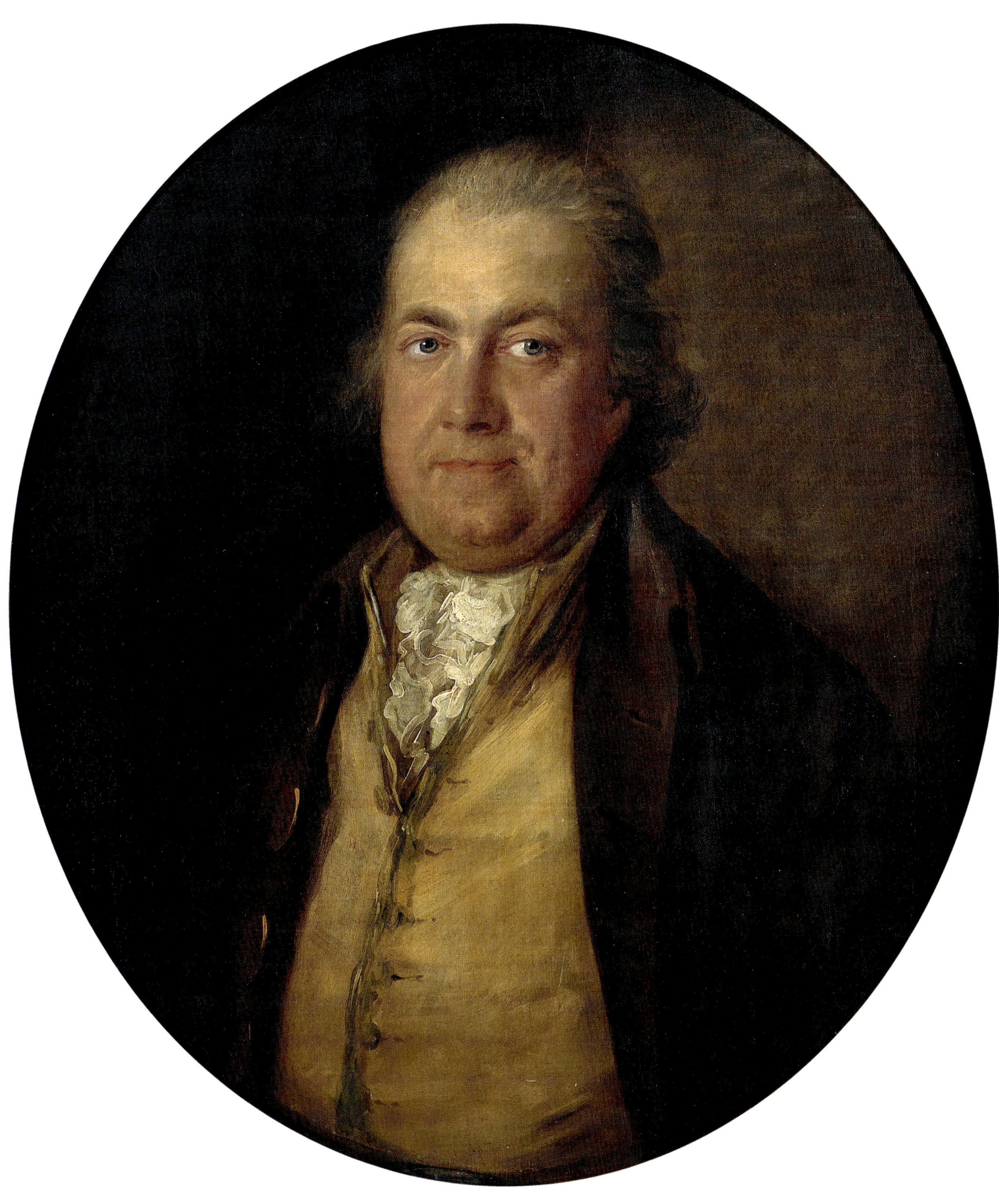

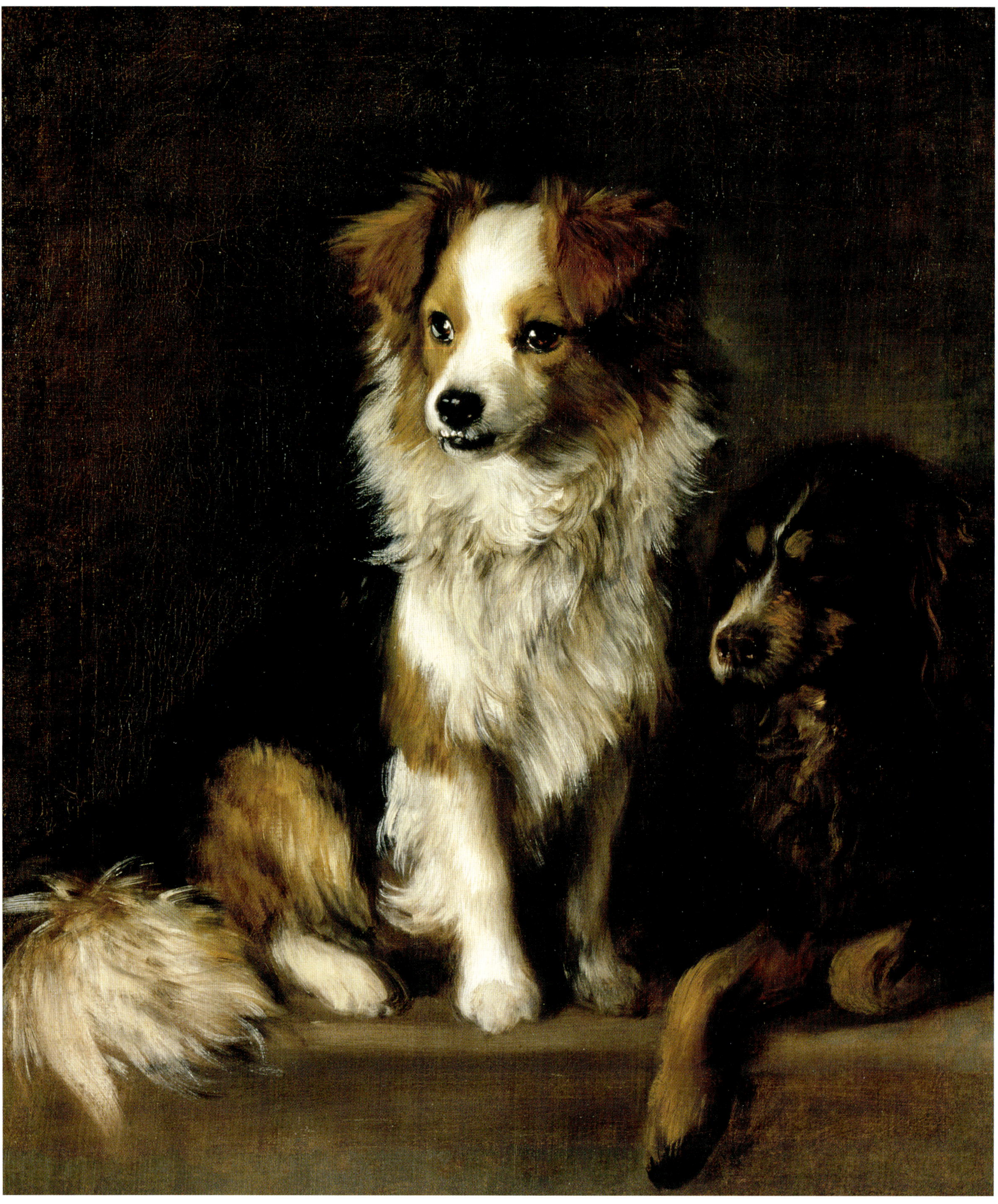

41

***Tristram and Fox* [?]**

c.1775–85

Oil on canvas, 610 x 508mm

Tate

The dogs shown in this portrait (which has been cut down on the right) can be identified with confidence as Gainsborough family pets, but we cannot be certain of their names. The Tristram and Fox depicted in an earlier chalk drawing (cat. 23) are clearly different animals, though it may well be that the Gainsboroughs used the same names for more than one pair of dogs. What appears in any case to be inarguable is that Gainsborough took this opportunity to create a study in contrasting canine temperaments. 'Fox' (his dog), the spitz shown in the centre, is alert and active; with its teeth bared, ears perked forward and eyes brightly focused, it seems to be reacting to, or possibly growling at, an unseen intruder. Margaret Gainsborough's spaniel-type 'Tristram', on the other hand, is not only darker in colour, but assigned an entirely different character: supine, passive, half-asleep, and completely oblivious to events. Based on what we know of Gainsborough and his wife from the artist's correspondence, it would make more sense if he identified her with the rather prickly left-hand dog, and himself with its lazier companion. Hence, it may well be that the spitz belonged to Margaret, and the spaniel to Thomas – or, if it was the other way around, that Gainsborough was amused by the fact that he and his wife were diametrically unlike their respective pets.

42

Susanna Gardiner, the Artist's Sister

1780–5
Oil on canvas, 756 x 629mm

Tate

Scholars have long debated whether this portrait is by Thomas Gainsborough or by his (and the sitter's) nephew, Gainsborough Dupont. Additionally, the layers of yellowy varnish that disfigure the surface of the canvas make it all the more difficult to arrive at a secure attribution. The apparent difference in quality between the sensitive characterisation of Susanna Gardiner's face and the weaker handling of her expensive bonnet – as compared with the same feature in the *Sarah Dupont* (cat. 38), for example – raises the possibility that both painters were involved. It would make sense if Gainsborough invited his nephew, as part of his training, to work on uncommissioned portraits of their relations.

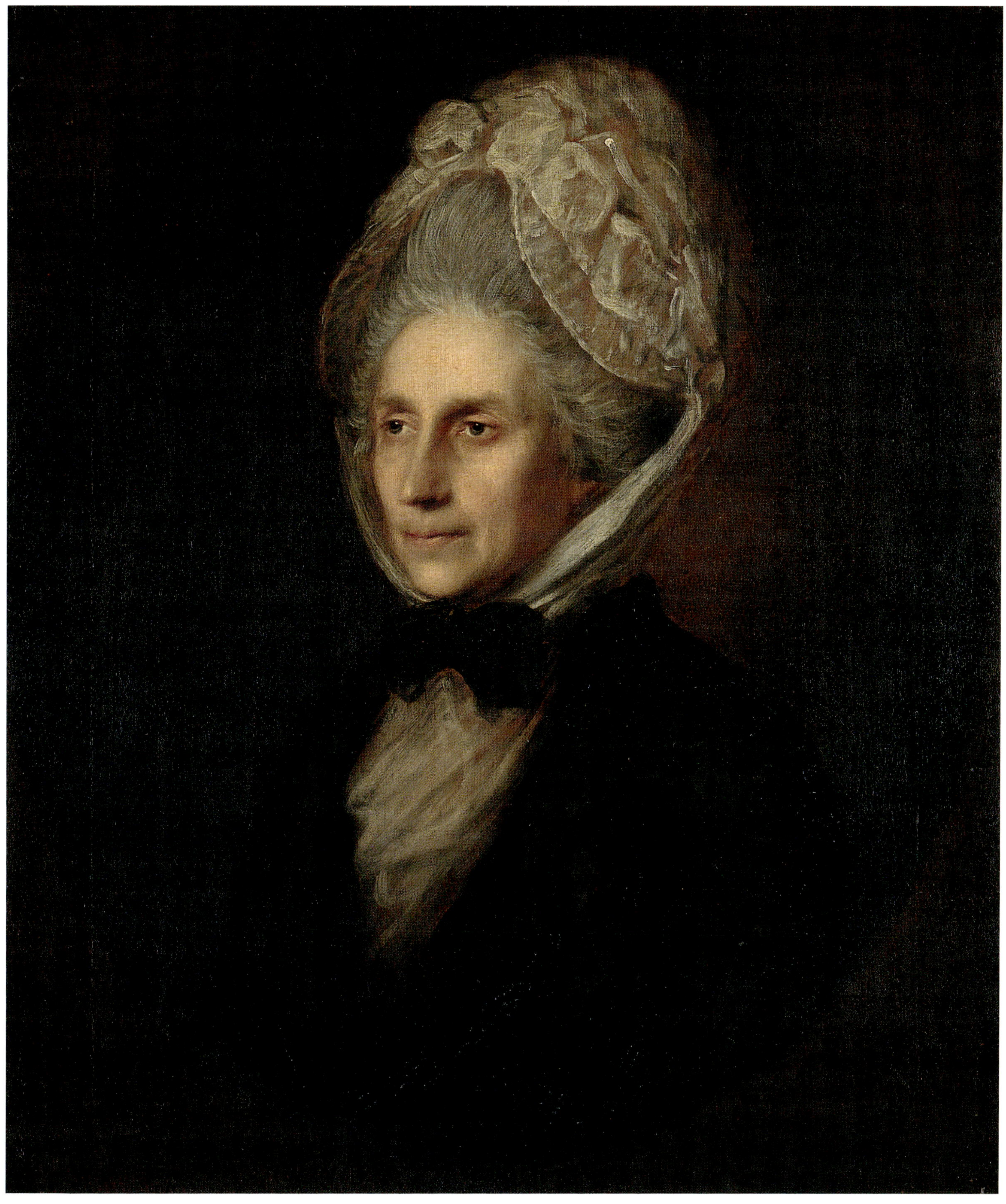

43

Study of an Elderly Woman, perhaps the Artist's wife

c.1780–5
Black chalk heightened with white chalk
on beige laid paper, 194 x 137mm
Reproduced larger than actual size

Yale Center for British Art, Paul Mellon Collection,
New Haven, CT

Based on information provided by Gainsborough's
great-niece Sophia Lane, the biographer Allan
Cunningham reported that the artist 'loved to sit
by the side of his wife during the evenings, and
make sketches of whatever occurred to his fancy'.[8]
This chalk study of an elderly woman wearing
a mob-cap, which looks to have been drawn by
candlelight, is likely to have been produced in
these leisurely domestic circumstances. The
sitter, seemingly caught unawares, may be
Gainsborough's wife Margaret, one of his sisters, or
another member of his largely female household.

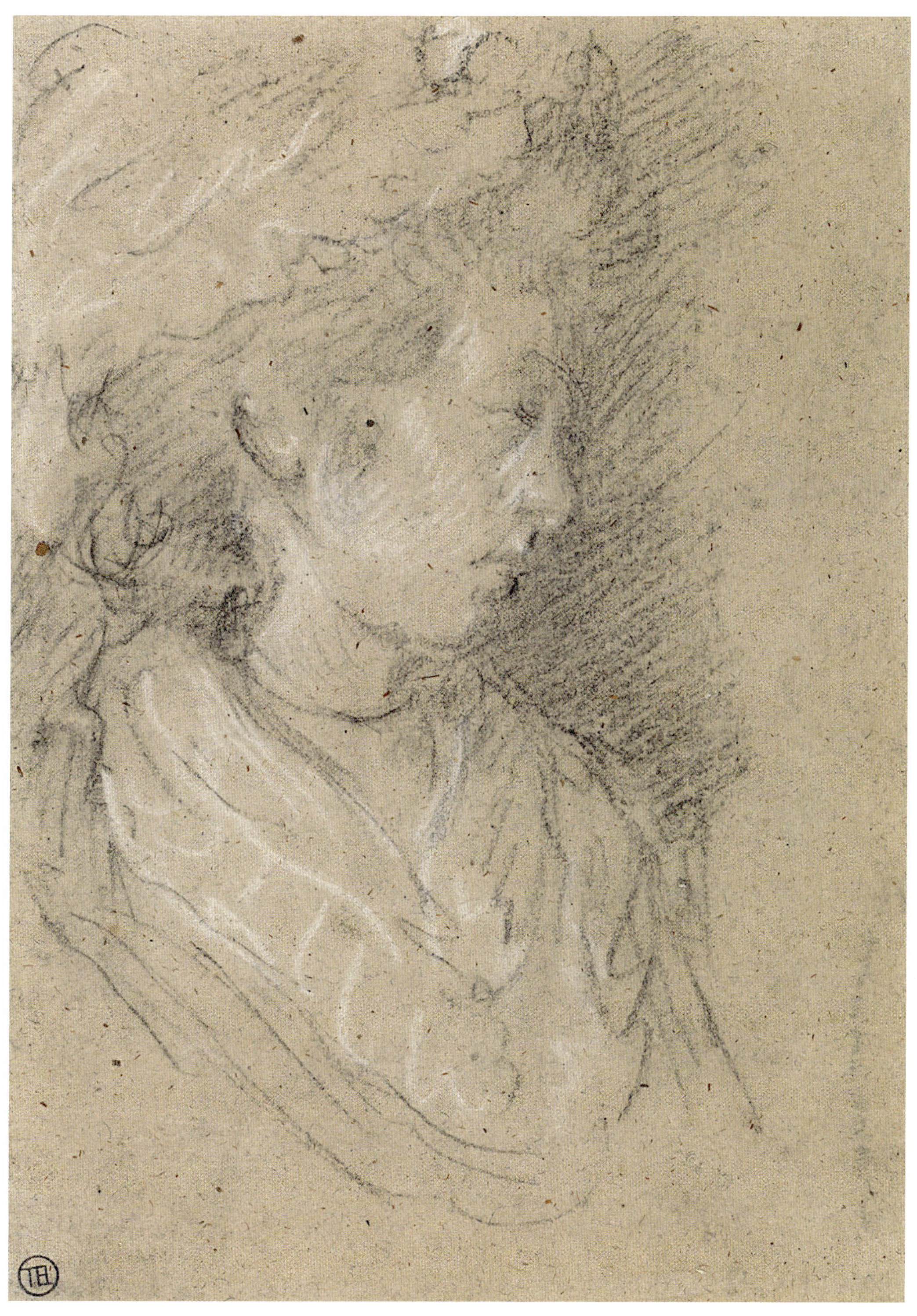

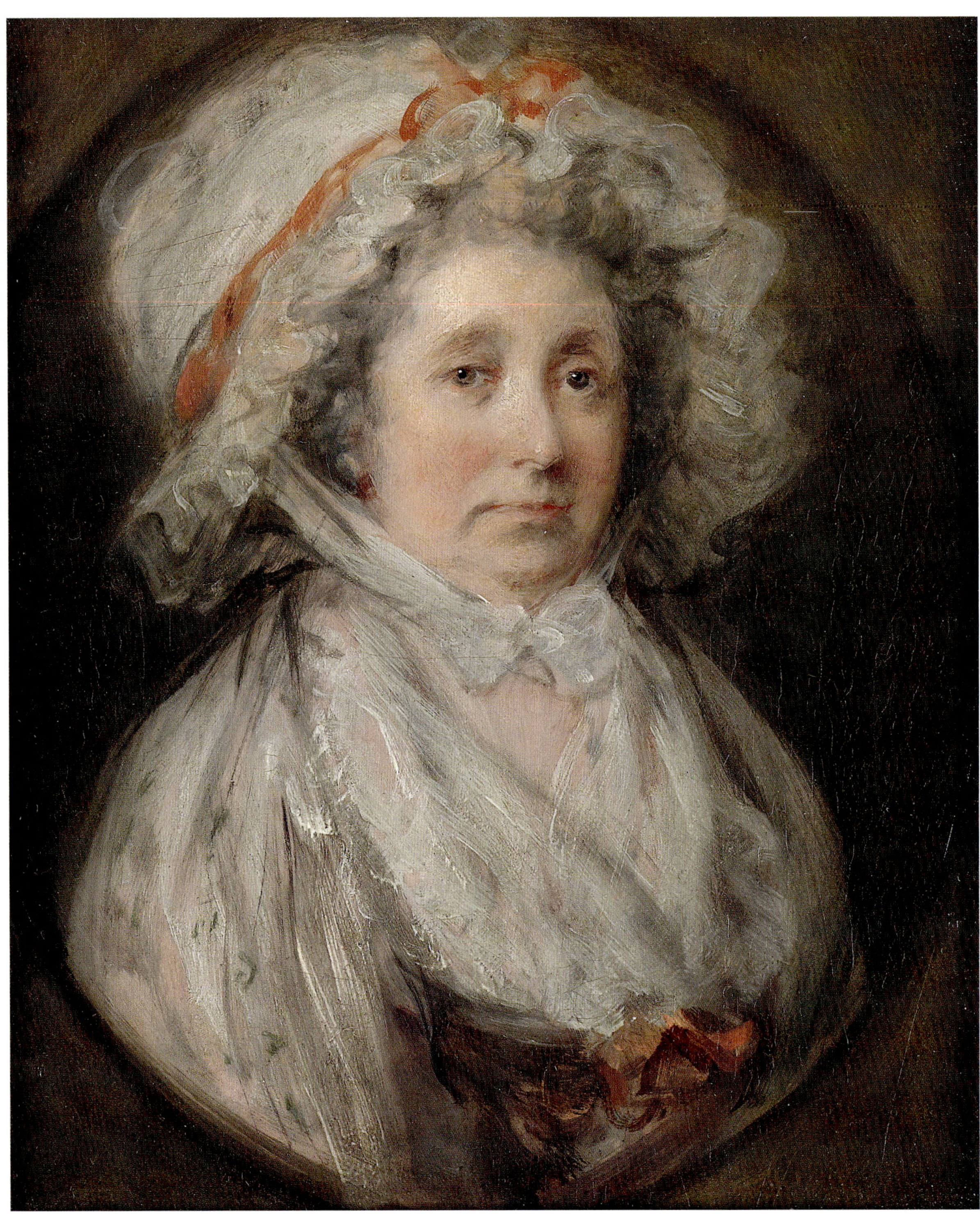

44

**Margaret Gainsborough,
the Artist's Wife**

mid to late 1780s
Oil on book board, 152 x 114mm
Reproduced larger than actual size

Gainsborough's House, Sudbury, Suffolk

For what was to be one of the last portraits he painted of his wife, Gainsborough employed a much-reduced version of the format that he had come to favour when depicting other members of his family. On so small a scale, a head-and-shoulders within an oval surround assumes the intimate character of a portrait miniature, Gainsborough's signature brushwork, too, takes on a different meaning, as a marker of his highly personal touch. Unlike most of Gainsborough's previous paintings of Margaret, this and the even smaller likeness from the mid 1780s (cat. 45) are unambiguously private in nature.

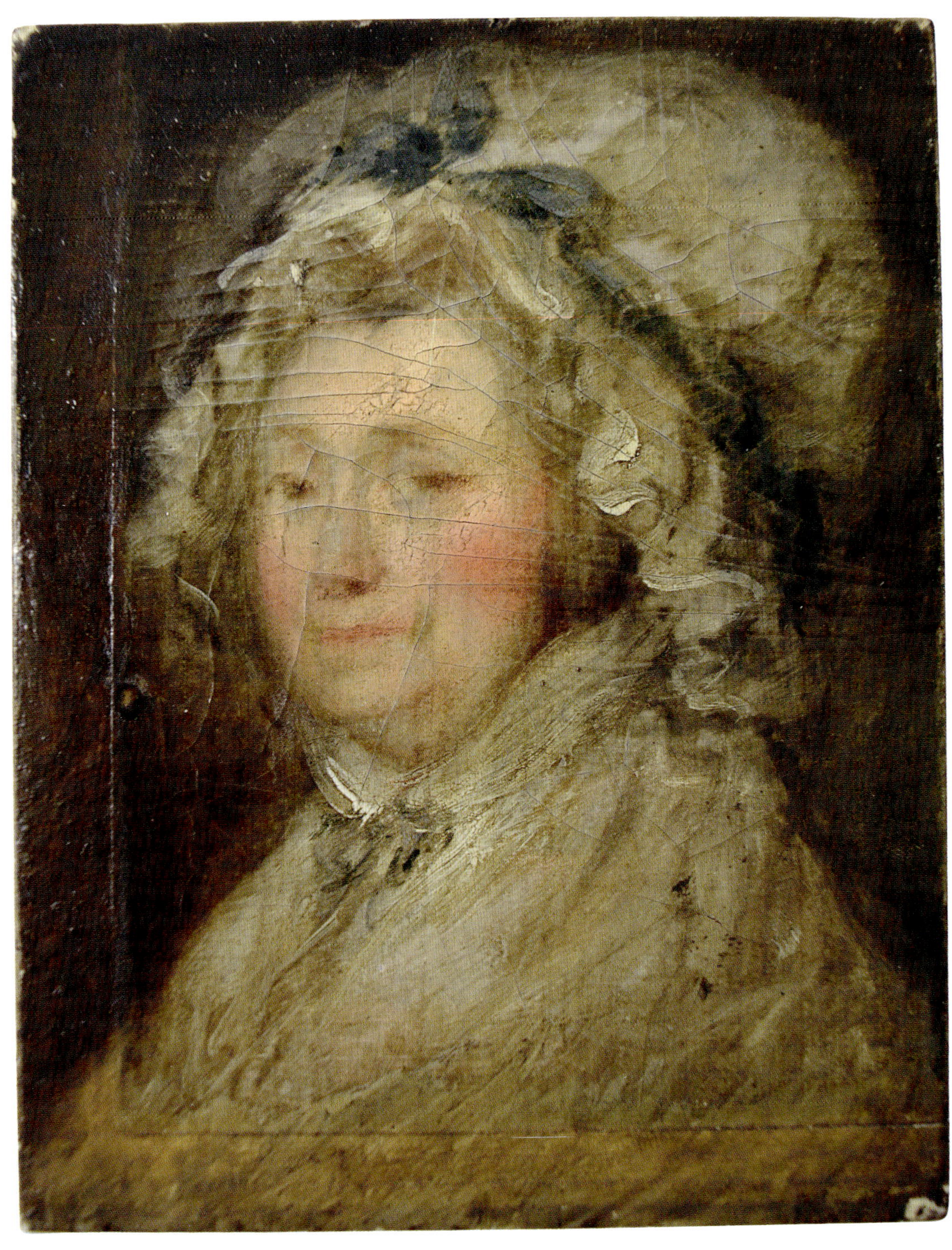

45

Margaret Gainsborough, the Artist's Wife

mid to late 1780s
Oil on paper laid down on panel, 112 x 85mm
Reproduced larger than actual size

Ipswich Borough Council (Colchester and Ipswich Museums),
Christchurch Mansion, Ipswich

The smallest of all Gainsborough's extant oils of his wife, this and the slightly larger example from around the same time (cat. 44) show her wearing a mob-cap with a large puffed crown, a style that came into fashion in London during the mid 1780s and that was typically worn in the home. Evidently, her husband was at pains to compliment Margaret's taste for fashionable dress, even as she entered upon advanced middle age, and even in the context of so informal and personal a likeness as this. The panel on which this portrait is painted has been formed from two pieces: a large rectangle lined with paper on front and back, which has been neatly inset into an unlined L-shaped strip of wood running along the left and bottom edges. Close technical examination suggests that the extra strip was added by a later hand, and painted to harmonise with Gainsborough's colouring and brushwork. The blurry character of the likeness implicitly invites its completion in the viewer's imagination – thus strengthening the sense of an emotive connection between the portrait's subject and its creator.

Self-portrait

c.1786
Oil on canvas, 762 x 635mm

Gainsborough completed his full-length of Thomas Edward Coke (later 1st Earl of Leicester) in 1786, and this self-portrait probably dates from around the same time. It may even have been painted at Holkham, Lord Coke's Norfolk seat. However, as William Whitley points out, no 'trustworthy evidence is known to exist concerning Gainsborough's visit to Holkham or what he did there'.[9] Instead we may be dealing with one of the self-portraits documented as remaining in the artist's studio at the time of his death, and possibly the picture that his daughter Margaret sent to the engraver Francesco Bartolozzi as a corrective to the painting (cat. 47) he was about to engrave (see page 75). The canvas's high level of finish may be indicative of the fact that it was executed for someone outside Gainsborough's family circle, either for a friend or for an admiring patron such as Lord Coke, at a time when Gainsborough had become one of England's most celebrated artists.

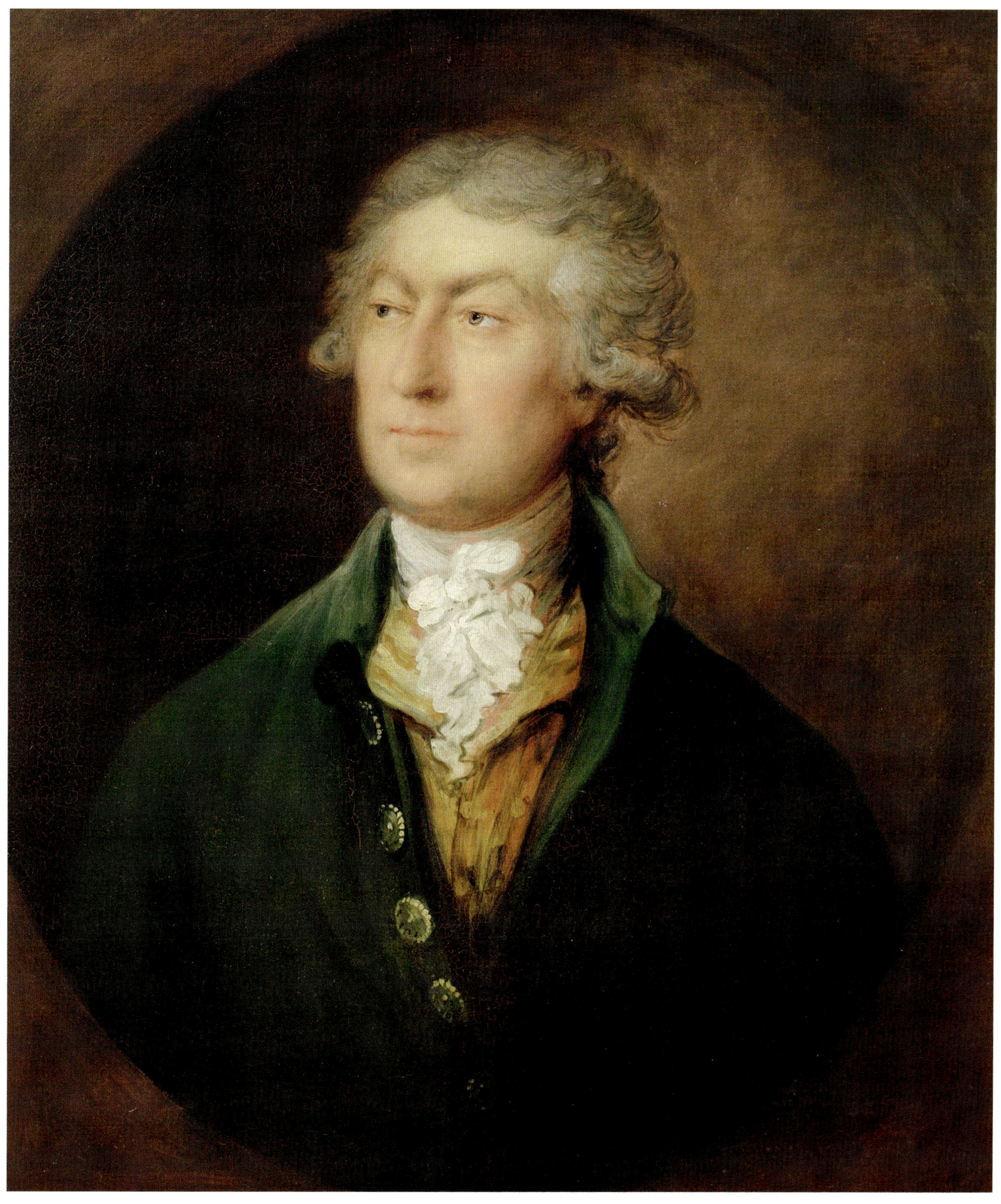

47

Self-portrait

*c.*1787
Oil on canvas, 773 x 645mm

Royal Academy of Arts, London

Gainsborough painted this self-portrait as a gift
for one of his closest friends, the German-born
composer Carl Friedrich Abel, who unfortunately
died before the picture was completed. The
following year, when he himself was terminally
ill, the painter left written instructions that this
unfinished '¾ sketch'[10] intended for Abel was
to be the only likeness of his features that he
would sanction to be engraved after his death
(figs 39 and 40) – in effect, nominating it as the
image by which he wished to be remembered.
One reason for his choice may been the picture's
painterly bravura – what the *Morning Herald* of
28 December 1788 described as its 'freedom &
bold stile'. But the image also conveys something
of the character that Philip Thicknesse ascribed
to Gainsborough, as a person who 'knows, as
well how to act, and think, like a gentleman, as
he does to contemn and despise those who dare
to treat him in any other light'.[11] The sharpness
of the scrutiny to which Gainsborough subjects
himself, and with which he confronts the viewer,
is certainly anything but modest or ingratiating.

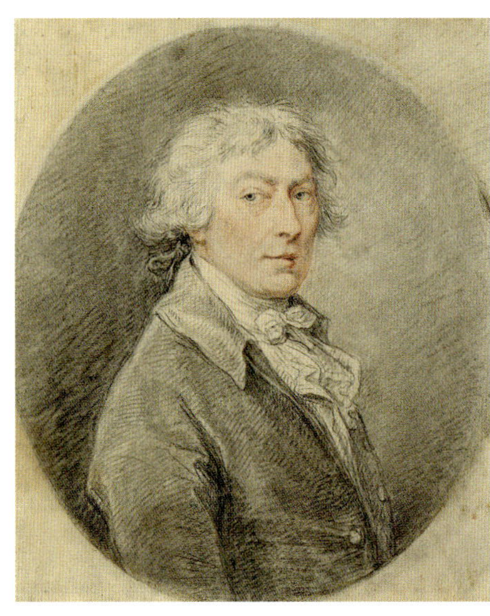

FIG. 39
**Francesco Bartolozzi
after Thomas Gainsborough**
Thomas Gainsborough, R.A.
1797
Black and red chalk with pencil
and grey wash, 210 x 165mm
National Portrait Gallery, London
Included in exhibition

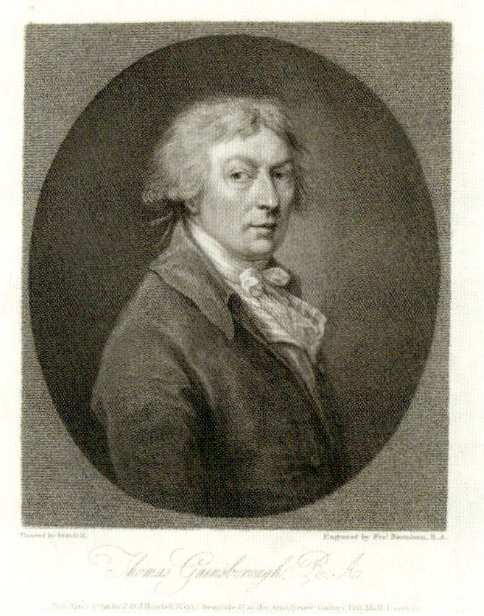

FIG. 40
**Francesco Bartolozzi
after Thomas Gainsborough**
Thomas Gainsborough, R.A.
1798
Stipple engraving, 252 x 201mm
National Portrait Gallery, London
Included in exhibition

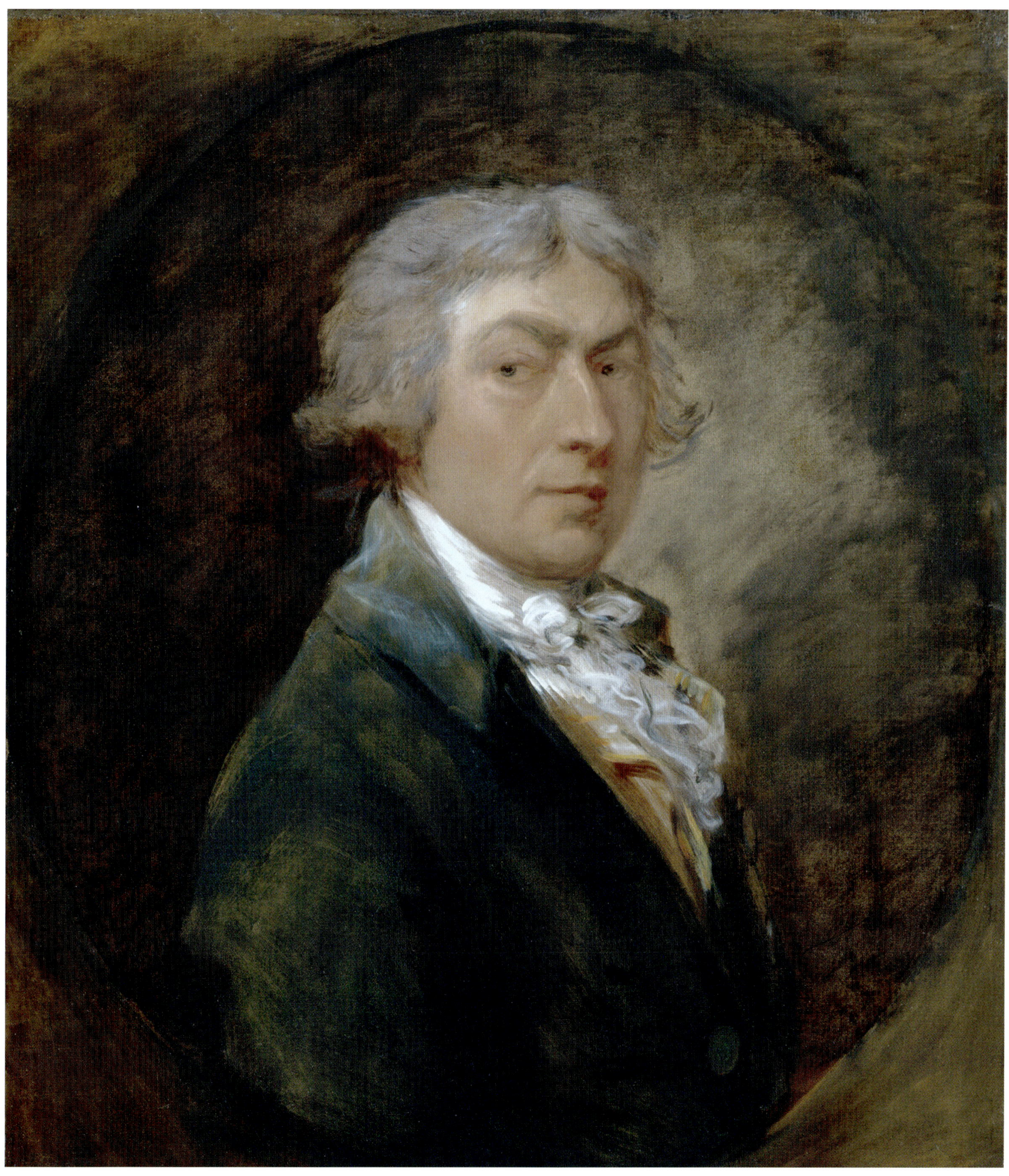

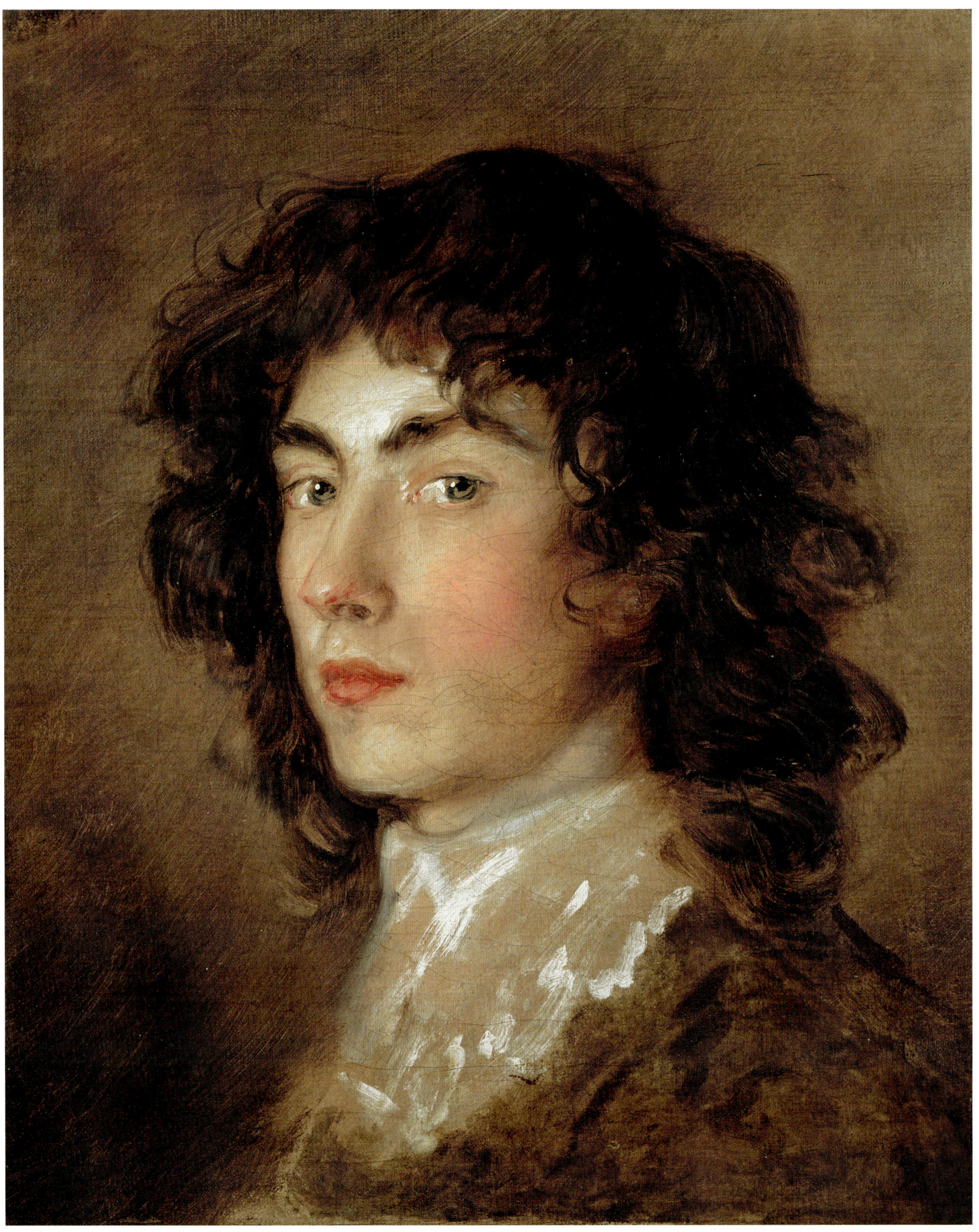

48

Gainsborough Dupont, the Artist's Nephew

*c.*1770–5
Oil on canvas, 445 x 362mm

Tate

Judging from its style and from the sitter's youthful appearance, this Van Dyckian oil sketch of Gainsborough Dupont must have been painted around the same time as the Waddesdon oval (cat. 26), that is to say, in the first half of the 1770s. Some fifty years later, however, Gainsborough's great-niece Sophia Lane identified it as the artist's 'last head, which was on his easel when he died' (see pages 36–9). If so – and there seems no reason to doubt the accuracy of Sophia's recollection – Gainsborough must have selected this small, incomplete portrait from the piles of old pictures cluttering up his studio, and elevated it to a position of remarkable prominence at a time when he was aware that he was dying, and had set about putting his affairs in order. His choice of an unfinished work to play the symbolically significant role of his own 'last picture' may well have been

the 61-year-old Gainsborough's deliberate way of signalling his regretful awareness that he was about to reach the end of his life without having realised the full extent of his talent – a sentiment he also expressed in his final conversation with his long-standing rival Sir Joshua Reynolds. But when on the easel in his Schomberg House painting room, the study of Dupont would also have communicated at least two other important messages to posterity. The first, looking back to the past, expressed Gainsborough's desire to be remembered alongside Van Dyck, the seventeenth-century Flemish master, whom he had taken as the highest object of his own emulation, and whose work he so deeply cherished. But the same gesture also encompassed the future, by designating Dupont, his nephew and only apprentice, as his appointed artistic heir.

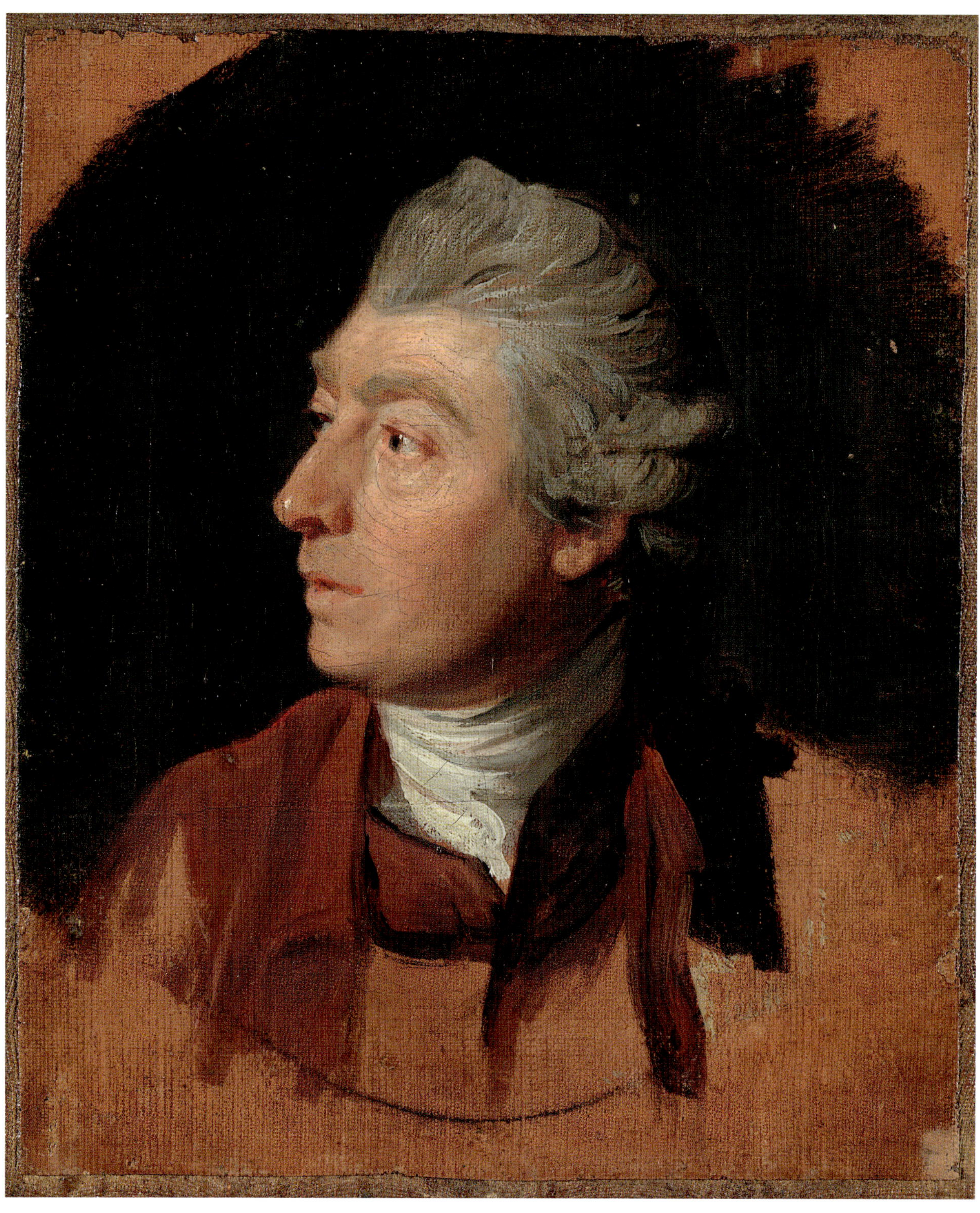

49

Johann Zoffany
Thomas Gainsborough

c.1772
Oil on canvas, 197 x 171mm

Tate

Johann Zoffany is likely to have painted this small study in oils of Gainsborough during a visit to Bath in the early winter of 1772. At that time, the German-born artist was preparing *The Portraits of the Academicians of the Royal Academy*, a large multi-figure conversation piece that he would exhibit at the Academy's forthcoming exhibition (now in the Royal Collection). But while Gainsborough initially agreed to sit for Zoffany's ambitious picture, shortly afterwards he must have changed his mind and asked to be omitted from the final composition – presumably having decided, like his fellow portraitist Nathaniel Dance, that he had no desire to appear in a picture that could not help but glorify Sir Joshua Reynolds, their chief competitor and the first President of the Academy. Apparently unbothered by this rather unfortunate episode, Zoffany later presented this likeness of the artist – possibly to Gainsborough himself, or to his widow after her husband's death. His immediate descendants prized this lively depiction as the most accurate likeness ever made of their celebrated forebear – truer even, they believed, than any of his own self-portraits. Given the pride Gainsborough took in his skills as the 'likeness man', one imagines that he would not have been best pleased by his family's preference for the Zoffany.

NOTES ON THE TEXTS

Private and Public Relations:
Gainsborough's Family Album
David H. Solkin

1 See Ben van Beneden, ed., *Rubens in Private: The Master Portrays his Family* (exh. cat., Rubenshuis, Antwerp, 2015, and Thames & Hudson, London, 2015).

2 Rubens's composition (the original oil is now in the Metropolitan Museum, New York) supplied the template for a host of eighteenth-century British portraits of promenading couples, perhaps the most famous example being Gainsborough's *Mr and Mrs William Hallett ('The Morning Walk')*, (1785, National Gallery, London).

3 For a discussion of the growing appreciation of unfinished portraits from the Renaissance through to the eighteenth century, see Andrea Bayer and Nicholas Cullinan, 'Portraiture and the Question of Focus' in Kelly Baum, Andrea Bayer and Sheena Wagstaff, eds, *Unfinished: Thoughts Left Visible* (exh. cat., Metropolitan Museum of Art, New York, 2016), pp.100–03. In this context it is worth recalling that Rubens left several portraits of his family members in an unfinished state, e.g. that of his brother Philippe Rubens, now in the Detroit Institute of Arts.

4 Charles Beale, *Notebook*, 1680-1, Heinz Archive and Library, National Portrait Gallery, MS 9535, quoted in Tabitha Barber, *Mary Beale: Portrait of a Seventeenth-Century Painter, her Family and her Studio* (exh. cat., Geffrye Museum, London, 2000), p.77.

5 Here it should be pointed out that two contemporary artists whom Gainsborough knew well, the portraitist William Hoare and the landscape watercolourist Paul Sandby, produced numerous drawings of their family members for their private pleasure. It is the predominance of oils that makes Gainsborough's 'family album' so distinctive.

6 Anthony Ashley Cooper, 3rd Earl of Shaftesbury, *Second Characters or the Language of Forms*, ed. Benjamin Rand (University Press, Cambridge, 1914), p.135; and idem, *Characteristicks of Men, Manners, Opinions, Times* (1711), 3 vols, ed. J.M. Robertson (Bobbs-Merrill, Indianapolis and New York, 1964), Vol.I, p.96.

7 Joseph Highmore taught Susanna to draw at an early age, and she would later go on to achieve considerable repute as both a poet and a book illustrator (under her married name Susanna Duncombe). The largest collection of her artistic works can be found in Tate Britain.

8 It is an indicator of the Gainsboroughs' advancing social status that two of the artist's uncles, Robert and Thomas, had had their portraits painted, in 1729 and 1731 respectively. The likeness of his uncle is one of a set of six family portraits commissioned from the German-born, Norwich-based artist John Theodore Heins. The group includes an image of Gainsborough's first cousin John, who helped the painter's father overcome the financial disaster occasioned by his bankruptcy. John's purchase of Gainsborough's House in Sudbury, Suffolk, made it possible for his uncle's family to continue to live there. For a discussion and illustrations of the early family portraits, see Hugh Belsey, *Gainsborough's Family* (exh. cat., Gainsborough's House Society, Sudbury, 1988). Belsey's catalogue has been an invaluable source for this essay and the *Gainsborough's Family Album* project as a whole.

9 See Susan Sloman, *Gainsborough in Bath* (Yale University Press, New Haven and London, 2002), p.191.

10 The portrait in question is that of *Mr and Mrs Andrews* (c.1750, National Gallery, London), which features a curious – and obvious – passage of unfinished painting, likely intended to represent a game bird, in Mrs Andrews' lap. It may well be that Gainsborough never got around to completing the picture, so the sitters, having lost patience, took possession of the painting as it stood. An alternative possibility, proposed by Tate curator Martin Myrone, is that a private joke may have been involved. See Michael Rosenthal and Martin Myrone, eds, *Gainsborough 1727–1788* (exh. cat., Tate, London, 2002), p.62.

11 It is worth pointing out, however, that X-rays have recently revealed that the *Susan Gardiner* (cat.10) was painted on top of a landscape. Gainsborough is unlikely to have reused an old canvas for a commissioned portrait.

12 The early copy, by an unknown hand, still belongs to St Catharine's College, Cambridge. The papers of historian William T. Whitley in the British Museum include a transcription from the Suffolk Notes compiled by the early nineteenth-century antiquarian David Elisha Davy regarding Henry Burrough: 'He soon wasted his wife's portion, being a man of insufferable vanity; he sent, unasked a picture of himself to Catharine Hall Combination [now St Catharine's College], where it yet hangs, August 8 1775, which was looked upon as a piece of great impertinence.'

13 One commission that may well have been inspired by the *Henry Burrough* came from the Reverend Tobias Rustat, Rector of Stutton, south of Ipswich, a contemporary of Burrough's, who had likewise studied at Cambridge. The very similar three-quarter portrait of Rustat (c.1757, Gainsborough's House, Sudbury) looks to be slightly later in date.

14 This suggestion has been made by Matthew Hargraves, see http://collections.britishart.yale.edu/vufind/Record/1670968

15 In 1779, for instance, Gainsborough refused payment for a framed portrait of Philip Ditcher, a doctor who had looked after the family in Bath, as a way of thanking him for his services. See his letter to Mary Ditcher of 31 July 1779, in John Hayes, ed., *The Letters of Thomas Gainsborough* (Yale University Press, New Haven and London, 2001), p.141.

16 For an exemplary study of eighteenth-century British family relations, which has richly informed my thinking on this topic, see Naomi Tadmor, *Family and Friends in Eighteenth-Century England: Household, Kinship, and Patronage* (Cambridge University Press, Cambridge, 2001).

17 The collection at Gainsborough's House includes two fragments of the portrait of an unidentified boy and girl, which has been dated to c.1744, though it may be somewhat later. The attribution to Gainsborough has met with general, but not universal, acceptance. See Hugh Belsey, *Gainsborough at Gainsborough's House* (Paul Holberton, London, 2002), pp.14–16.

18 For example, see Michael Levey, *Gainsborough: The Painter's Daughters Chasing a Butterfly*, Painting in Focus series, no. 4 (National Gallery, London, 1975), unpaginated; Lora Rempel, *The Matter of Style: Thomas Gainsborough, the Portrait in a Landscape, and the Mark of the Modern Painter*, 1997 (unpublished PhD dissertation, City University of New York), p.77; Sloman, 2002, pp.33–6; and Ann Bermingham in this volume, p.47.

19 See Ann Bermingham, this volume p.47.

20 For instance, see Judy Egerton, *National Gallery Catalogues – The British School* (National Gallery, London, 1998), p.92.

21 *Ipswich Journal*, 20 October 1759. The full text of the advertisement reads as follows: 'To be sold, opposite the Shire Hall, Ipswich. On Monday, Tuesday next the 22nd, 23rd inst. All the HOUSEHOLD GOODS OF MR THOMAS GAINSBOROUGH, with some PICTURES, original DRAWINGS in the Landskip way, by his own hand, which as he is desirous of leaving among his friends, will have the lowest prices set upon them.' I take the word 'Landskip' to refer to both the pictures *and* the drawings, not, as other scholars have assumed, to the drawings alone.

22 Samuel Richardson, *The Apprentice's Vade Mecum; or Young Man's Travel Companion* (Edward Exshaw, Dublin, 1734), p.38.

23 Jean André Rouquet, *The Present State of the Arts in England* (J. Nourse, London, 1755), p.38.

24 Because they present their sitters facing in the same direction, the National Portrait Gallery and the Gemäldegalerie portraits of Gainsborough and his wife are most unlikely to have been conceived with a view to hanging them side by side. But husband and wife pendants could also be displayed on opposite walls, or at either end of a table; in the case of our two pictures, another intriguing possibility is that they were positioned one above the other. It is also conceivable that Gainsborough wished to encourage potential patrons to view each composition individually, as templates for independent likenesses that they might be persuaded to commission. The less than companionable relationship between these two ostensible companion pieces may invite the inference of marital discord, but this invitation should probably be declined, even if we know that the painter's marriage was not without its problems.

25 [Philip Thicknesse], *Sketches and Characters of the most Eminent and most Singular Persons now Living. By Several Hands* (John Wheble, Bristol, 1770), p.97.

26 Letter from William Whitehead to Viscount Nuneham, 6 December 1758, in the possession of the Hon. Mrs C. Gascoigne, quoted in Sloman, 2002, p.38.

27 Ozias Humphry, 'Memoir' (unpublished), Royal Academy of Arts, Humphry papers HU/1/20–40, between ff.36 and 37, quoted in Sloman, 2002, p.57.

28 For examples of early Bath-period commissioned pictures that broadly conform in type to the National Portrait Gallery and Gemäldegalerie portraits of the artist and his wife, see (for the self-portrait), e.g. *William Villiers, 3rd Earl of Jersey* and *George, Lord Villiers, later 4th Earl of Jersey* (1758, private collection); *Robert Price* (1758 or earlier, whereabouts unknown); or the *Christopher Griffith Senior* (1759; Restoration House, Rochester). And (for the portrait of Margaret Gainsborough) see, e.g, *Mrs Philadelphia Lee* (1758–9; private collection); *A Lady of the St Quintin Family* (1759, private collection); or *Barbara Brown, Lady Mostyn* (1759, Albany Institute of History and Art, Albany, NY). All these works are in Sloman, 2002, pp.40–5. For a further related comment on this issue, see note 24 above.

29 Rempel, 1997, p.10.

30 Sir Joshua Reynolds, *Discourses on Art* [1769–90], ed. Robert R. Wark (Yale University Press, New Haven and London, 1975), *Discourse XIV* (1788), pp.257–8.

31 See note 26.

32 Reynolds/Wark, 1975, p.258.

33 Thomas Gainsborough to William Hoare [1773], in Hayes, 2001, p.113.

34 For an extremely useful introduction to the issues raised by unfinished paintings in the early modern period, see Nico Van Hout, *The Unfinished Painting* (Ludion, Antwerp, 2012); also the essays by Van Hout and others in Baum *et al.*, 2016.

35 Thomas Gainsborough to William Jackson, 2 September 1767, in Hayes, 2001, p.42.

36 Thomas Gainsborough to James Unwin, 25 May 1768, ibid., p.53.

37 The ledgers recording transactions channelled through Gainsborough's account at Hoare's Bank, Fleet Street, record a series of fairly regular payments to Dupont, ranging from £17 to £100, starting 31 December 1774 and continuing until the ledgers come to an end in 1783. A full transcription with annotations can be found in Sloman, 2002, pp.204–12.

38 Susan Sloman deserves full credit for recently identifying the subject of this portrait as Dupont, and for rediscovering the evidence concerning its production and reception. I am greatly indebted to her article, '"A Divine Countenance": Gainsborough's Portrait of his Nephew Rediscovered', *Burlington Magazine*, Vol.146, no.1214, (May 2004), pp.319–22.

39 Philip Thicknesse, *A Sketch of the Life and Paintings of Thomas Gainsborough*, esq. (London, 1788), pp.49, 54–5. Thicknesse never forgave Gainsborough for failing to complete his full-length portrait, thus offering us a salutary reminder that in eighteenth-century Britain unfinished likenesses were generally regarded as unsatisfactory and inadequate.

40 Philip Thicknesse to John Cooke, 14 April [1773], quoted in Robert R. Wark, 'Thicknesse and Gainsborough: Some New Documents', *Art Bulletin*, Vol.40, no.4 (December 1958), p.332.

41 This is how Gainsborough styled himself in a letter to the Hon. Constantine Phipps, 13 February 1772; see Hayes, 2001, p.94.

42 Sloman, 2004, p.322, persuasively argues that Thicknesse must have given the portrait of Dupont to Lord Bateman by 1775 at the latest.

43 This was not the first occasion when Gainsborough gave a public demonstration of his ability to produce a portrait at speed. In his *Sketch* (pp.16–17), Thicknesse recalled how, shortly after Gainsborough's arrival in Bath, the artist had sketched Thicknesse's head in one fifteen-minute sitting, claiming that this incomplete portrait had served as a 'decoy duck' that helped generate commissioned work. The next recorded instance of Gainsborough executing a finished portrait

at speed involves the 762 x 635mm (30 x 25") 'head' of the writer and musician Ignatius Sancho, which, according to a note attached to the back of the canvas, was 'painted at Bath in one hour and forty minutes, Nov. 29, 1768'; see Ignatius Sancho, *The Letters of Ignatius Sancho*, eds Paul Edwards and Polly Rewt (Edinburgh University Press, Edinburgh, 1994), Appendix II, pp.266–7 (I am grateful to Susan Sloman for this reference). The Sancho portrait now belongs to the National Gallery of Canada, Ottawa. Later, Gainsborough may have painted even faster: according to the Linley family, with whom the artist was on intimate terms, his portrait of Samuel Linley (*c*.1777; Dulwich Picture Gallery) was painted in 48 minutes. See *A Nest of Nightingales* (exh. cat., Dulwich Picture Gallery, London, 1988), p.88.

44 According to Rouquet, 1755 (pp.34–5), Kneller 'painted with an amazing quickness, without any appearance of study, and oftentimes at the first stroke. This set them [English portraitists] all upon painting quick… Several were so affected, so as not to cover the whole canvas, that is in those parts where its teint [sic] and colour might answer the purpose, because Sir Godfrey Kneller had done so.' It is hard to think of a mid-eighteenth-century British portraitist more deserving of this description than Gainsborough.

45 Roger de Piles, *The Principles of Painting*, 2nd edn (Charles Marsh, London, 1743), p.177.

46 This passage comes from an anonymous obituary of Gainsborough in the *Morning Chronicle*, 8 August 1788, quoted by David Brenneman in *The Critical Response to Thomas Gainsborough's Painting: A Study of the Contemporary Perception and Materiality of Gainsborough's Art*, (unpublished PhD dissertation Brown University, Ann Arbor, 1995), p.35. My discussion of Gainsborough's engagement with Van Dyck owes much to Brenneman's thesis.

47 Susan Sloman, 'Gainsborough's *Blue Boy*', *Burlington Magazine*, Vol.155, no.1321, (April 2013), pp.231–7.

48 Here I am taking the liberty of borrowing freely from my own article, 'Gainsborough's Classically Virtuous Wife', *British Art Journal*, Vol.II, no.2 (Winter 2000/01), pp.75–7.

49 'Mira' [pseud. for Eliza Haywood], *The Wife*, 3rd edn (H. Gardner, London, 1773), p.8.

50 Joseph Spence, *Polymetis: or, an Enquiry concerning the Agreement between the Works of the Roman Poets, and the Remains of the Antient Artists* (R. and J. Dodsley, London, 1747), p.57. For the identification of Spence's text as Gainsborough's likely source, and the implications of this discovery for our understanding of the image, see the welcome modification of my own earlier reading by Hilary S. Brown, 'Gainsborough's Classically Ambivalent Wife', *British Art Journal*, Vol. III, no.1 (Autumn 2001), p.78.

51 Thomas Gainsborough to his sister Mary Gibbon, 10 June [1776], in Hayes, 2001, p.131.

52 William T. Whitley, *Thomas Gainsborough* (Smith, Elder & Co., London, 1915), p.10, cites an article by one Alexander Fraser, published thirty-five years previously in *The Portfolio* magazine. Speaking of the Burr family, then of Glasgow (Margaret's mother was a Burr), Fraser noted, 'They have, or had until lately, a most delicately touched small cabinet portrait of Mrs Gainsborough by her husband, the tradition in the family being that he annually for many years painted her portrait on the anniversary of his marriage day.' The small picture referred to by Fraser may be cat. 36, 37, 44 or 45, or another work, now lost.

53 This is how Thomas described Margaret in a letter of 25 October 1763 to his friend James Unwin (Hayes, 2001, p.23), in which he wrote of how she had helped him recover from the bout of venereal disease

occasioned by his recent encounter with a prostitute during a visit to London.

54 William T. Whitley, letter to *The Times*, 28 February 1936. According to Whitley, 'Mrs Lane, who was Mrs Gainsborough's favourite niece, and was frequently at Schomberg House during Gainsborough's last illness, says in an existing letter to her daughter, written in 1829: – "His last head, which was on his easel when he died, was one of his nephew, Gainsborough Dupont, which is now in my possession".' Two years later, Mrs Lane tried to sell the picture at Christie's (26 February 1831, lot 54), where it was described as 'the last picture Gainsborough ever painted, very spirited'. However, the work was returned to her after it failed to reach its reserve of £10 – a low level no doubt calculated on the basis of the canvas's small size and its unfinished state. Sophia's son Richard later disposed of the picture to the artist George Richmond. The letter to which Whitley refers is actually from Sophia Lane's daughter (relaying information supplied to her by her mother) to the biographer Allan Cunningham; it is held in the National Art Library, 86.GG.19, unpaginated.

55 The information about the placement of the self-portraits comes from the *Public Advertiser*, 13 August 1788; and for Gainsborough's instructions regarding his posthumous imagery, see Hayes, 2001, p.175.

56 This is how the picture was described, presumably based on information supplied by its then owner Sophia Lane (née Gardiner), when it went for sale at Christie's in 1831; see note 54 above.

57 Pliny the Elder, *The Historie of the World: Commonly Called, The Naturall Historie of C. Plinius Secundus*, trans. Philemon Holland, 2 vols (John Grismond, London, 1634), Vol.II, Book 35, p.550.

58 Reynolds/Wark, [1769–90] 1975, pp.251–2.

59 Whitley, 1915, p.307. Whitley, who can usually be relied upon for his accuracy, does not give the source of this information, for which I have found no evidence beyond the statement in Gainsborough's letter inviting Reynolds to visit him; here he asks him to come 'look at my things', including his large fancy picture of *The Woodman* (destroyed). See Thomas Gainsborough to Sir Joshua Reynolds [July 1788], in Hayes, 2001, p.176.

60 William Jackson, *The Four Ages; together with Essays on Various Subjects* (Cadell, Davies, London, 1798), p.161.

61 Joseph Farington, *The Diary of Joseph Farington* [1793–1821], Vol.X, ed. Kathryn Cave (Yale University Press, New Haven and London, 1982), p.3799. Farington's source was William Pearce, one of Gainsborough's closest lifelong friends and a pallbearer at his funeral, who – unlike Jackson – was at the artist's bedside when he died.

62 Susan Sloman (2004, p.320) deserves the credit for observing that the *Dupont* (now in the Tate, (cat. 48) is modelled on the head of Lord Bernard Stuart in the full-length double portrait of *Lord John Stuart and his Brother, Lord Bernard Stuart* (*c*.1638, National Gallery, London), which Gainsborough copied on more than one occasion (including fig. 14). His full-size copy of the entire composition belongs to the Saint Louis Art Museum, Missouri.

63 Coupled with the placement of Gainsborough's self-portraits so that they faced the wall, the elevation of the *Dupont* to a position of such prominence would have reinforced the point of the uncle being eclipsed by his nephew.

Daughters and Sisters: Gainsborough's
Portraits of Mary and Margaret
Ann Bermingham

1   Gbenga Adesina, 'How to Paint a Girl', from *New Generation of African Poets: A Chapbook Box Set (Tatu)*, ed. Kuame Dawes and Chris Abani (Akashic Books, New York, 2016), quoted in the *New York Times Magazine*, 10 July 2016, p.19. I owe a debt of gratitude to my colleagues: Susan Sloman for her very helpful reading of an earlier draft of this essay, Lucy Peltz for her photographs of the Whitbread portrait of Mary and Margaret, and David Solkin for his generous sharing of information and observations, and for his care as an editor. Thanks to Mark Rose for his close and critical readings of this essay, which I wish to dedicate to Professor Henri Zerner.

2   As Marcia Pointon demonstrates throughout *Hanging the Head: Portraiture and Social Formation in Eighteenth-Century England* (Yale University Press, New Haven and London, 1993), a portrait is a cultural artefact, not a simple reflection of the sitter. As such, it exhibits cultural and historical ideas and attitudes.

3   Ellis Waterhouse catalogues eleven portraits of Mary and Margaret, either single or double. See Ellis Waterhouse, 'Preliminary Checklist of Portraits by Thomas Gainsborough', *Walpole Society*, 1948–50, Vol.33 (1953), pp.42–4. Hugh Belsey in *Gainsborough's Family* (exh. cat., Gainsborough's House Society, Sudbury, 1988), fig. 20, plates 16 & 17 includes several additional single portraits of Mrs Gainsborough and Margaret Gainsborough. The dates when Mary and Margaret were born have been established by David Tyler in 'The Gainsborough Family: Births, Marriages and Deaths Re-examined', *Gainsborough's House Review*, 1992/3, p.42. Also see his 'Thomas Gainsborough's Daughters', *Gainsborough's House Society Annual Report*, 1991/2, p.50. My essay is indebted to Mr Tyler for his extensive research into the lives of Mary and Margaret Gainsborough.

4   See Susan Sloman's meticulously researched account of *Gainsborough in Bath* (Yale University Press, New Haven and London, 2002).

5   Ibid., p.36.

6   Susan Sloman, 'Mrs Margaret Gainsborough: "A Prince's Daughter"', *Gainsborough's House Review*, 1995/6, pp.47–55. Also see Sloman, 2002, pp.23–31. Sloman was the first to examine the documents related to the Beaufort annuity and to establish beyond a doubt Margaret Burr's patrimony.

7   Joseph Farington, *The Diary of Joseph Farington* [1793–1821], Vol. IV, ed. Kenneth Garlick and Angus Macintyre (Yale University Press, New Haven and London, 1979), p.1152.

8   Allan Cunningham, *The Lives of the Most Eminent British Painters, Sculptors and Architects*, 5 vols (John Murray, London, 1829–33), Vol.I, pp.323–4. Cunningham's source was Gainsborough's niece Sophia Lane (née Gardiner).

9   Thomas Gainsborough to Mary Gibbon, 22 September 1777, in John Hayes, ed., *The Letters of Thomas Gainsborough* (Yale University Press, New Haven and London, 2001), p.135.

10 Sloman, 2002, pp.120–1.

11 See David Tyler, 'Thomas Gainsborough's Days in Hatton Garden', *Gainsborough's House Society Annual Report 1992/3*, pp.27–32; and Michael Rosenthal and Martin Myrone, eds, *Thomas Gainsborough, 1727–1788* (Tate, London, 2002), p.60; or Lindsay Stainton and Bendor Grosvenor,

'Tom will be a Genius': New Landscapes by the Young Thomas Gainsborough (Philip Mould Ltd, London, 2009), p.28.

12 Stainton and Grosvenor, p.28.

13 Thomas Gainsborough to James Unwin, 25 October 1763, in Hayes, 2001, p.23.

14 Ibid., 1 March 1764, pp.26, 28, n.10.

15 Thomas Gainsborough to Mary Gibbon, 26 December 1775, in Hayes, 2001, p.130.

16 Philip Thicknesse, *A Sketch of the Life and Paintings of Thomas Gainsborough,* esq. (Printed for the author, London, 1788), pp.33–4.

17 Thomas Gainsborough to James Unwin, 10 July 1770, in Hayes, 2001, p.78.

18 Idem., 25 May 1768, ibid., p.53.

19 Thomas Gainsborough to William Jackson, 4 June [1770?] in Hayes, 2001, p.68.

20 Ibid. This interpretation of the wagon motif was first proposed by Michael Levey, 'The Genius of Gainsborough', *Christie's International Magazine*, October 1990, p.2.

21 The confusion starts with Philip Thicknesse, who incorrectly described Mary as the younger daughter in his memoir of the artist (*Thicknesse*, London, 1788, pp.49–50) . Gainsborough's first biographer, George Williams Fulcher (*Life of Thomas Gainsborough*, Longman, Brown, Green and Longmans, London, 1856, p.116) perpetuated the error by following Thicknesse's account. The error may also have been related to the fact that Margaret was, with her mother, joint executrix of her father's will. She was also her older sister's caretaker in later life, and was called 'Mrs Gainsborough', a courtesy title. William Whitley's standard biography (*Thomas Gainsborough*, John Murray, London, 1915) misidentifies the girls throughout. On p.80 he takes a reference to 'Miss Gainsborough' in a letter as referring to Margaret, and calls Mary 'the younger daughter' (pp.123, 404). However, in a letter to *The Times*, 9 March 1922, Whitley acknowledged his error after having visited Mary and Margaret's graves in Hanwell.

22 Stainton, op. cit., p.21.

23 Michael Levey, 'The Painter's Daughter's chasing a Butterfly', *Painting in Focus*, no. 4, 1975, National Gallery, London. Also see Amal Asfour and Paul Williamson, *Gainsborough's Vision* (Liverpool University Press, Liverpool, 1999), pp.89–92. A similar gesture and sentiment appears in plate 1, *La Chasse au Papillon*, in Jacques Stella's *Les Jeux et plaisirs de l'enfance* (Paris, 1657). Stella's book is filled with images of children at play that were repeated by later eighteenth-century artists, such as François Boucher and Hubert-François Gravelot (Gainsborough's teacher). See for instance Gravelot's *L'Exercice de l'Infanterie* (Paris, 1766) reproduced in Vera Salomons, *Gravelot* (John & Edward Bumpus Ltd, London, 1911).

24 Hingeston's son, quoted in Fulcher, 1856, p.48, recalled that Gainsborough had been a close friend of his father's, whose 'residence bears testimony alike to his skill as a painter and his kindness as a man, for the panels of several of the rooms are adorned with the productions of his genius. In one, is a picture of Gainsborough's two daughters, when young; they are engaged in chasing a butterfly; the arrangement of the figures, and the landscape introduced into the back ground, are of the most charming description. There are several other drawings, all in good preservation, and delineated in his happiest manner.' In many cases it would seem that Gainsborough valued his male friends as much as his family. His letters to James

Unwin and William Jackson are especially revealing of the artist's activities, his ambitions and his sometimes ambivalent feelings about his marriage and the members of his immediate family. The only female correspondent to whom he confides family business and affections is his sister, Mary Gibbon.

25 As Asfour and Williamson observe (1992, p.92), Hingeston's *Discourse upon the Divine Covenants: or, an Enquiry into the Origin and Progress of Religion, Natural and Revealed* (1771) describes nature as a 'series of providential emblems', a belief accommodated by Gainsborough's use of the butterfly and thistle. The portrait's moralising imagery, alluding to the dangers of the world, would also seem of a piece with a general nonconformist mindset and with Gainsborough's Dissenter background. At the end of his life he identified his brother Humphrey with Presbyterianism, his sister Mary with 'rank' Methodism, and himself, by that time, with Church of England. See Thomas Gainsborough to Mary Gibbon, 13 November 1775, in Hayes, 2001, p.128.

26 Mary's left hand and the area immediately behind it show some loss of colour or pigment, which suggests the presence of a ribbon or bow there at one time.

27 The portrait has received rough treatment; at one time it was cut in half, and then later rejoined. The Victoria and Albert Museum (http://collections.vam.ac.uk/item/O17303/the-painters-two-daughters-oil-painting-gainsborough-thomas-ra/) explains: 'The history of the painting is somewhat obscure, but according to tradition, it passed from Margaret Gainsborough to John Jackson, RA, and was then divided vertically into two halves, one going to W.C. Macready, the actor, and the other to John Forster, the friend and biographer of Dickens. Forster, as is recorded, ultimately acquired Macready's portion, which he reunited with his own, the joined painting coming to the Museum in 1876 … however … the backgrounds of the two halves do not entirely tally, and Mary's left arm seems out of alignment with the rest of her torso, the upper arm being over-painted to connect with the raised forearm on the right hand side of the painting.' For a reconstruction of the figures' original alignment, see fig. 33, p.109 in this book.

28 It is assumed that Gainsborough painted directly on to the canvas because so few preparatory drawings relating to his portraits exist. The ones that do are usually related to works from the late Suffolk/early Bath period, which are painted on a larger scale than his early Suffolk portraits.

29 The appearance of this painting, prior to its dismemberment, was described in 1824 as follows: 'This picture represents portraits of his two daughters, in the garb of peasant girls, on the confines of a corn-field, dividing their gleanings. They appear to be of the age of about eight and nine, and are the size of life. The painting is pure, & the characters are nature, clothed with the utmost simplicity of art; unfortunately both [this work and an early circular landscape] are left in part unfinished'; see William Henry Pyne, 'Gems of Art', *Somerset House Gazette, and Literary Museum*, Vol.II, no.XLIV (August 1824), p.272.

30 On Dutch seventeenth-century portraits and fancy pictures of children, see Jan Baptist Bedaux and Rudi Ekkart, *Pride and Joy: Children's Portraits in the Netherlands, 1500–1700* (Ludion, Ghent and Amsterdam, 2000) and E. de Jongh, *Portretten van echt en trouw: Huwelijk en gezin in de Nederlandse kunst van de zeventiende eeuw* (Frans Hals Museum, Haarlem, 1986). I am grateful to Ann Jensen Adams for these references. On the impact of French fancy

painting on British artists in the 1730s and 1740s, see Martin Postle, *Angels and Urchins: The Fancy Picture in 18th-Century British Art* (exh. cat., Djanogly Art Gallery, Nottingham, 1998), p.13.

31 Stainton and Grosvenor, 2009, p.20; Brian Allen, *Francis Hayman* (Yale University Press, New Haven and London, 1987), pp.39–45. Lawrence Gowing was the first to suggest that one of these supper-box paintings might be attributed in part to Gainsborough. See his 'Hogarth, Hayman and the Vauxhall Decorations', *Burlington Magazine,* Vol. 95, no. 598 (January 1953), p.11. I am grateful to Brian Allen for confirming the relationship between Hayman's *The Play of See-Saw* and a similar image in Gravelot, 1766.

32 Elizabeth E. Barker and Alex Kidson, *Joseph Wright of Derby in Liverpool* (Walker Art Gallery, Liverpool, 2007), p.65.

33 See Postle, 1997, p.87.

34 Allen, 1987, p.29. It should be noted that Allen (pp.92–3) was able to confirm the fact that Gainsborough assisted Hayman by painting the landscape backgrounds for portraits such as *Elizabeth and Charles Bedford with a St Bernard Dog* (private collection). As Hayman's assistant, Gainsborough no doubt absorbed his teacher's fancy-picture approach to portraiture.

35 See Pointon, 1993, pp.177 ff; James Christian Steward, *The New Child: British Art and the Origins of Modern Childhood, 1730–1830* (University of Washington Press, Seattle, WA, 1995); Anne Higonnet, *Pictures of Innocence: The History and Crisis of Ideal Childhood* (Thames & Hudson, New York, 1998), pp.15–31.

36 It is just possible that the portrait of the Mary fastening a bow in Margaret's hair and the image of the girls with a cat were intended to suggest the senses of sight and touch. If so, Gainsborough would be following the example of Mercier and Hayman, both of whom in the 1740s and 1750s created series depicting the five senses. See Allen, 1987, pp.142–4.

37 Thomas Gainsborough to James Unwin, 15 September 1763 and 25 October 1763, in Hayes, 2001, pp.19, 22.

38 Margaret recalled to Farington the great pleasure Gainsborough derived from his rides through the Bath countryside, explaining that 'While he resided at Bath [he used to] ride frequently, after he had received his morning sitters'. See Farington/ Garlick and Mcintyre, p.1149.

39 Judy Egerton, *National Gallery Catalogues – The British School* (National Gallery, London, 1998), p.96, no.5.

40 This is confirmed by an X-ray taken of the work in the late twentieth century; see fig. 34, p.114.

41 Compositional drawings for other portraits from this time suggest that Gainsborough was still not wholly at ease painting directly on the canvas when working on a large scale. See, for example, the study for an unexecuted full-length of his wife and daughters (cat. 14), and the two studies, one in the British Museum and the other in Gainsborough's House, for the portrait of Ann Ford (1760, Cincinnati Museum of Fine Arts). For the British Museum sketch, see John Hayes, *The Drawings of Thomas Gainsborough*, 2 vols (Yale University Press, New Haven and London, 1970), cat. 16, p.114, plate 327; the second example is reproduced is Hugh Belsey, *Gainsborough at Gainsborough's House* (Paul Holberton, London, 2002), cat. 17, p.51.

42 Thomas Gainsborough to James Unwin, 1 March 1764, in Hayes, 2001, pp.25–6.

43 See Michael Rosenthal, 'Thomas Gainsborough's *Ann Ford*', *Art Bulletin*, Vol. 80, no. 4 (December 1998), pp.649–65. The portrait now belongs to the Cincinnati Art Museum.

44 Farington, [1793–1821]/ Garlick and Mcintyre, p.1149.

45 Beechey's report appears in Whitley, 1915, p.110. For the reception of Gainsborough's landscapes during the Bath period, see Sloman, 2002, pp.117–24. The catalogue for the posthumous sale of Gainsborough's works at Schomberg House reveals that apart from the works that were not put up for sale – mainly family portraits and a small number of landscapes, there were 52 Old Master paintings, 10 copies of old master paintings by himself, 5 fancy pictures by himself, and 36 landscape paintings by himself. Only one portrait by Gainsborough (a large oval of the Duke and Duchess of Cumberland with Lady Elizabeth Luttrell, now in the Royal Collection) is listed in the sale catalogue. See *A Catalogue of the Pictures and Drawings of the Late Mr. Gainsborough*, London, 30 March 1789, pp.1–4 (and lot 70).

46 Thomas Gainsborough to William Jackson, 4 June [1770?] in Hayes, 2001, p.68.

47 As his substantial pricing of his Bath landscapes and his exhibition of them in London suggests, Gainsborough may have imagined that he could turn the fortunes of the genre around and make it a profitable one.

48 Thomas Gainsborough to William Jackson, 4 June [1770?], in Hayes, 2001, p.68.

49 The style of Margaret's dress conforms to what we see in Gainsborough's portrait of Elizabeth Tudway (Philadelphia Museum of Art). The portrait was billed by the artist in July 1773; see Rosenthal and Myrone, 2002, p.154. The distinguished historian of dress, Professor Aileen Ribeiro, believes that the dress of Mary and Margaret is 'fanciful' in that it 'approximates to the lines of fashion but is generalised and incorporates aspects of "historical" and "oriental" features. Historical in the way the dresses are lifted up à la Van Dyck, oriental re the fringed sashes …' On the basis of the sisters' costumes, she dates the work to about 1774. I am grateful to Professor Ribeiro for her insights.

50 The production pattern of the portraits of Mary and Margaret departs from conventional eighteenth-century British practice. Portraits were usually painted to mark an important passage in life, such as a young boy's breeching (moving into long trousers) or his leaving home to attend school, or a person's marriage, and even an individual's death.

51 The Schomberg House sale began on 30 March 1789 and ended on the last day of May. Christie's sale of works belonging to the artist's widow took place on 2 June 1792. It was Philip Thicknesse (1788, p.61) who reported that Mrs Gainsborough had many of Mary's drawings, but without having any securely attributable works, it is nearly impossible for art historians to identify drawings by her. Drawings in the style of Gainsborough from the collection of Henry Briggs, a close friend of Margaret's in her later life at Acton, and from the collection of Sophia Lane, a cousin and the executrix of Margaret's will, might be places to start in searching for work plausibly by Mary, as Margaret gave both of them a large number of artworks. See Tyler, 1788, 1991/2, pp.53–8.

52 Whitley, 1915, p.312.

53 Ibid., pp.312, 353. In 1779 Gainsborough wrote to his sister Mary Gibbon that he wanted for nothing and lived on £1,000 a year. This is quoted in Fulcher, 1856, p.110, but the letter appears to be lost and

is not in Hayes, 2001. If Mrs Gainsborough and her daughters were used to an income of £1,000 a year, they might not have considered £10,000 that comfortable a sum to live on.

54 Thomas Gainsborough to Mary Gibbon, 21 October 1780, in Hayes, 2001, p.144. As Gainsborough explains in his letter, if caught and convicted, Mary could have been subject to transportation.

55 Whitley, 1915, p.311.

56 Ibid., p.80. Here Whitley confuses the birth order of Mary and Margaret, and therefore wrongly claims that it was Margaret who suffered from the fever. Palmer's letter had simply referred to 'Miss Gainsborough', the form of address customarily applied to the first-born, unmarried daughter.

57 Quoted in Belsey, 1988, p.37.

58 Quoted in Tyler, 1991/2, p.55.

59 Thomas Gainsborough to Mary Gibbon, 10 June [1776], in Hayes, 2001, p.131.

60 Idem., 26 December 1775, ibid., p.130.

61 Fulcher, 1856, p.118.

62 Pyne, 1824, p.272.

63 Walter Armstrong, *Gainsborough and His Place in English Art* (Charles Scribner's Sons, New York, 1904), p.196.

64 It should be noted that while Mrs Gainsborough's paternity conveyed prestige, it also brought with it the shame of illegitimacy. This irony may have played a part too in the girls' self-esteem, and perhaps explains, in particular, Margaret's social awkwardness and eccentricities.

65 David Tyler has given the most complete account of this period in their lives. According to him, at Acton they were befriended by Henry Briggs and his nephew of the same name. Margaret rented their house for £30 per annum from the elder Mr Briggs and developed a fond interest in the 19-year-old nephew, who was an amateur artist. Two years before her death, Margaret made a deed of gift of artworks to Henry the younger, 'in consideration of the friendship and regard I have towards my very good friend'. See Tyler, 1991/2, pp.53–7.

66 After Margaret's death Mary became the charge of her cousin Sophia Lane. The sisters are buried together in the churchyard of St Mary's, Hanwell. This was not their parish church, nor even the churchyard where their parents were buried. For this reason David Tyler, 1991/2, pp.53–7) has speculated that Margaret may have taken her own life.

67 Whitley, 1915, p.238, reproduces a letter from Gainsborough Dupont to Thicknesse asking him not to publish his 'Sketch' of the life of Gainsborough, 'attacking her [Mrs Gainsborough] and my uncle's reputation' and promising to take legal action against Thicknesse should he do so.

68 Fulcher, 1856, pp.117–18.

69 On these twentieth-century accounts of Gainsborough's daughters, see Hugh Belsey and Christopher Wright, *Gainsborough Pop: Gainsborough's Pictures Through the Popular Imagination 1760– 2000* (Gainsborough's House Society and Paul Holberton, London, 2002). Also see Charles Spencer, *Cecil Beaton: Stage and Film Designs* (Academy Editions, London, 1975), pp.54–9. In his diary Beaton assumes that, after a happy childhood in the Bath countryside, the bright lights of London went to the girls' heads and they became 'snobbish' and 'dotty old maids'. Cecil Beaton, *The Strenuous Years: Diaries 1948–55* (Weidenfeld & Nicolson, London, 1973), p.79.

70 The painting was given by Gainsborough to Walter Wiltshire, a public carrier in Bath, who transported

the artist's paintings to London without charge and who gave him a grey horse for his country rides. Cunningham (1829–32, p.331) says that the wagon held the whole family, including Gainsborough, and that the grey horse appears as the lead horse. The earliest source to identify the painter's daughters as two of the young women in the scene appears to be E. Finden, *The Royal Gallery of British Art* (1838–51, J. Hogarth, London, unpaginated). Either

Edward or William Finden interviewed Wiltshire's son (then aged eighty-two) about the picture in 1841. Fulcher, 1856, p.70, claims that the wagon contains Mary who is seated and Margaret who is shown climbing in. Since that time these identifications have generally been accepted by art historians. See for example, Paul Spencer-Longhurst and Janet M. Brooke, *Thomas Gainsborough: The Harvest Wagon* (Birmingham Museum and Art Gallery, Birmingham,

1995). Michael Rosenthal's eagle eye has spied gold buckles on Margaret's shoes (see *The Art of Thomas Gainsborough: 'A Little Business for the Eye'*, Yale University Press, New Haven and London, 1999, p.213) – a harbinger of things to come.

Women of Consequence:
Mrs Gainsborough and Mrs Gibbon
Susan Sloman

1   Jenny Uglow, *Hogarth: A Life and a World* (Faber & Faber, London, 1997), p.475.
2   John Hayes suggested Panton Betew might have been the silversmith with whom the young Gainsborough lodged (John Hayes, *The Landscape Paintings of Thomas Gainsborough*, 2 vols. (Yale University Press, New Haven and London, 1982, Vol.I, pp.29–30) but Betew was born in 1722. Elizabeth, née Pantin and her second husband Benjamin Godfrey are more likely candidates, but other silversmiths have been proposed.
3   Mrs Gainsborough's birth date is often given as 1728, but the inscription on the family grave at Kew states that she died on 17 December 1798 'in the 72nd year of her age' (i.e. at 71), see David Tyler, 'The Gainsborough Family: Births, Marriages, and Deaths re-examined', *Gainsborough's House Review 1992/93*, p.47. See also note 19 below for a suggested birth date.
4   John Bensusan-Butt , *Thomas Gainsborough in his Twenties:. A Memorandum Based on Contemporary Sources*, 3rd edn (Colchester, 1993), pp.26–7, 38–9.
5   Thomas Gainsborough to James Unwin, 1 March 1764, in John Hayes, *The Letters of Thomas Gainsborough*, (Yale University Press, New Haven and London, 2001), p.16.
6   Christopher Gibbon made a will in November 1759 and died on 6 April 1760 (Bensusan-Butt, 1993, pp.25–6, 39).
7   Georg Christoph Lichtenberg, *Lichtenberg's Visits to England: as described in his letters and diaries*, ed., trans. & anno. Margaret L. Mare and W.H. Quarrell (Clarendon Press, Oxford, 1938), letter 17, dated 13 October 1775, p.94.
8   Nicola Phillips, *Women in Business, 1700–1850* (Boydell Press, Woodbridge, 2006), pp.131–4, 143.
9   It has been pointed out that the pose for Margaret Gainsborough's portrait is taken from a classical figure of *Juno Matrona* (fig. 13), virtuous wife and haughty scold. See Hilary S. Brown, 'Gainsborough's classically ambivalent wife', *British Art Journal*, Vol.III, no.1 (Autumn 2001), p.78.
10 Ellis Waterhouse, *Gainsborough* (Spring Books, London, 1966; 1st edn, 1958), no.606, p.89; Susan Sloman, *Gainsborough in Bath* (Yale University Press, New Haven and London, 2002), p.59, fig. 48.
11 Brown, 2001, p.78, remarks on the evident 'tenderness and sympathy' of the portrait.
12 Allan Cunningham, *The Lives of the Most Eminent British Painters, Sculptors, and Architects*, 5 vols, (John Murray, London, 1829–33), Vol.I, p.327.
13 National Archives, Kew, PROB11/1169. Margaret Gainsborough is named as executrix, with Samuel Kilderbee of Ipswich appointed to assist her.
14 David Tyler, 'Thomas Gainsborough's Days in Hatton Garden', *Gainsborough's House Society Annual Report 1992/93*, p.45.
15 Thomas Gainsborough to Richard Stevens, 2 October 1767, in Hayes, 2001, p.49.
16 Thomas Gainsborough to Mary Gibbon, 10 June [1776], ibid., p.131.
17 Susan Sloman, 'Mrs Margaret Gainsborough, "A Prince's Daughter"', *Gainsborough's House Review*, 1995/6, pp.47–58.
18 William T. Whitley, *Thomas Gainsborough* (Smith, Elder & Co., London, 1915), pp.9–10. David Tyler (in a private communication to the author) notes that Mrs Gainsborough's niece Mary Burr married James Scott in Edinburgh on 29 August 1800.
19 Sloman, 2002, p.25 and notes 16, 20, p.222. Margaret Burr may be the person of that name born 7 October 1727 and baptised at St James's, Westminster on 15 October 1727 as the child of William and Margaret Burr, http://www.familysearch.org
20 Information communicated by David Tyler. Both children were baptised at St Cuthbert's, Edinburgh: Margaret on 26 March 1805, Gainsborgh on 6 December 1806.
21 Letter from Mr and Mrs Scott dated 18 January 1821 among privately owned papers formerly on loan to Gainsborough's House, Sudbury, MS LPI/1/8.
22 Thomas Gainsborough to Mary Gibbon, 22 September 1777, Hayes, 2001, p.135. Gainsborough tells his sister that his wife 'cannot come at the Knowledge of my Price' for landscapes, but that he has to pass all portrait income to her.
23 Thomas Gainsborough to Philip, Viscount Royston, 21 July 1763, and to Percival Beaumont, 27 January 1765, in ibid., pp.14, 36.
24 George, Prince of Wales to Prince Frederick Augustus, from Windsor Castle, 15 October 1782 in Arthur Aspinall, ed., *The Correspondence of George, Prince of Wales 1770–1812*, 8 vols (Cassell, London, 1963–71) Vol.I, no.66, p.93. The picture is untraced.
25 Oliver Millar, *Later Georgian Pictures in the Collection of Her Majesty the Queen*, 2 vols (Phaidon, London, 1969), I, p.xxiv; Joseph Farington, *The Diary of Joseph Farington*, Vol.IV, ed. Kenneth Garlick and Angus Macintyre (Yale University Press, New Haven and London, 1979), pp.1146–7, entry for 25 January 1799.
26 Oliver Millar, *Gainsborough, Paul Sandby and Miniature-Painters in the Service of George III and His Family* (exh. cat., Queen's Gallery, London, 1970), no. 58, pp.29–30.
27 Thomas Gainsborough to Mary Gibbon, 22 September 1777, in Hayes, 2001, p.135.
28 At this date, pictures that were for sale were marked with an asterisk in the Royal Academy catalogues. None of Gainsborough's landscapes or fancy pictures was marked in this way.
29 Thomas Gainsborough to James Unwin, 13 November 1757, in Hayes, 2001, pp.178–9; Sloman, 1995/6, p.53.
30 British Library, Add. MS 44,025, f.7; Add. MS 44,024, f.31. These may have been half-yearly payments of Mrs Hone's annuity; Mrs Gainsborough's was paid in this way.
31 Daphne Foskett, *Miniatures, Dictionary and Guide* (Antique Collectors' Club, Woodbridge, 1990), p.569. Hone lived at St James's Place from 1764 to 1773 and at 94 Pall Mall from 1774 to 1780. See Algernon Graves, *The Society of Artists of Great Britain 1760–1791, The Free Society of Artists 1761–1783* (George Bell & Algernon Graves, London, 1907), pp.123–4; Algernon Graves, *The Royal Academy of Arts: A Complete Dictionary of Contributors*, 8 vols (Graves & Bell, London, 1905–6), Vol.IV, pp.142–3.
32 Philip Thicknesse, *A Sketch of the Life and Paintings of Thomas Gainsborough*. (London, 1788), p.16.
33 Susan Sloman, 'Gainsborough and "The Lodging House Way"', *Gainsborough's House Society Annual Report 1991/2*, p.23 and note 8, p.38.
34 Martin Postle, *Angels and Urchins: The Fancy-Picture in 18th-century British Art* (exh. cat., Djanogly Art Gallery, Nottingham, 1998), no.58, p.80 and no.16, p.64.
35 Ibid., no.43, pp.74–5. A particularly fine seventeenth-century precedent is the mezzotint, *Boy Drawing a Cast of the Farnese Hercules* by Wallerant Vaillant. Gainsborough's daughters are shown drawing a cast of the Farnese Flora.
36 See John Newman, 'Reynolds and Hone: "The Conjuror" Unmasked', in Nicholas Penny, ed., *Reynolds* (Royal Academy in association with Weidenfeld & Nicolson, London, 1986), pp.344–54.
37 Bensusan-Butt, 1993, pp.38–9; Deborah Simonton, 'Milliners and *Marchandes de Modes*: Gender, Creativity and Skill in the Workplace', in Deborah Simonton, Marjo Kaartinen and Anne Montenach' eds, *Luxury and Gender in European Towns, 1700–1914* (Routledge, New York and Abingdon, 2015), p.33.
38 Bensusan-Butt, 1993, p.39.
39 Simonton, 2015, p.32.
40 Bensusan-Butt, 1993, p.35. Reinhold was then organist at St Peter's, Colchester. His portrait by Zoffany is in the collection of the Garrick Club, London.
41 Bensusan-Butt, 1993, p.25.
42 Sloman, 2002, p.205.
43 Unless the non-standard sized profile portrait of a woman by Gainsborough sold at Christie's, 9 December 2009 (lot 233), represents Mrs Gibbon. The format suggests it is of a family member or close friend, but its provenance is unknown.
44 Thomas Gainsborough to Dr Rice Charlton, 24 June 1779, in Hayes, 2001, p.139.
45 Ibid.
46 Ibid.
47 Thomas Gainsborough to Mary Gibbon, 12 September 1777, ibid., p.134.
48 Thomas Gainsborough to James Unwin, 15 September

1763, ibid., p.21.

49 Anthony Pasquin [pseud. for John Williams], *Memoirs of the Royal Academicians; Being an Attempt to Improve the National Taste* (H.D. Symonds, London, 1796), p.92.

50 Bensusan-Butt, 1993, p.39; Simonton, 2015, p.33. Simonton adds the name of Elizabeth Reeve to Bensusan-Butt's list of Colchester apprentices.

51 Sloman, 1991/2, p.44.

52 Ibid.

53 John William Fletcher, *Thirteen Original Letters written by the late Rev John Fletcher* (Campbell and Gainsborough and S. Hazard, Bath, 1791). A copy of the print after Vaslet in the British Museum, Q,3.53, bears the publication date 20 June 1791 and the name of the publishers, Campbell and Gainsborough. John Jones had previously engraved Gainsborough's portraits of the actor John Henderson (1783) and dancer Giovanna Baccelli (1784); see Henry Percy Horne, *An Illustrated Catalogue Engraved Portraits and Fancy Subjects Painted by Thomas Gainsborough, R.A., …* (Eyre and Spottiswoode, London, 1891) no. 38, p.18, no.7, p.12.

54 British Museum, Banks Trade Card collection, D,2.410.

55 Mrs Gibbon gave weekly financial support to her brother John (see Thomas Gainsborough to Sarah Dupont, 29 September 1783, in Hayes, 2001, p.155).

56 Thomas Gainsborough to Dr Rice Charlton, 24 June 1779, ibid., p.139.

57 Thomas Gainsborough to William Jackson, 8 July 1779, ibid., p.140, and to Mary Ditcher, 31 July 1779, ibid., p.141; Whitley, 1915, p.253.

58 Richard Wendorf, *Sir Joshua Reynolds: The Painter in Society* (National Portrait Gallery Publications, London, 1996), p.131.

59 Alex Kidson, *George Romney 1734–1802* (National Portrait Gallery Publications, London, 2002), p.27.

60 Whitley, 1915, p.146, quoting the *London Chronicle*, 1777 (day and month not noted).

61 Aileen Ribeiro, *The Art of Dress: Fashion in England and France 1750 to 1820* (Yale University Press, New Haven and London, 1995) p.202.

62 Aileen Ribeiro, *Clothing Art: The Visual Culture of Fashion 1600–1914* (Yale University Press, New Haven and London, 2016) p.219.

63 The sequence of occupancy of Schomberg House is more fully explained in Susan Sloman, *Gainsborough in London* (forthcoming).

64 *Morning Herald*, 18 November 1784.

65 Bath Record Office, City Rate Midsummer to Michaelmas 1781, BC5/70/19; *Morning Herald*, 2 June 1783. For Mrs Gibbon at the Circus in the 1770s and 1780s, see Sloman, 2001, p.44. She may also have been associated with 2 Circus, which is apparently the address on a letter to her from her brother Thomas, dated 21 October 1780 (Hayes, op. cit., p.144).

66 For a plan of this property and its relationship with 17 Circus, see Walter Ison, *The Georgian Buildings of Bath from 1700 to 1830* (Kingsmead Press, Bath, 1980), p.98, fig. 24.

67 Bath Record Office, City Rate Christmas 1785 to Lady Day 1786, BC5/70/25; Minchin's advertisement, *Bath Chronicle*, 25 October 1787; Trevor Fawcett, *Bath Commercialis'd: Shops, Trades and Market at the 18th-Century Spa* (Ruton, Bath, 2002) p.41.

68 Miss Minchin's advertisement, *Bath Chronicle*, 21 November 1793, shows that she now ran the company at 19 Circus. For this house and the Miss Gardiners, see Sloman, 1991/2, p.42, note 74, and p.44.

69 Sloman, 1991/2, p.33.

70 *Morning Herald*, 18 November 1784. In 1785 the partnership between Mr and Mrs Dyde and James Hartshorn was dissolved, see *Morning Post*, 28 November 1785.

71 The hat worn by Fanny Burney in her portrait of 1784–5 by Edward Francisco Burney (National Portrait Gallery, London) appears to be a balloon hat.

72 M.H. Spielmann, 'Note on Gainsborough and Gainsborough Dupont', *The Walpole Society*, Vol.5 (1915–17), p.105

73 The landscape prints and Dupont's involvement are the subject of a chapter in Sloman, *Gainsborough in London* (forthcoming).

74 Uglow, p.695.

75 *St James's Chronicle*, 11–14 October 1766. Mary Worlidge's advertisement states that nine parts of the Antique Gems series had been issued by her husband before his death. The whole set was published in 1768.

76 See David Alexander, *Affecting Moments: Prints of English Literature Made in the Age of Romantic Sensibility, 1775–1800* (exh. cat., University of York, York, 1992), pp.20–1, 30–1.

77 Thomas Gainsborough to an unknown recipient, 15 June 1788, in Hayes, 2001, p.175.

78 Sharp's engraving after the Reynolds of John Hunter was published on 1 January 1788.

79 Andrew W. Tuer, *Bartolozzi and His Works*, 2 vols (Field & Tuer, London, 1882–5), Vol.II, cat. 1792, p.138. Miss Gainsborough's undated letter was then in the possession of Algernon Graves.

80 Farington, [1793–1821]/ Garlick and Mcintyre, 1979 p.1537, entry for 11 April 1801.

81 Ibid., p.1146, entry for 25 January 1799.

82 Original copies of the *Morning Herald* of 4 August 1788 with Henry Bate's obituary no longer seem to survive. The text, as reprinted in the *Morning Chronicle*, 5 August 1788, is referred to here; a further reprint appeared in the *London Chronicle*, 2–5 August 1788.

Catalogue

1 Thomas Gainsborough to William Mayhew, 13 March 1758, in John Hayes, ed., *The Letters of Thomas Gainsborough* (Yale University Press, New Haven and London, 2001), p.10.

2 George Williams Fulcher, ed. by Edmund Syer Fulcher, *Life of Thomas Gainsborough, R.A.* (Longman, Brown, Green, and Longmans, London, 1856), p.141.

3 Ibid., pp.152–3.

4 See, for example, the portrait of Andrea Palladio engraved by Bernard Picart after Sebastiano Ricci, frontispiece to Andrea Palladio, *The Architecture of A. Palladio, in four books*, trans. Giacomo Leoni John Watts, (London, 1715), Vol.I.

5 Thomas Gainsborough to the Hon. Edward Stratford, 21 March 1771, in Hayes, 2001, p.83.

6 Christie's, 7 July 1838, lot 171.

7 For the full report by Sawicka and Lenk, see http://courtauld.ac.uk/wp-content/uploads/2015/06/Report-Gainsborough-by-A-Sawicka-and-S-Lenk.pdf

8 Allan Cunningham, *The Lives of the Most Eminent British Painters, Sculptors, and Architects*, 5 vols (John Murray, London, 1829–33), Vol.I, p.339.

9 William T. Whitley, *Thomas Gainsborough* (John Murray, London, 1915), p.268.

10 Thomas Gainsborough to an unknown recipient, 15 June 1788, in Hayes, 2001, p.175.

11 [Philip Thicknesse], *Sketches and Characters of the most Eminent and most Singular Persons now Living. By Several Hands* (John Wheble, Bristol, 1770), p.97.

SELECT BIBLIOGRAPHY

Brian Allen, *Francis Hayman* (Yale University Press, New Haven and London, 1987)

Amal Asfour and Paul Williamson, *Gainsborough's Vision* (Liverpool University Press, Liverpool, 1999)

Hugh Belsey, *Gainsborough's Family* (Gainsborough's House Society, Sudbury, 1988)

Hugh Belsey, *Gainsborough at Gainsborough's House* (Paul Holberton, London, 2002)

John Bensusan-Butt, *Thomas Gainsborough in His Twenties: A Memorandum Based on Contemporary Sources*, 3rd edn (Colchester, 1993)

David Brenneman, *The Critical Response to Thomas Gainsborough's Painting: A Study of the Contemporary Perception and Materiality of Gainsborough's Art* (unpublished PhD dissertation, Brown University, Ann Arbor, 1995)

Hilary S. Brown, 'Gainsborough's Classically Ambivalent Wife', *British Art Journal*, Vol.III, (Autumn 2001), p.78

Judy Egerton, *National Gallery Catalogues – The British School* (National Gallery, London, 1998)

Joseph Farington, *The Diary of Joseph Farington* [1793–1821] Kenneth Garlick, Angus Macintyre and Kathryn Cave, eds., 17 vols. (Yale University Press, New Haven and London, 1978–98)

George Williams Fulcher, ed. by Edmund Syer Fulcher, *Life of Thomas Gainsborough R.A.* (Longman, Brown, Green and Longmans, London 1856)

John Hayes, *The Drawings of Thomas Gainsborough*, 2 vols (Yale University Press, London, 1971)

John Hayes, *The Landscape Paintings of Thomas Gainsborough*, 2 vols (Yale University Press, London, 1982)

John Hayes, ed., *The Letters of Thomas Gainsborough* (Yale University Press, New Haven and London, 2001)

Marcia Pointon, *Hanging the Head: Portraiture and Social Formation in Eighteenth-century England* (Yale University Press, New Haven and London, 1993)

Martin Postle, *Angels and Urchins: The Fancy Picture in 18th-century British Art* (Djanogly Art Gallery, Nottingham, 1998)

Lora Rempel, *The Matter of Style: Thomas Gainsborough, the Portrait in a Landscape, and the Mark of the Modern Painter* (unpublished PhD dissertation, City University of New York, 1997)

Kate Retford, *The Art of Domestic Life: Family Portraiture in Eighteenth-century England* (Yale University Press, New Haven and London, 2006)

Sir Joshua Reynolds, *Discourses on Art* [1769–90], ed. Robert R. Wark (Yale University Press, New Haven and London, 1975)

Aileen Ribeiro, *The Art of Dress: Fashion in England and France 1750 to 1820* (Yale University Press, New Haven and London, 1995)

Michael Rosenthal, *The Art of Thomas Gainsborough: 'A Little Business for the Eye'* (Yale University Press, New Haven and London, 1999)

Michael Rosenthal and Martin Myrone, eds, *Gainsborough 1727–1788* (Tate Publishing, London 2002)

Jean André Rouquet, *The Present State of the Arts in England* (J. Nourse, London, 1755)

Susan Sloman, *Gainsborough in Bath* (Yale University Press, New Haven and London, 2002)

Susan Sloman, '"A Divine Countenance": Gainsborough's Portrait of his Nephew Rediscovered', *Burlington Magazine*, Vol.146, no.1214, 2004, pp.319–22

David H. Solkin, 'Gainsborough's Classically Virtuous Wife', *British Art Journal*, Vol.II, no.2, (Winter 2000/01), pp.75–7

David H. Solkin, *Art in Britain 1660–1815* (Yale University Press, New Haven and London, 2015)

Lindsay Stainton and Bendor Grosvenor, *'Tom will be a Genius': New Landscapes by the Young Thomas Gainsborough* (Philip Mould Ltd, London, 2009)

James Christen Steward, *The New Child: British Art and the Origins of Modern Childhood, 1730–1830* (University of Washington Press, University Art Museum and Pacific Film Archive, University of California, Berkeley, 1995)

Naomi Tadmor, *Family and Friends in Eighteenth-Century England: Household, Kinship, and Patronage* (Cambridge University Press, Cambridge, 2001)

[Philip Thicknesse], *Sketches and Characters of the most Eminent and most Singular Persons now Living. By Several Hands* (John Wheble, Bristol, 1770)

Philip Thicknesse, *A Sketch of the Life and Paintings of Thomas Gainsborough* (London, 1788)

David Tyler, 'Thomas Gainsborough's Daughters', *Gainsborough's House Society Annual Report 1991/2*, pp.50–64

David Tyler, 'Thomas Gainsborough's Days in Hatton Garden', *Gainsborough's House Society Annual Report 1992/3*, pp.27–32

Ellis Waterhouse, *Gainsborough* (Spring Books, London, 1966; 1st edn. 1958)

William T. Whitley, *Thomas Gainsborough* (John Murray/ Smith, Elder & co., London, 1915)

LIST OF LENDERS

Andrew Clayton-Payne

Anthony Mould

Arp Museum Bahnhof Rolandseck / Collection Rau for UNICEF

The Art Institute of Chicago

Ashmolean Museum of Art and Archaeology, University of Oxford

The British Museum, London

Corcoran Gallery of Art, Washington D.C.

The Courtauld Gallery

The Earl of Leicester and the Trustees of the Holkham Estate

Fitzwilliam Museum, Cambridge

Gainsborough's House, Sudbury, Suffolk

Gemäldegalerie, Staatliche Museen zu Berlin

Guildhall Art Gallery, City of London

The Henry Barber Trust, The Barber Institute of Fine Arts, University of Birmingham

Ipswich Borough Council - Colchester and Ipswich Museums

Kupferstichkabinett, Staatliche Museen zu Berlin

Memphis Brooks Museum of Art, Memphis, TN

The National Gallery, London

National Gallery of Ireland, Dublin

Private Collections

Restoration House Collection, Rochester, Kent

Royal Academy of Arts, London

Tate

USC Fisher Museum of Art, Los Angeles

Victoria and Albert Museum, London

Waddesdon (Rothschild Family)

Worcester Art Museum, Worcester, MA

Yale Center for British Art, Paul Mellon Collection, New Haven, CT

INDEX

PICTURE CREDITS

The National Portrait Gallery would like to thank the copyright holders for granting permission to reproduce works illustrated in this book. Every effort has been made to contact the holders of copyright material, and any omissions will be corrected in future editions if the publisher is notified in writing.

Cat 1 Corcoran Collection (Edward C. and Mary Walker Collection) CGA.37.18. Image courtesy of the National Gallery of Art, Washington

Cat 2 The National Gallery, London. Acquired under the acceptance-in-lieu scheme at the wish of Sybil, Marchioness of Cholmondeley, in memory of her brother, Sir Philip Sassoon, 1994. © The National Gallery, London

Cat 3 Gainsborough's House, Sudbury, Suffolk

Cat 6 Image © The Trustees of the British Museum

Cat 7 © National Gallery of Ireland. Presented, Sir Hugh Lane, 1914. Photo © National Gallery of Ireland

Cat 8 Guildhall Art Gallery, City of London

Cat 9 The National Gallery, London. Henry Vaughan Bequest, 1900. © The National Gallery, London

Cat 10 Yale Center for British Art, Paul Mellon Collection

Cat 12 National Portrait Gallery, London. Accepted in lieu of tax by H.M. Government and allocated to the gallery, 1965. © National Portrait Gallery, London

Cat 13 Gemäldegalerie, Staatliche Museen zu Berlin. Photo © bpk / Gemäldegalerie, SMB / Volker-H. Schneider

Cat 14 Kupferstichkabinett, Staatliche Museen zu Berlin. Photo © bpk / Kupferstichkabinett, SMB / Dietmar Katz

Cat 15 Victoria and Albert Museum, London. Bequeathed by John Forster. Image © Victoria and Albert Museum, London

Cat 16 The National Gallery, London. Bought, 1923. © The National Gallery, London

Cat 17 Ashmolean Museum of Art and Archaeology (University of Oxford). Purchased with the assistance of a gift in memory of Helen, Henry and Marius Winslow and the Victoria and Albert Museum Purchase Grant Fund, 1975. WA1975.72. © Ashmolean Museum of Art and Archaeology (University of Oxford)

Cat 18 Gainsborough's House, Sudbury, Suffolk

Cat 19 Worcester Art Museum, Massachusetts, USA. Museum Purchase, 1917.181. Photo © Bridgeman Images

Cat 20 © The Henry Barber Trust, The Barber Institute of Fine Arts, University of Birmingham

Cat 21 Private collection, on loan to Gainsborough's House, Sudbury, Suffolk

Cat 22 USC Fisher Museum of Art, Los Angeles, Elizabeth Holmes Fisher Collection

Cat 23 Private Collection. Photo © Christie's Images/ Bridgeman Images

Cat 24 Tate: Presented by the family of Richard J. Lane 1896. Image © Tate, London 2018

Cat 25 Victoria and Albert Museum, London. Bequeathed by Claude D. Rotch. Image © Victoria and Albert Museum, London

Cat 27 Tate: Presented by Miss Marjorie Gainsborough Gardiner 1965. Image © Tate, London 2018

Cat 28 Yale Center for British Art, Paul Mellon Collection

Cat 31 Image courtesy of Sotheby's

Cat 32 Memphis Brooks Museum of Art, Memphis, Tennessee; Gift of Mr. and Mrs. Morrie A. Moss 61.173

Cat 33, 34 The Samuel Courtauld Trust. The Courtauld Gallery, London

Cat 35 Tate: Bequeathed by Sir Otto Beit 1945. Image © Tate, London 2018

Cat 36 Arp Museum Bahnhof Rolandseck/ Collection Rau for UNICEF. Photo: Peter Schälchli, Zurich

Cat 38 The Art Institute of Chicago, Charles H. and Mary F. S. Worcester Collection; through prior gift of Mr and Mrs Denison B. Hull, Mr and Mrs William Kimball, and Mrs Charles McCulloch, 1987.139. Image © 2018. The Art Institute of Chicago / Art Resource, NY / Scala, Florence

Cat 39 Given by Charles Fairfax Murray, 1918. The Syndics of the Fitzwilliam Museum, University of Cambridge. © Fitzwilliam Museum, Cambridge

Cat 40 Restoration House Collection, Rochester, Kent

Cat 41 Tate: Presented by the family of Richard J. Lane 1896. Image © Tate, London 2018

Cat 42 Tate: Presented by Miss Marjorie Gainsborough Gardiner 1965. Image © Tate, London 2018

Cat 43 Yale Center for British Art, Paul Mellon Collection

Cat 44 Gainsborough's House, Sudbury, Suffolk

Cat 45 Courtesy of Ipswich Borough Council - Colchester and Ipswich Museums

Cat 46 By kind permission of the Earl of Leicester and the Trustees of the Holkham Estate. Photo courtesy of Bridgeman Images

Cat 47 Royal Academy of Arts, London. Given by Miss Margaret Gainsborough, 1808 © Royal Academy of Arts, London

Cat 48 Tate: Bequeathed by Lady d'Abernon 1954. Image © Tate, London 2018

Cat 49 Tate: Presented by the family of Richard J. Lane 1896. Image © Tate, London 2018

Fig 1 The Metropolitan Museum of Art, New York. Gift of Georgiana W. Sargent, in memory of John Osborne Sargent, 1924

Fig 2 National Portrait Gallery, London. Purchased, 1912

Fig 3 National Gallery of Victoria, Melbourne, Felton Bequest, 1947

Fig 4 Art Gallery of South Australia, Adelaide. Gift of the Art Gallery of South Australia Foundation 1994

Fig 5, 6 National Gallery of Victoria, Melbourne, Felton Bequest, 1947

Fig 7 Victoria Art Gallery, Bath and North East Somerset Council / Bridgeman Images

Fig 8 Photo © Birmingham Museums Trust

Fig 9, 10 Photo © bpk / Gemäldegalerie, SMB / Volker-H. Schneider

Fig 12 © Courtesy of the Huntington Art Collections, San Marino, California. Photo © 2015 Fredrik Nilsen

Fig 15 Tate: Bequeathed by Lady d'Abernon 1954. Image © Tate, London 2018

Fig 16 © The Henry Barber Trust, The Barber Institute of Fine Arts, University of Birmingham

Fig 17 The National Gallery of Ireland, Dublin. Bequeathed, Sir Hugh Lane, 1918

Fig 20 Tate: Presented by the Friends of the Tate Gallery 1962. Image © Tate, London 2018

Fig 21 Scottish National Gallery, Edinburgh. Bequest of Lady Murray of Henderland 1861. Photo: National Galleries of Scotland

Fig 23 Given by Charles Fairfax Murray, 1911. The Syndics of the Fitzwilliam Museum, University of Cambridge

Fig 24 William Linley Bequest, 1835. By Permission of Dulwich Picture Gallery, London

Fig 25 Royal Collection Trust / © Her Majesty Queen Elizabeth II 2018

Fig 27 Acquired by Sterling and Francine Clark, 1943. Image courtesy of the Clark Art Institute, Williamstown, Massachusetts, USA

Fig 28 National Museums Northern Ireland / Mary Evans

Fig 29 Scottish National Gallery, London. Bequest of Robert Graham of Redgorton, 1859. Photo: National Galleries of Scotland

Fig 30 Image © The Trustees of the British Museum

Fig 33 Victoria and Albert Museum, London. Bequeathed by John Forster. Image © Victoria and Albert Museum, London

Fig 34 Image courtesy of Philip Klausmeyer, Worcester Art Museum

Fig 40 National Portrait Gallery, London. Purchased with help from the Friends of the National Libraries and the Pilgrim Trust, 1966

All works are © National Portrait Gallery, London, unless otherwise noted.

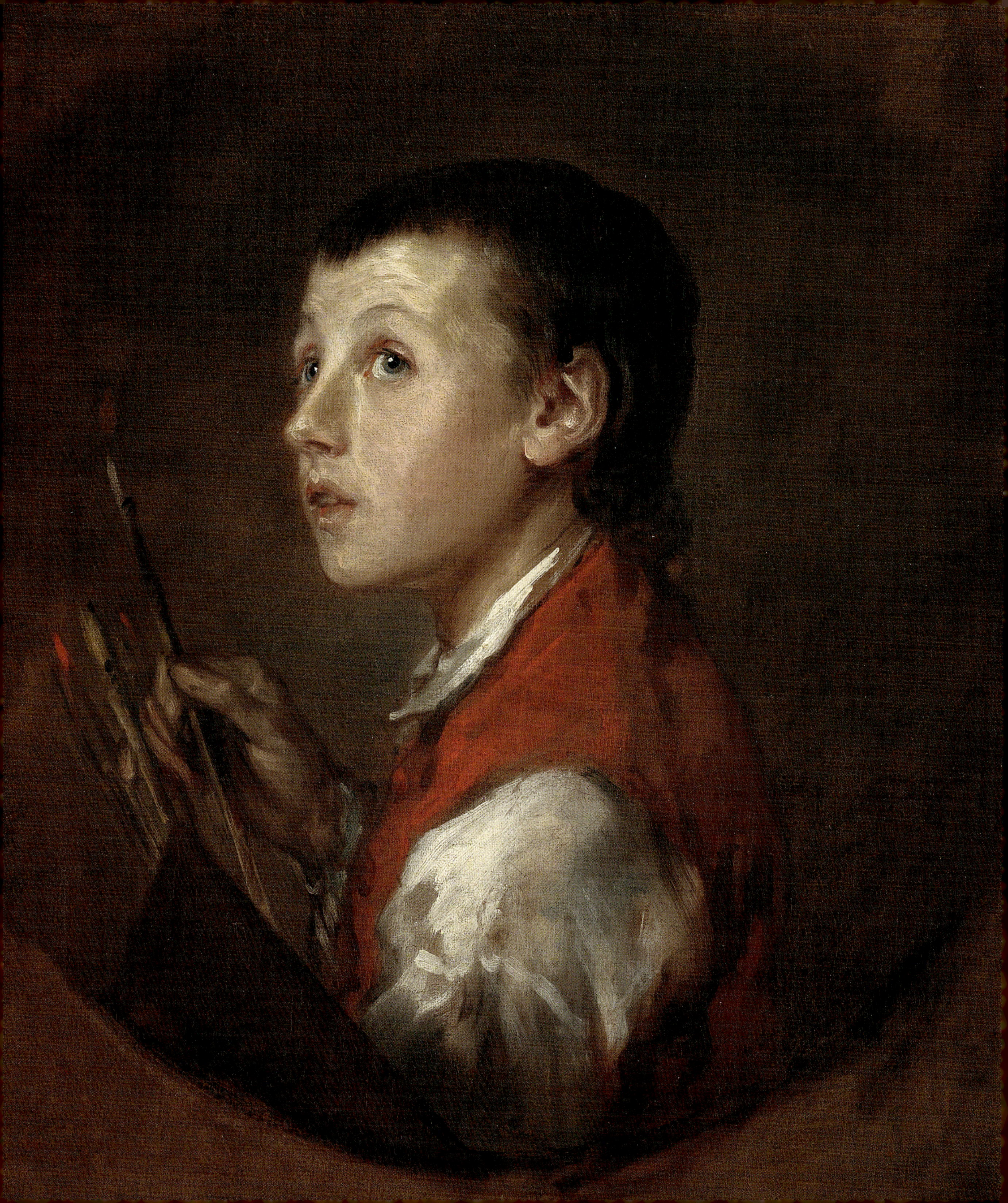

Published in Great Britain by
National Portrait Gallery Publications.
National Portrait Gallery,
St Martin's Place, London WC2H 0HE

Published to accompany the exhibition:
Gainsborough's Family Album
National Portrait Gallery, London,
22 November 2018 to 3 February 2019
Princeton University Art Museum,
23 February to 9 June 2019

This exhibition has been made possible as a result of the Government Indemnity Scheme. The National Portrait Gallery, London, would like to thank HM Government for providing indemnity and the Department for Digital, Culture, Media and Sport and Arts Council England for arranging indemnity.

Every purchase supports the National Portrait Gallery, London.
For a complete catalogue of current publications, please visit our website at
www.npg.org/publications

Supported by a Publications Grant from the Paul Mellon Centre for Studies in British Art

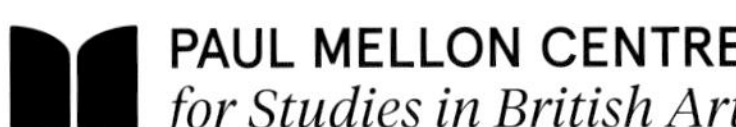

ISBN 978 1 85514 790 4

A catalogue record for this book is available from the British Library
10 9 8 7 6 5 4 3 2 1

Head of Commercial: Anna Starling
Publishing Manager: Kara Green
Editor: Amelia Collins
Picture Researcher: Mark Lynch
Production Manager: Ruth Müller-Wirth

Design: Ocky Murray